Gauvin Alexander Bailey

Der Palast von Sans-Souci in Milot, Haiti
The Palace of Sans-Souci in Milot, Haiti

Panofsky-Professur 2017
am Zentralinstitut für Kunstgeschichte München

Gauvin Alexander Bailey

Der Palast von Sans-Souci in Milot, Haiti (ca. 1806–1813)
Das vergessene Potsdam im Regenwald

The Palace of Sans-Souci in Milot, Haiti (ca. 1806–1813)
The Untold Story of the Potsdam of the Rainforest

ZENTRALINSTITUT
FÜR KUNSTGESCHICHTE

DEUTSCHER KUNSTVERLAG

Die Panofsky-Professur
am Zentralinstitut für Kunstgeschichte

»1957–8 was in Munich.« Vor genau 60 Jahren kam der zu diesem Zeitpunkt 24-jährige englische Kunsthistoriker Michael Baxandall für ein Gaststudium nach München. Aus seiner Autobiographie werden die Gründe für diese Entscheidung nicht wirklich deutlich.[1] Zuvor hatte er in Basel ein Jahr Deutsch gelernt und für den Lebensunterhalt an einer internationalen Schule Englisch unterrichtet. Möglicherweise war bereits das Interesse für die Skulptur der Frühen Neuzeit in Deutschland ausschlaggebend, ein Themenfeld, zu dem Baxandall dann ab 1965 publizieren sollte. Vielleicht spielte auch die kunsthistorische Tradition Münchens und Baxandalls Interesse an Heinrich Wölfflins ›Kunstgeschichte des Sehens‹ eine Rolle bei der Ortswahl gerade von Basel und München. Hans Sedlmayr jedenfalls, der zu diesem Zeitpunkt für die aktuelle Münchner Kunstgeschichte einstand und 1951 auf den Lehrstuhl der Ludwig-Maximilians-Universität berufen worden war, sollte sich für den jungen Engländer methodisch als Enttäuschung entpuppen. Die Folge war die Entdeckung des Zentralinstituts: »Es gab auch noch eine andere Bibliothek, das Zentralinstitut für Kunstgeschichte am Königsplatz, und nach einer Weile ging ich – wie eine Reihe anderer Studenten, die mit Sedlmayr nicht zu recht kamen – regelmäßig dorthin.«

Die Universitätsveranstaltungen, unter anderem auch zur deutschen Gegenwartsliteratur, scheinen noch anderes geboten zu haben: »Ich hatte ein dünnes, blasses Mädchen in den

The Panofsky Professorship
at the Zentralinstitut für Kunstgeschichte

"1957–8 was in Munich." Exactly 60 years ago the English art historian Michael Baxandall came to Munich as a visiting student. He was 24 years old. In his autobiography, the reasons behind this decision are never really explained.[1] Baxandall had previously spent a year learning German in Basel, where he supported himself by teaching English at an international school. Perhaps he was encouraged by what was already a nascent interest in sculpture in Early Modern Germany, a field in which he would start publishing in 1965. Perhaps the tradition of art history in Munich and an interest in Heinrich Wölfflin's "Art History of Seeing" also played a role in his decision to go specifically to Munich and Basel. However, Hans Sedlmayr, who at the time was representative of art history in Munich and had taken a professorship at the Ludwig-Maximilian-Universität, apparently turned out to be a methodological disappointment for the young Englishman. The result was Baxandall's discovery of the Zentralinstitut: "There was an alternative library, the Central Institute for Art History in the Königsplatz, and after a time I based myself there instead, like other students not at ease with Sedlmayr."

University courses, including even courses on German contemporary literature, appear to have offered something else for Baxandall: "I had met a thin, pale girl in his lectures whom I found waif-like and poignant. I was touched by the anxious intensity on her face when she listened to Schnabel, or to

Vorlesungen von Ernst Schnabel getroffen, die mich irgendwie fesselte. Ich war von der Intensität ihres Gesichtsausdrucks, mit der sie Schnabel wie dann auch mir lauschte, gefesselt [...]«. Allerdings endete diese Attraktion mit einem modischen Schockerlebnis genau in dem Moment, als die Beziehung mit einem Abendessen auf die nächste Stufe gehoben werden sollte: »Ich erinnere mich an das Entsetzen, als ich sie mit diesem sie vollkommen verändernden Hut ankommen sah – grauer Filz, grün gefasster Rand, Federn: niedlich-völkisch.« In der Rückschau reflektiert Baxandall über seine heftige Reaktion und das abrupte Beziehungs-Ende: »Ein akademisches Jahr in einem anderen Land macht einen nicht so eingehend mit diesem vertraut, wie man gerne annehmen würde.«

Ein Blick auf Michael Baxandall und seine Erfahrungen in München kann verdeutlichen helfen, was mit der Panofsky-Professur am Zentralinstitut für Kunstgeschichte München beabsichtigt ist, die seit 2016 vergeben wird und die nach dem 1933 aus Deutschland in die USA emigrierten Kunsthistoriker Erwin Panofsky (1892–1968) benannt ist.

Der ›Umweg‹ über Baxandall soll daran erinnern, dass es bei der Professur um prominent von Panofsky vertretene, aber keineswegs mit diesem abgeschlossene Ideen und Perspektiven geht. Panofsky entwarf eine der methodischen Grundlegungen des Faches Kunstgeschichte, die das Verhältnis von Bildwerk, Text und kulturellem Kontext zu fassen versucht. Michael Baxandall hat in den 1970er und 80er Jahren an einer fundamentalen Erweiterung dieses Verständnisses gearbeitet, indem er zeigte, wie mit Hilfe von Texten historische Seherfahrungen, Erwartungshorizonte und ästhetische Kriterien zu rekonstruieren sind. Die Panofsky-Professur am Zentralinstitut zeichnet international herausragende Kunsthistorikerinnen und Kunsthistoriker aus, die solche inhaltlichen und methodischen Erweiterungen und Neuausrichtungen des Faches angehen.

me ..." However, this attraction ended with a fashion disaster, at the very moment when a dinner was supposed to take the relationship to the next level: "The memory is of the horror of seeing her arrive in this totally transforming hat – grey felt, green trimming, feathers: cute-völkisch." Looking back, Baxandall reflects on his strong reaction and the abrupt end of the relationship: "An academic year spent in another country does not take one as far into it as one would like to think it is doing."

A look at Michael Baxandall and his experiences in Munich can help to illuminate the purpose of the Panofsky professorship at the Zentralinstitut für Kunstgeschichte in Munich, which has been awarded since 2016 and is named after the art historian Erwin Panofsky (1892–1968), who emigrated from Germany to the U.S. in 1933.

This "detour" through Baxandall should remind us that the professorship is about ideas and perspectives prominently represented by Panofsky but in no way limited to him. Panofsky laid out one of the methodological foundations of the discipline of art history, which attempted to grasp the relationship between artwork, text, and cultural context. In the 1970s and 1980s, Michael Baxandall worked out a fundamental expansion of this understanding, in that he showed how historical experiences of seeing, horizons of expectation, and aesthetic criteria can be reconstructed with the help of texts. The Panofsky professorship at the Zentralinstitut honors exceptional international art historians whose work addresses such methodological expansions and new directions of the discipline.

The historical challenge posed by the name Panofsky for Munich is quite clear. In 1967, when Panofsky was awarded the *Pour le Mérite* at the ZI, it was a deeply ambivalent event for the scholar who had been displaced from Nazi Germany.[2]

Dabei ist uns die historische Herausforderung, die gerade der Name Panofsky an München stellt, sehr bewusst: Dass und wie 1967 im ZI der Orden *Pour le Mérite* an ihn überreicht wurde, war für den aus Nazi-Deutschland Vertriebenen eine mehr als ambivalente Erfahrung.[2] Und noch Baxandall vermerkte bei aller Anerkennung für das Zentralinstitut: »Viele Leute mit Urteilsvermögen mögen München nicht.« Es bleibt zu hoffen, dass die kunsthistorischen Aktivitäten in der Stadt und die heutigen Erfahrungen am ZI einen Teil dazu beitragen, dies zu ändern.

Im Jahr 2017 spielten für unsere Einladungen Fragen des kulturellen Austauschs und des weiträumigen Zirkulierens von Ideen, Personen, Formen und Materialien eine wichtige Rolle: Gauvin Alexander Bailey, Professor and Bader Chair in Southern Baroque Art an der Queen's University in Kanada, kam als Panofsky-Professor ans ZI. Caroline Fowler, Princeton University, die zur globalen Zirkulation von Papier in der Frühen Neuzeit arbeitet, und Marlene Schneider, Universität des Saarlandes, mit einem Projekt zur Künstlermobilität im 18. Jahrhundert konnten als Panofsky Fellows eingeladen werden.

Dies war allein dank der großzügigen Förderung durch den Verein der Freunde des Zentralinstituts für Kunstgeschichte e.V. CONIVNCTA FLORESCIT möglich. Allen Beteiligten gilt unser herzlicher Dank.

Ulrich Pfisterer

1 Michael Baxandall, *Episodes. A Memorybook*, London 2010, S. 99–110.
2 Christopher S. Wood: Panofsky in Munich, 1967, in: *Modern Language Notes* 131 (2016), S. 1236–1257.

And even Baxandall, for all his appreciation for the ZI, still noted that "[m]any discerning people dislike Munich." Let us hope that the current art-historical activities in the city and at the ZI contribute to changing this.

In 2017, questions of cultural exchange and of the far-reaching circulation of ideas, people, forms, and materials played an important role in the invitations. Gauvin Alexander Bailey, Professor and Bader Chair in Southern Baroque Art at Queen's University in Canada, came to the ZI as Panofsky Professor. Invited as fellows were Caroline Fowler of Princeton University, who works on the global circulation of paper in the Early Modern period, and Marlene Schneider of the University of Saarland, with a project on the mobility of artists in the 18th century.

This was only possible thanks to the generous support of the CONIVNCTA FLORESCIT, the Society for the Friends of the Zentralinstitut für Kunstgeschichte. Our sincerest thanks is due to all of the participants.

Ulrich Pfisterer

1   Michael Baxandall, *Episodes. A Memorybook*, London 2010, pp. 99–110.

2   Christopher S. Wood: Panofsky in Munich, 1967, in: *Modern Language Notes* 131 (2016), pp. 1236–1257.

Karl Ritter, Palast von Sans
Souci, *Naturhistorische Reise
nach der westindischen Insel
Hayti* (Stuttgart, 1836).
Bayerische Staatsbibliothek,
It.sing. 883 m

Karl Ritter, Palace of Sans
Souci, *Naturhistorische Reise
nach der westindischen Insel
Hayti* (Stuttgart, 1836).
Bayerische Staatsbibliothek,
It.sing. 883 m

Gauvin Alexander Bailey

Der Palast von Sans-Souci in Milot, Haiti (ca. 1806–1813)
Das vergessene Potsdam im Regenwald

Et quel château ! Un château des mille et une nuits !
[Aimé Césaire, *La tragédie du Roi Christophe* 3. Akt, 1. Szene][1]

Was aber Ti Noël am meisten überraschte, war die Entdeckung, dass diese fabelhafte Welt, dergleichen die französischen Gouverneure des Kaps niemals gekannt hatten, eine Welt der Neger war.
[Alejo Carpentier, *Das Reich von dieser Welt*, Teil III, Buch 2][2]

Der opulente barocke Palast von Sans-Souci (ca. 1806–13), den König Henry I. Christophe von Haiti als Teil eines Residenz-Komplexes auf beinahe acht Hektar Land hatte errichten lassen, ist eines der spektakulärsten Gebäude seiner Zeit in der westlichen Hemisphäre – und zugleich eines der wissenschaftlich am schlechtesten bearbeiteten [Abb. 1, 14, 15]. Nachdem der Palast 1842 von einem Erdbeben beschädigt worden war, ragen heute nur mehr Ruinen aus Ziegeln und Steinen hoch auf – und dominieren gleichwohl immer noch das bescheidene Städtchen Milot, einstmals eine koloniale Plantage 45 Auto-Minuten von der Hafenstadt Cap-Haïtien entfernt. Der Palast liegt am Fuße des 969 m hohen Berges Laferrière, der von der atemberaubenden Citadelle Laferrière (1804–20) bekrönt wird. Diese ›Wolkenburg‹ ist von Milot aus

Gauvin Alexander Bailey

The Palace of Sans-Souci in Milot, Haiti (ca. 1806–1813)
The Untold Story of the Potsdam of the Rainforest

Et quel château ! Un château des mille et une nuits !
[Aimé Césaire, *La tragédie du Roi Christophe* Act III, scene 1][1]

But what surprised Ti Noël most was the discovery
that this marvellous world, the like of which the
French governors of the Cap had never known,
was a world of Negroes.
[Alejo Carpentier, *The Kingdom of this World*, Part III, book 2][2]

King Henry I Christophe of Haiti's opulent Baroque Palace of Sans-Souci (ca. 1806–13), part of a complex occupying nearly eight hectares of land, is one of the most spectacular yet least-studied buildings of its era in the Western Hemisphere [Figs 1, 14, 15]. Its towering brick and stone ruins, damaged by an 1842 earthquake, still dominate the modest agricultural town of Milot (a 45-minute drive from Cap-Haïtien), once a colonial plantation. The palace also sits at the foot of the 969-metre high Laferrière Peak, surmounted by the staggering Citadelle Laferrière (1804–20), a castle in the clouds invisible from Milot but built during the same campaign and probably by many of the same people [Figs. 2, 10]. Begun the same year as Haitian independence (1804) by a man who would become America's first black king (r. 1811–20) the Ci-

Abb. 1 Henry Christophe, Joseph (?) Faraud, Joseph-Antoine Dardan und anderen zugeschrieben: Palast von Sans-Souci, Milot, Haiti (ca. 1806–1813)
Fig. 1 Attributed to Henry Christophe, Joseph (?) Faraud, Joseph-Antoine Dardan, and others: Palace of Sans-Souci, Milot, Haiti (ca. 1806–1813)

nicht sichtbar, wurde aber vermutlich während derselben Kampagne und überwiegend von denselben Arbeitern errichtet [Abb. 2, 10]. Im Jahr der Unabhängigkeit Haitis (1804) von einem Mann begonnen, der der erste schwarze König Amerikas (reg. 1811–20) werden sollte, wurden die Citadelle und Sans-Souci gemeinsam gebaut, um zu demonstrieren, dass Haiti sich in einer feindseligen Welt aus Monarchien und Reichen behaupten konnte.

Obwohl der Palast von Sans-Souci eine Hauptattraktion während der touristischen Glanzzeit Haitis in den 1940er und 50er Jahren war und seit 1982 zum UNESCO-Welterbe gehört, war er nie Gegenstand einer wissenschaftlichen Einzelstudie und es ranken sich viele Mythen und Spekulationen um dieses Bauwerk, dessen Wurzeln bis ins frühe 19. Jahrhun-

Abb. 2 Henry Christophe, Joseph (?) Faraud und anderen zugeschrieben: Citadelle Laferrière, Haiti (1804–1820)

Fig. 2 Attributed to Henry Christophe, Joseph (?) Faraud, and others: Citadelle Laferrière, Haiti (1804–1820)

tadelle, like Sans-Souci, was built to demonstrate Haiti's capacity to confront a hostile world in which most nations were still monarchies or empires. Although a major attraction during Haiti's tourism heyday in the 1940s–50s and a UNESCO World Heritage Site since 1982, the Palace of Sans-Souci has never been the subject of a concentrated scholarly study and it has generated a particularly fertile web of myth and speculation going back to the early nineteenth century. Its architect, builders, and prototypes, like those of the Citadelle, are particularly shrouded in mystery, a situation worsened by the absence of archival documents directly related to the palace's construction. In fact hard facts about the architectural patronage of Roi Christophe, as he is popularly known in Haiti today, are thin on the ground and even its earliest visitors

dert zurückreichen. Seine Architekten, Erbauer und Prototypen sind – ähnlich wie diejenigen der Citadelle – geheim-
nisumwoben und dieser Umstand lässt sich mangels Archiv-
materialen zum Bau des Palastes auch nur schwer beheben.
In der Tat sind belastbare Fakten zu den Architektur-Aufträ-
gen von Roi Christophe, wie er heute in Haiti volkstümlich
genannt wird, rar. Und selbst noch in jüngster Zeit bekam
man beim Besuch der Stätte anstelle von glaubwürdigen In-
formationen eine starke Dosis der berühmten haitianischen
Gerüchteküche *teledyòl* verabreicht: Noch 1923 nannte die
New York Times den Palast ein »Voodoo-Schloss« und begründete seine architektonischen Wunder mit »Schwarzer
Magie«, ungeachtet der Tatsache, dass König Henry ein from-
mer Katholik war und Anhänger der Vodun-Religion verfol-
gen ließ.[3] Die Assoziation mit dem Übernatürlichen war tatsächlich so gegenwärtig, dass die Citadelle und Sans-Souci
den kubanischen Schriftsteller Alejo Carpentier 1949 dazu in-
spirierten, die Idee des *real maravilloso* zu entwickeln: eine der
Grundlagen des Magischen Realismus. Die Gebäude sind
durch Autoren wie Carpentier und Derek Walcott in den
1940ern, Aimé Cesaire in den 1960ern und Edwidge Danticat
in den 1990ern zu einem bedeutenden Motiv der karibischen
und lateinamerikanischen Literatur geworden. Sie sind
zudem ein wiederkehrendes Thema in der haitianischen und
afroamerikanischen Malerei von den 1930ern bis in die Ge-
genwart und wurden von Künstlern wie William Edouard
Scott und Sénèque Obin aufgegriffen.[4]

Und doch sind die Mythen, die den Palast und die Citadelle
umranken, nicht ohne Wert, zeugen die diversen *Oral Histories* doch von der anhaltenden Bedeutung und globalen Reich-
weite dieses Komplexes. Sie evozieren zugleich ein interna-
tionales Netzwerk historisch bedeutender Gestalten, darunter
Napoleon und Ludwig XVIII. von Frankreich, Friedrich der
Große von Preußen, Zar Alexander I. von Russland, Georg III.

were treated to a heavy dose of Haiti's famed *teledyòl* or rumour mill. As recently as 1923 the staid *New York Times* called it a "Voodoo Castle" and attributed its architectural marvels to "black magic," ignoring the fact that King Henry was a devout Catholic and persecuted Vodun.[3] Indeed their associations with the supernatural were so pervasive that the Citadelle and Sans-Souci inspired Cuban writer Alejo Carpentier in 1949 to develop the idea of *lo real maravilloso*, a foundation of Magic Realism, and the buildings have become a major motif in Caribbean and Latin American literature from writers such as Carpentier and Derek Walcott in the 1940s to Aimé Cesaire in the 1960s and Edwidge Danticat in the 1990s. They are also a recurrent subject in Haitian and African-American painting from the 1930s to the present day by the likes of William Edouard Scott and Sénèque Obin.[4]

Yet the mythmaking is not without value: these oral histories testify to the enduring importance and global reach of this complex and they evoke an international cast of characters including Napoleon and Louis XVIII of France, Frederick the Great of Prussia, Tsar Alexander I of Russia, George III of England, revolutionary leader Jean-Jacques Dessalines, naturalist Joseph Banks, portraitist Richard Evans (assistant to Sir Thomas Lawrence), and British abolitionists Thomas Clarkson and William Wilberforce, not to mention anonymous groups ranging from ex-slave labourers, German mercenaries, renegade French officers, British merchants and spies, and Dahomeyan warriors. These stories locate Sans-Souci and the Citadelle at the crossroads of Empire, which is precisely where they stood: although little-known outside Haiti today the Citadelle and Sans-Souci were among the most visited and talked-about buildings in the Western Hemisphere when they were first opened to foreigners in the decades following Henry's death in 1820, fascinating and horrifying visitors in equal measure. Indeed, although they are rarely recognised as such

von England, den Revolutionsführer Jean-Jacques Dessalines, den Naturforscher Joseph Banks, den Porträtisten Richard Evans (Assistent von Sir Thomas Lawrence), und die britischen Abolitionisten Thomas Clarkson und William Wilberforce – ganz abgesehen von anonymen Gruppen, zu denen ehemalige Arbeitssklaven, deutsche Söldner, abtrünnige französische Offiziere, britische Händler und Spione und dahomeyische Krieger zählen. Diese Geschichten verorten Sans-Souci und die Citadelle an der Wegscheide von Weltreichen und genau dort müssen diese Gebäude auch lokalisiert werden: Obwohl heute außerhalb Haitis kaum bekannt, gehörten die Citadelle und Sans-Souci seit ihrer Öffnung für Ausländer in den Jahrzehnten nach Henrys Tod im Jahre 1820 zu den meistbesuchten und -erwähnten Gebäuden in der westlichen Hemisphäre. Für ihre Besucher waren sie zugleich Objekte der Faszination und des Schreckens. Tatsächlich stellen Sans-Souci und die Citadelle – auch wenn selten als solches anerkannt – das erste große Bauprojekt im unabhängigen Lateinamerika dar. Realisiert wurde es Jahrzehnte bevor etwas Vergleichbares in den spanisch- oder portugiesisch-sprachigen Gebieten Amerikas errichtet wurde, die ihre Unabhängigkeit zum Großteil etwa zwischen 1810 und 1822 erlangten. Es datiert auch deutlich früher als viele der berühmten öffentlichen Monumente der ersten unabhängigen amerikanischen Nation, von Thomas Jeffersons Universität von Virginia (1817–28) und Benjamin Latrobes Kathedrale von Baltimore (1821 vollendet) bis zum ursprünglichen US-Kapitol in Washington (1793–1826).[5]

Einer der Gründe für die Folklore, die Sans-Souci umgibt, ist ihr Bauherr König Henry (nach englischer Art mit »y« geschrieben), der selbst in einer Ära, der es nicht an überdimensionierten Egos mangelte, eine Ausnahmeerscheinung darstellte [Abb. 3]. Sein Leben und sein Aufstieg ›vom Tellerwäscher zum Millionär‹ eignen sich hervorragend als Stoff

Abb. 3 Richard Evans, Porträt Henry Christophes. Öl auf Leinwand,
ca. 1814. Josefina del Toro Fulladosa Collection, Alfred Nemours Collection,
University of Puerto Rico, Río Piedras Campus
Fig. 3 Richard Evans, Portrait of Henry Christophe. Oil on canvas, ca. 1814.
Josefina del Toro Fulladosa Collection, Alfred Nemours Collection,
University of Puerto Rico, Río Piedras Campus

Sans-Souci and the Citadelle comprise the first major building project of Independent Latin America—decades before
anything comparable was built in Spanish and Portuguese-

für Erzählungen – es verwundert also nicht, dass sich ihn bislang so viele Schriftsteller zu eigen machten.[6] 1767 als Sohn versklavter oder befreiter schwarzer Eltern auf der englischen Insel Granada zur Welt gekommen, wurde Henry Christophe – so sein Geburtsname – als Kabinenjunge auf einem französischen Marineschiff angeworben und auf Saint-Domingue abgesetzt, wie Haiti während der Kolonialzeit hieß. Dort wurde er von einem Zuckerplantagenbesitzer gemischter Abstammung mit Namen Badèche als Stallbursche und Küchengehilfe angestellt, bevor er von Admiral *comte* d'Estaing eingezogen wurde, um an der französischen Expedition nach Savannah (1778–79) im amerikanischen Unabhängigkeitskrieg teilzunehmen.[7] Nach seiner Rückkehr arbeitete er als Koch und schließlich als *maître d'hôtel* einer Herberge mit dem verheißungsvollen Namen *Auberge de la Couronne* in Cap-François (Cap-Haïtien), deren Mitinhaber sein Dienstherr war. Beim Ausbruch der Französischen Revolution schrieb er sich in die koloniale Artillerie ein und heiratete 1793 Marie-Louise Coidavid, die Tochter seines alten Arbeitgebers und seine zukünftige Königin. Zwar wird in den meisten Geschichten behauptet, Christophe sei ein Sklave gewesen, jedoch ist es wahrscheinlicher, dass er rechtlich ein freier Schwarzer war, dessen frühe Arbeitsjahre einer Art Indentur gleichkamen. Als Revolutionär diente Henry als einer der hochrangigsten Generäle unter Toussaint Louverture. Nachdem dieser 1802 nach Frankreich deportiert wurde, schloss er sich dem General (und späteren Kaiser) Dessalines an, um der französischen Armee am 18. November 1803 eine schwere Niederlage zu bereiten. Nach Dessalines Ermordung durch einen Hinterhalt im Jahre 1806 wurde die junge Nation zweigeteilt: Die südliche Hälfte (der Großteil der kolonialzeitlichen westlichen und südlichen Distrikte) wurde zur Republik unter dem Rivalen General Alexandre Pétion (1770–1818) mit Sitz in Port-au-Prince, während der ehemalige nördliche

speaking America, most of which gained independence between roughly 1810 and 1822. It is also earlier than some of the most renowned public monuments of the first independent American nation, from Thomas Jefferson's University of Virginia (1817–28) and Benjamin Latrobe's Baltimore Cathedral (completed 1821) to the original US Capitol in Washington (1793–1826).[5]

One of the reasons Sans-Souci is so surrounded by folklore is that the patron, King Henry (spelt in the English manner with a "y"), was one of the most outsized personalities of an era when they were hardly thin on the ground [Fig. 3]. His rags-to-riches life story makes for particularly good copy, which is why he has attracted so many writers.[6] Born to enslaved or freed black parents on the English island of Grenada in 1767 the then Henry Christophe was enlisted as a cabin boy on a French naval vessel and discharged in Saint-Domingue, as Haiti was called in colonial times, where he was employed by a mixed-race sugar plantation owner named Badêche to work as a stable hand and apprentice cook before being conscripted by Admiral *comte* d'Estaing to take part in the French expedition to Savannah (1778–79) during the American War of Independence.[7] Upon his return he worked as a cook and eventually *maître d'hôtel* of the auspiciously-named Auberge de la Couronne in Cap-François (Cap-Haïtien), of which his master was a co-owner. With the outbreak of the French Revolution he enlisted in the colonial artillery and in 1793 he married Marie-Louise Coidavid, the daughter of his old employer and his future queen. Although most histories claim that Christophe was a slave, it is more likely that he was legally a free person of colour, although his early years of employment amounted to little more than indentured servitude. As a revolutionary Henry served as one of the top generals under Toussaint Louverture and after that leader was deported to France in 1802 he joined General (and later Emperor)

Distrikt unter die Diktatur Henrys (seit 1807 Präsident auf Lebenszeit) geriet, bis dieser am 28. März 1811 das Königreich ausrief. Seine Selbstkrönung im Stile Napoleons fand am 2. Juni in einer eigens dafür errichteten Kathedrale auf dem Champs de Mars in Cap-Haïtien statt, dem ehemaligen Cap-François, das er in Cap-Henry umbenannte.[8]

Im Verlauf der folgenden neun Jahre stellte Henry die Citadelle und den Palast von Sans-Souci fertig. Außerdem schuf er eine Konstellation von Edelmännern – vier Prinzen, sieben Herzöge, 22 Grafen, 36 Barone, und 14 *chevaliers* – sowie eine kirchliche Hierarchie, angeführt von Toussaints bevorzugtem Geistlichen, dem französischen Priester Corneille Brelle, nun Grand Almoner des Königs und Erzbischof von Haiti. Zugleich begründete er eine rigorose Hofkultur, inspiriert von denjenigen Ludwigs XIV. und Napoleons, samt einer verwirrenden Anzahl von Livreen und Kostümen, die vor Goldstickereien, Epauletten und hoch aufragenden Federbüschen strotzten, sowie Kronjuwelen, Medaillen, Münzen und ein ausgefeiltes Zeremonialsystem.[9] 1811 gab er ein aufwendiges Wappenbuch für den Adel (das *Armorial Général du Royaume d'Hayti*) in Auftrag, mit 91 einzigartigen Wappen für sich selbst und seine neue Aristokratie [Abb. 4].[10] Henry verstand genau, was Ludwig XIV. und sein Minister Colbert 150 Jahre zuvor gemeint hatten, als sie die sogenannte *gloire* des Reiches mit Hofritualen, Architektur und Luxusobjekten förderten.[11] König Henrys Gebäude, Kostüme, und sonstige Ausstaffierungen wurden zwar von zeitgenössischen Kommentatoren als geschmacklos und amateurhaft verspottet – weiße Autoren waren darauf aus, ihn als Narr darzustellen und haitianische Republikaner hielten seinen Hof für rückständig und despotisch – tatsächlich trifft auf sie jedoch das genaue Gegenteil zu. So bemerkt Clive Cheesman hinsichtlich des *Armorial Général*, dass »der Eindruck einer des Wissens und der sorgfältigen Abwägung [sei]« und Frédérick Mangones

Baron de Faraud

Abb. 4 Wappen von Joseph (?), baron de Faraud, aus dem Armorial Général du Royaume d'Hayti (1812; 1814): 62. London, Royal College of Arms, Ms JP 177

Fig. 4 Arms of Joseph (?), baron de Faraud, from the Armorial Général du Royaume d'Hayti (1812; 1814): 62. London, Royal College of Arms, Ms JP 177

Dessalines decisively to defeat the French army at the Battle of Vertières on 18 November 1803. After Dessalines' murder in an ambush in 1806 the new nation split in half, its southern part (most of the colonial Western and Southern Districts) a republic under rival General Alexandre Pétion (1770–1818) based in Port-au-Prince and the former Northern District under Henry's dictatorship (as President for Life from 1807) until, on 28 March 1811, he declared it a kingdom. His self-

traf eine ähnliche Aussage zu Henrys Architektur: »Der König umgibt sich immer mit qualifizierten Experten und besteht immer auf Vortrefflichkeit in allen Dingen«.[12] Als Werke der Architektur sind die Citadelle und Sans-Souci Gebäude allerersten Ranges, anspruchsvoller als alles, was die Franzosen jemals im Atlantikraum bauten.

Henry war davon überzeugt, dass nur ein Königreich mit entsprechender *gloire* Haiti im Ansehen der Welt heben könne, und forderte damit Pétions bescheidenere Republik direkt heraus.[13] Mittels der Insignien der europäischen Zivilisation erhoffte sich Henry die Widerlegung der vorherrschenden Annahme, Ex-Sklaven seien nur der »Barbarei und Ignoranz gegenüber der europäischen Kunst der Vernunft« fähig, wie Doris Garraway es formulierte.[14] Berüchtigt ist seine Selbstbetitelung als »Henry, von Gottes Gnaden und dem Konstitutionellen Gesetz des Staates, König von Haiti, Souverän von Tortuga, Gonâve und anderen benachbarten Inseln, Zerstörer der Tyrannei, Erneuerer und Wohltäter der Haitianischen Nation, Erschaffer ihrer Moralischen, Politischen und Militärischen Institutionen, Erstgekrönter Monarch der Neuen Welt, Verteidiger des Glaubens, und Gründer des Königlichen und Militärischen Ordens von Saint-Henry«.[15] Letzteren schuf er nach dem Vorbild des französischen Ordens von Saint-Esprit, ausgestattet mit einem brillantenverzierten Kreuz, darauf sein Gesicht und das Motto »*Je renais de mes cendres*«, eine Erinnerung an Christophes berüchtigtste Widerstandshandlung gegen Napoleon, die Inbrandsetzung von Cap-François im Jahre 1802.[16] Er engagierte Evans zwischen ca. 1814 und ca. 1817 – einerseits für Porträts von sich selbst und seiner Familie, die Henry in Abgrenzung zu seinen Höflingen und in Anlehnung an Georg III. in schlichter English-Regency-Kleidung zeigen [Abb. 3], und andererseits um ihn in seiner neugegründeten *Académie de dessin et de peinture* zu beschäftigen (inspiriert von

coronation, Napoleon style, took place on 2 June in a purpose built cathedral on the Champs de Mars in Cap-Haïtien, the former Cap-François, which he renamed Cap-Henry.[8]

Over the next nine years Henry would complete the Citadelle and the Palace of Sans-Souci and he would also create a constellation of nobles—four princes, seven dukes, 22 counts, 36 barons, and 14 *chevaliers*—and an ecclesiastical hierarchy led by Toussaint's favourite cleric, the French priest Corneille Brelle, now Grand Almoner to the King and Archbishop of Haiti. Likewise he would establish a rigorous court culture inspired by those of Louis XIV and Napoleon alike, complete with a bewildering array of liveries and costumes bristling with gold embroidery, epaulets, and lofty feather plumes, as well as crown jewels, medals, and coins and an elaborate system of ceremonial.[9] In 1811 he commissioned a lavish armorial for the nobility (the *Armorial Général du Royaume d'Hayti*) with 91 unique heraldic shields for himself and his new aristocracy [Fig. 4].[10] Henry perfectly understood what Louis XIV and his minister Colbert had meant 150 years earlier when they promoted what they termed as the *gloire* of their realm though court ritual, architecture, and luxury goods.[11] Although commentators tended to scoff at King Henry's buildings, costumes, and other accoutrements as being tawdry and amateurish—white writers were only too keen to depict him as a buffoon and Haitian republicans considered his court to be retrograde and despotic—they are fascinating precisely because they are not. As Clive Cheesman remarks about the *Armorial Général*, "the impression is rather one of knowledgeable and careful deliberation," and Frédérick Mangones made a similar point about his architecture: "the king always surrounded himself with qualified experts and always insisted on excellence in all matters."[12] As architecture the Citadelle and Sans-Souci are world-class, more sophisticated than anything the French ever built in the Atlantic.

der französischen *Académie de peinture et de sculpture*, 1648).[17] Da er eingeborenen haitianischen Soldaten misstraute, nahm Henry Sklavenhändler unter Vertrag, die eine 4000-Mann starke, farbenprächtige afrikanische Gendarmerie aus Dahomey einschifften: die *Royals-Dahomets*, welche fortan als persönliche Leibwache, innerstaatliche Polizei und Geheimdienst dienten. Mitglieder der Elite der Truppe wurden als *Royals-Bonbons* bezeichnet – sehr zur Belustigung der Gegner Haitis.[18]

Obwohl er ein Tyrann war, bemühte sich König Henry ernsthaft um die Reformierung seines Landes. Wie Napoleon erließ er ein ganzes Ensemble ziviler, landwirtschaftlicher und kommerzieller Gesetze, insbesondere den sogenannten *Code Henry* (1812), unterstützt von einem souveränen Gerichtshof und zehn Bezirksgerichten, und den *Code Rural*, dessen Rechtsprechung sich auf die landwirtschaftliche Produktion erstreckte (ehemalige Sklaven arbeiteten weiterhin auf den Plantagen, erhielten jedoch ein Viertel ihrer Ernte als Sold). Joseph Banks (1743–1820), Präsident der Royal Society und Botaniker auf Kapitän Cooks erster Reise, erachtete den *Code Rural* als »würdig, in goldenen Lettern geschrieben zu werden; nichts, was ich jemals gesehen habe, das für denselben Zweck von weißen Männern geschrieben wurde, ist es wert, damit verglichen zu werden«.[19] König Henry baute zudem Krankenhäuser und ermöglichte seinem Volk ein kostenloses Gesundheitswesen. Er legte Wert auf Bildung und gründete zahlreiche nationale Schulen, königliche Akademien und berufliche sowie militärische Hochschulen, von denen manche mit englischen Lehrern ausgestattet waren, die Wilberforce und Clarkson organisiert hatten (wie etwa Pastor William Morton). Sein Ziel war es, eine professionelle und handwerkliche Klasse auf Haiti aufzubauen.[20] Henry half auch dabei, seine am Boden zerstörte Nation vor dem finanziellen Ruin zu bewahren, indem er haitianische Produkte wie

Henry was convinced that only a kingdom with its atten-
dant *gloire* could raise Haiti in the world's estimation, a direct
challenge to Pétion's more modest republic.[13] Through the
trappings of European civilisation Henry hoped to counter
the predominant presumption that ex-slaves were capable
only of "savagery and ignorance of the European arts of reason," as Doris Garraway put it.[14] He notoriously styled himself
"Henry, by the Grace of God and the Constitutional Law of
the State, King of Haiti, Sovereign of Tortuga, Gonâve and
other adjacent Islands, Destroyer of Tyranny, Regenerator and
Benefactor of the Haitian Nation, Creator of her Moral, Po-
litical and Martial Institutions, First Crowned Monarch of
the New World, Defender of the Faith, and Founder of the
Royal and Military Order of Saint-Henry."[15] He created the
Order of Saint-Henri on the model of the French Order of
Saint-Esprit featuring a cross encrusted with brilliants bearing his face and the motto "*Je renais de mes cendres,*" a reminder
of Christophe's most infamous act of defiance against Napoleon when he set Cap-François ablaze in 1802.[16] He hired
Evans between ca. 1814 and ca. 1817 to paint portraits of himself and his family—Evans' portraits demonstrate that unlike
his courtiers Henry dressed in plain English Regency costume
in imitation of George III [Fig. 3]—and to staff his newly-
founded *Académie de dessin et de peinture* (inspired by the
French *Académie de peinture et de sculpture*, 1648).[17] Distrusting
Haitian-born soldiers, Henry contracted with slave traders to
bring in a 4,000-strong, colourfully-garbed African gendarmerie from Dahomey called the *Royals-Dahomets* to serve as his
personal bodyguard, internal police force, and spy service, the
most elite of which were called the *Royals-Bonbons*—much to
the amusement of Haiti's enemies.[18]

Although a tyrant King Henry was also seriously committed to reforming his country. Like Napoleon he promulgated
a whole ensemble of civil, maritime, rural, and commercial

Kaffee und Mahagoni förderte und einen robusten Handel mit England und den USA anregte, weniger als ein Jahrzehnt nach der Revolution. Bereits 1811 exportierte England Waren im Wert von £ 1.200.000 in das Königreich, darunter die Einrichtungsgegenstände für Henrys Bauten.[21] Earl Griggs und Clifford Prater notierten, dass »[a]nstelle des spektakulären und primitiven Despoten, als der er so oft in Büchern über ihn dargestellt wird, Christophe ein weiser und weitsichtiger Monarch [war], der sich dem Wohl seiner Bevölkerung widmete«.[22] Alexander I. von Russland, mit dem Henry korrespondierte, war einer der wenigen Herrscher der Zeit, die die fortschrittliche Seite von Henrys Regime erkannten. So merkte er an, dass es »höchst überraschend und wahrhaft erfreulich war zu sehen, wie er es [sein Reich] inmitten von Unwissenheit und Finsternis auf den Säulen der Bildung unter christlichen Auspizien gründete« und dass er hoffe, »ein neues Imperium« zu erblicken, »das den Weißen hinsichtlich allem, was Groß und Gut war, gleichkomme«.[23]

Die Architektur von Cap-François vor der Unabhängigkeit

Der Palast von Sans-Souci und die Citadelle Laferrière werden häufig mit fantastischen Begriffen versehen, als Gebäude, die auf unwahrscheinliche Weise im Dschungel eines exotischen schwarzen Königreiches ohne jegliche Kultur oder Infrastruktur auftauchten. Diese Sichtweise war ein Nebenprodukt des Rassismus der ersten europäischen und nordamerikanischen Besucher, die nicht selten versuchten, einen Beweis für die Unfähigkeit der Schwarzen zur Selbstregierung zu erbringen – Henrys Königstitel wurde oft in Anführungszeichen gesetzt, so als wäre er eine Figur in einem Maskenspiel –, und die seine Projekte, inklusive der architektonischen, als kindisch und vulgär abtaten.[24] Aber diese Monu-

laws, notably the so-called *Code Henry* (1812) supported by a sovereign court of justice and 10 district courts and the *Code Rural*, with jurisdiction over agricultural production (ex-slaves still worked the plantations but in exchange for a quarter of their harvest as payment). Joseph Banks (1743–1820), president of the Royal Society and botanist on Captain Cook's first voyage, deemed that it was "worthy to be written in letters of gold; nothing that I have ever seen which was written for the same purposes by white men is worthy to be compared to it."[19] King Henry also built hospitals and offered free healthcare to his people and placed special importance on education, founding numerous national schools, royal academies, and royal colleges, both professional and military, some staffed by British teachers organised by Wilberforce and Clarkson (such as the Reverend William Morton) with the goal of creating a Haitian professional and artisanal class.[20] Henry also helped rescue his shattered nation from financial ruin, promoting Haitian products such as coffee and mahogany and encouraging a robust trade with Britain and the United States less than a decade after the Revolution: already in 1811 Britain exported £1,200,000 worth of goods to the kingdom, including furnishings for Henry's buildings.[21] As Earl Griggs and Clifford Prater noted "[i]nstead of the spectacular and savage despot so often found in books dealing with him, Christophe [was] a wise and farsighted monarch dedicated to the welfare of his people."[22] Alexander I of Russia, with whom Henry corresponded, was one of the few world leaders of that time to recognise the progressive side of the King's regime, remarking that "to see him, in the midst of ignorance and darkness, founding it on the pillars of education under Christian auspices was more surprising and truly delightful" and that he hoped to see "a new Empire rivalling the whites in all that was great and good."[23]

Abb. 5 René-Gabriel Rabié, Fassade, Pfarrkirche von Notre-Dame-de-l'Assomption, Cap-François (heute Cap-Haitien), 1771–1774. Aus Moreau de Saint-Mery, *Recueil*, 1791, Tafel 6. Bibliothèque Nationale de France. CP 149, 4, 23

Fig. 5 René-Gabriel Rabié, Façade, Parish church of Notre-Dame-de-l'Assomption, Cap-François (now Cap-Haitien), 1771–1774. From Moreau de Saint-Mery, *Recueil*, 1791, pl. 6. Bibliothèque Nationale de France. CP 149, 4, 23

mente entstanden keineswegs aus einem Vakuum heraus: Tatsächlich hatte es auf Saint-Domingue seit über 70 Jahren eine blühende Architekturtradition gegeben, begründet von weißen, schwarzen sowie Baumeistern gemischter Abstammung. Gegen Ende des achtzehnten Jahrhunderts war Saint-Domingue die reichste Kolonie der Welt, und Cap-François (gegr. 1670; Bevölkerung um 1789: 18.500) war ihre Vorzeigestadt – ein Ort prachtvoller Steinarchitektur, eleganter Privathäuser, von importierten Ulmen gesäumter öffentlicher Plätze, weitläufiger französischer Gärten und Brunnen.[25] In der Größe vergleichbar mit Dijon oder Boston, besaß es die größte Kirche des französischen Atlantikreiches, Notre-Dame

Architecture in Cap-François before Independence

The Palace of Sans-Souci and the Citadelle Laferrière are often discussed in fantastical terms as buildings which appeared improbably in the jungle of an exotic black kingdom lacking culture or infrastructure. This perspective was a by-product of the racism of the first European and North American visitors, most of whom were committed to proving that black people were incapable of self-government—the "King" of King Henry was often put in quotation marks as if he were a figure in a masquerade—and they dismissed his projects, including architectural ones, as being childlike and vulgar.[24] But these monuments did not arise out of a vacuum: indeed a flourishing tradition of architecture had existed in Saint-Domingue for at least 70 years among white, black, and mixed-race builders alike. At the end of the eighteenth century Saint-Domingue was the world's richest colony, and Cap-François (founded 1670; population 18,500 by 1789) was its showcase city, a place of grand stone architecture, elegant private homes, public squares lined with imported elm trees, vast formal gardens, and fountains.[25] The size of Dijon or Boston it had the French Atlantic Empire's largest church, Notre-Dame de l'Assomption (1772–1774), a replica of François Mansart's Church of the Minimes in Paris [Figs. 5, 6]; the largest barracks in the French West Indies (1752–56; 1781) [Figs. 7, 8]; a grand Government House in the style of Louis XV (formerly a Jesuit residence, 1738–48); a theatre known as La Comédie (1766) boasting a full programme of performances and dances; a spacious hospital to the south of town also in the style of François Mansart (mostly 1777–82); and formal gardens with forested groves based on André Le Nôtre's at Versailles (1774).

The most ambitious project was the Place Royale (now Place Toussaint Louverture, begun 1780), a public square enclosed in uniform facades in the manner of Jules Hardouin-

de l'Assomption (1772–74, ein Nachbau von François Mansarts Kirche der Minimes in Paris) [Abb. 5, 6]; die größte Kaserne in Französisch-Westindien (1752–56; 1781) [Abb. 7, 8]; ein prächtiges Regierungsgebäude im Stil Ludwigs XV. (eine ehemalige Jesuitenresidenz, 1738–48); ein Theater, bekannt als La Comédie (1766), das sich eines vollen Programms aus Schauspiel und Tanz rühmen konnte; ein geräumiges Krankenhaus im Süden der Stadt, ebenfalls im Stil von François Mansart (hauptsächlich 1777–82); und französische Gärten mit bewaldeten Hainen, basierend auf denjenigen André Le Nôtres in Versailles (1774).

Das ehrgeizigste Projekt war allerdings der Place Royale (heute Place Toussaint Louverture, 1780 begonnen), ein öffentlicher Platz umschlossen von einheitlichen Fassaden im Stile von Jules Hardouin-Mansarts Place Louis-le-Grand in Paris (heute Place Vendôme, 1685; 1699–1708), mit einem sockelartigen Brunnen im Zentrum und drei Triumphbögen im römischen Stil, entworfen vom königlichen Ingenieur-Architekten René-Gabriel Rabié (bl. 1739–85; Letztere wurden nie fertiggestellt).[26] Der Platz wurde von seinem Kollegen, dem Ingenieur-Architekten Jean-Pierre Calon de Felcourt (bl. 1752–86) in Kollaboration mit Jean Artau (bl. 1770er – ca. 1803) geplant, einem zivilen Architekten, der eine große Werkstatt in Cap-François führte, deren Schreinersklaven die Fassaden entwarfen. Der Platz hatte dieselben Dimensionen wie der nahegelegene Place de Clugny (heute der *marché de fer*), sein südliches Ende sollten zwei neue selbststehende *îlots* (Häuserblöcke) bilden, und das Land weiter südlich mit einer schattigen Promenade aus Laubbäumen bepflanzt werden. Wie bei den *places royales* in Frankreich basierten die Fassaden auf einer klassischen, dreiteiligen Struktur aus zwei Stockwerken mit hohen rechteckigen Fenstern und Türen, Kolossalordnungspilastern, und einem dreieckigen Pediment über dem zentralen Risalit.[27] Bis heute überlebt hat nur der

Abb. 6 René Gabriel Rabié, Fassade, Pfarrkirche (heute Kathedrale) von
Notre-Dame-de-l'Assomption, Cap-Haitien, Erdgeschoss 1771–1774;
obere Abschnitte und Türme nach 1842
Fig. 6 René Gabriel Rabié, Façade, Parish church (now Cathedral) of
Notre-Dame-de-l'Assomption, Cap-Haitien, ground floor 1771–1774;
upper sections and towers after 1842

Mansart's Place Louis-le-Grand in Paris (now Place Vendôme,
1685; 1699–1708), with a plinth-like fountain at the centre and
three Roman-style triumphal arches designed by royal engineer architect René-Gabriel Rabié (fl. 1739–85; the latter were
never completed).[26] The square was planned by fellow engineer architect Jean-Pierre Calon de Felcourt (fl. 1752–86) in
collaboration with Jean Artau (fl. 1770s–ca. 1803), a civilian
architect who ran a large workshop in Cap-François staffed
with carpenter slaves, who designed the facades. The square
had the same dimensions as the nearby Place de Clugny (now
the *marché de fer*), its southern rank was to be formed of two

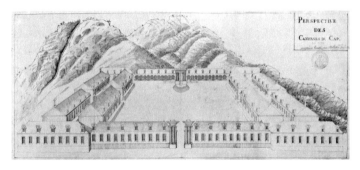

Abb. 7 René-Gabriel Rabié, Die Kaserne in Cap-François, Saint-Domingue, 1752, 1781 vergrößert (Zeichnung von 1783). Archives Nationales d'Outre-Mer, Aix-en-Provence, F3 296 E2

Fig. 7 René-Gabriel Rabié, The Barracks at Cap-François, Saint-Domingue, 1752, enlarged 1781 (drawing of 1783). Archives Nationales d'Outre-Mer, Aix-en-Provence, F3 296 E2

Brunnen mit seinen ionischen Säulen und der klassischen Urne, der aus dem Gedränge der Holzstände und Planen eines chaotischen Kleidermarkts hervorlugt [Abb. 9].[28]

Das größte öffentliche Gebäude in Cap-François, Rene-Gabriel Rabiés Große Kaserne (Grandes Casernes) hinter dem Regierungsgebäude und an den Champs de Mars angrenzend, ahmt ebenfalls den barocken Klassizismus der Metropole nach, diesmal den Innenhof von Les Invalides in Paris (1671–79) von Libéral Bruand und Hardouin-Mansart [Abb. 7, 8]. Das ursprüngliche Erscheinungsbild des Gebäudes ist in dem Originalplan und Aufriss von 1752, einer Zeichnung in Vogelperspektive von 1782, welche die Renovierungsarbeiten von 1781 durch den Architekten und Hydraulikexperten Charles-François Hesse (1748–1801) zeigt, und einem Stich, der von dem Anwalt Médéric Louis Élie Moreau de Saint-Méry in seiner gefeierten Chronik des kolonialen Saint-Domingue veröffentlicht wurde (1791), erhalten geblieben.[29] Allerdings ist es auch eines der sehr wenigen noch existierenden öffentlichen Gebäude aus der französischen Kolonialzeit:

Abb. 8 René-Gabriel Rabié, Die Kaserne, Cap-Haitien, 1752, 1781 vergrößert, im 19. Jahrhundert und 1917 restauriert. Ehemaliger Haupteingang und Kapelle im Westflügel. Heute das Hôpital Universitaire Justinien
Fig. 8 René-Gabriel Rabié, The Barracks, Cap-Haitien, 1752, enlarged 1781, restored 19th century and 1917. Former main entrance and chapel in the western wing. Now the Hôpital Universitaire Justinien

new self-standing *îlots* (city blocks), and the land further south was to be planted with a shady promenade of deciduous trees. As in *places royales* in France the facades were based on a classical tripartite structure of two storeys with high rectangular windows and doors, giant order pilasters, and a triangular pediment over the central ressaut.[27] All that survives today is the fountain with its Ionic columns and classical urn, peeking out from the crush of wooden stalls and tarpaulins of what is now a chaotic clothing market [Fig. 9].[28]

The largest public building in Cap-François, Rene-Gabriel Rabié's Great Barracks (Grandes Casernes) behind Government House and adjacent the Champs de Mars, also emulated the Baroque classicism of the metropole, this time the court-

Der Großteil des (westlichen) Hauptflügels ist intakt und wurde in das Hôpital Universitaire Justinien integriert. Die zehn ursprünglichen Blöcke der Kaserne, aus Quadermauerwerk bestehend, ermöglichten die Unterbringung von 1.624 Soldaten und 70 Offizieren, und bargen einst 80 Schlafsäle für Soldaten, 75 für Offiziere, 12 Küchen, eine Kapelle, zwei Gefängnisse und zwei Isolationszellen.[30] Moreau schrieb, dass die Große Kaserne »in den berühmtesten Städten des Königreiches als schön angesehen würde«.[31]

Die Große Kaserne nimmt direkten Bezug auf Les Invalides, besonders mit ihren mit skulptierten *trophées* beladenen Gaubenfenstern und den langen, den Hof umgebenden Pfeiler-Arkaden. Jedoch besitzt sie einen feineren Dekor, der stärker mit dem Stil Ludwigs XV. übereinstimmt, insbesondere am Eingangspavillon, der ursprünglich eine Kapelle war. Von Zwillingstreppenaufgängen aus zugänglich, umrahmte er einen monumentalen Grottenbrunnen (heute ein offener Bogen) mit halbrunden Stufen, rund 12 m hohen, eingebundenen dorischen Säulen und Pilastern, einem Gebälk mit Triglyphen und Zahnschnitt, sowie einer niedrigen Attika, die früher das Wappen Frankreichs und allegorische Flussgottheiten zeigte. Der originale Wasserhahn des Brunnens – der einstmals aus dem Mund eines *Mascaron* hervortrat – funktioniert immer noch.[32] Die ehemalige Kapelle, heute ein Vestibül, ist im Inneren mit gepaarten dorischen Pilastern und Gesimsen auf den Innenseiten der Bögen behauen. Von den Giebeln auf den flankierenden Galerien mit ihren *trophées* ist nichts erhalten, die Arkaden jedoch sind intakt geblieben. Die Kaserne überstand die Revolution, weil sie nützlich war: Stehende Heere brauchten eine Unterkunft, auch wenn die Kaserne aufgrund der Stadtbrände von 1793 und 1802 ständig repariert werden musste.[33] Der britische Besucher William Woodis Harvey, der 1827 nach Haiti reiste, bezeugte den guten Zustand der Großen Kaserne: »[Die Garnison] bei Cap

Abb. 9 Zentraler Brunnen, ehemaliger Place-Royale
(heute Place Toussaint Louverture), Cap-Haitien, 1789
Fig. 9 Central fountain, former Place-Royale
(now Place Toussaint Louverture), Cap-Haitien, 1789

yard of Les Invalides in Paris (1671–79) by Libéral Bruand and
Hardouin-Mansart [Figs 7, 8]. The building's original appearance is preserved in the original 1752 plan and elevation, a
1782 bird's-eye view drawing showing the 1781 renovations
by architect and hydraulics expert Charles-François Hesse
(1748–1801), and an engraving published by barrister Médéric

François belegte für gewöhnlich die geräumige Kaserne, die zur Zeit der Franzosen gebaut wurde, da diese eines der wenigen Gebäude war, das der Zerstörung entging, als die Stadt niederbrannte«.[34]

Vier Sorten von Architekten und Handwerkern arbeiteten in Cap-François unter den Franzosen. Die namhafteste Gruppe waren die königlichen Ingenieur-Architekten vom *corps royal du Génie*, beinahe alle geborene Franzosen, die gemäß dem rigorosen Programm des berühmtesten aller Ingenieur-Architekten, Sébastien Le Prestre, *maréchal* de Vauban (1633–1707), ausgebildet worden waren; dieses bestand aus Zeichenkunst, architektonischem Entwerfen, Steinschnitt, Perspektivlehre, Zimmererhandwerk, Ingenieurwesen und Mathematik.[35] Seit 1748 studierten Ingenieur-Architekten an der *École royale du génie de Mézières* in den Ardennen, einer offiziellen, geisteswissenschaftlichen Akademie für Ingenieur-Architekten, dem militärischen Äquivalent zur Königlichen Akademie für Architektur in Paris (1671).[36] Bücher stellten einen essentiellen Teil der Ausbildung der Ingenieur-Architekten dar: Die gängigsten waren Schriften der Antike und der Renaissance von Vitruv, Serlio, Vignola, und Palladio; Traktate aus der Ära Ludwigs XIV. von François Blondel, Augustin-Charles D'Aviler, Claude Perrault, und Pierre Bullet; sowie Bände des achtzehnten Jahrhunderts über die Stereotomie, wie Amédée François Fréziers *La théorie de la pratique de la coupe des pierres et des bois ... ou Traité de Stéréotomie* (Straßburg und Paris, 1737), einem beliebten Buch zur Vorbereitung auf die Gildenmeisterprüfung.[37] In den Kolonien waren Ingenieur-Architekten viel stärker auf Kupferstiche und gedruckte Bücher angewiesen als ihre Kollegen in Frankreich, sodass der barocke Klassizismus von Paris und Versailles dort aufblühte, lange nachdem dieser Stil in der *métropole* aus der Mode gekommen war – wie wir bereits anhand der Großen Kaserne und des Place Royale sehen konnten. Die

Louis Élie Moreau de Saint-Méry in his celebrated chronicle of colonial Saint-Domingue (1791).[29] However it is also one of the very few French colonial public buildings to survive today: most of the main (western) wing is intact and has been incorporated into the Hôpital Universitaire Justinien. Capable of accommodating 1,624 troops and 70 officers, its original ten blocks once held 80 dormitories for soldiers, 75 for officers, 12 kitchens, a chapel, two prisons, and two isolation chambers, and it was built of ashlar masonry.[30] Moreau wrote that the Great Barracks "would be considered beautiful in the most renowned cities of the kingdom."[31]

The Great Barracks directly evoked the Invalides, particularly in its dormer windows piled with sculpted *trophées* and the long arcade on piers surrounding the courtyard. However it has more delicate decorative features more in keeping with the style of Louis XV, notably in the entrance pavilion, which was originally the chapel. Accessed by twin staircases, it framed a monumental grotto fountain (now an open arch) with its own semicircular steps, 40 foot-high engaged Doric columns and pilasters, an entablature with triglyphs and a band of dentils, a low attic once containing the arms of France and allegorical river gods. The fountain's original spigot—once emerging from the mouth of a *mascaron*—is still functional.[32] The former chapel, now a vestibule, is dressed on the inside with paired Doric pilasters and mouldings on the interiors of the arches. Nothing is left of the gables on the flanking galleries with their *trophées*, but the arcades are intact. The barracks survived the Revolution because they were useful: standing armies needed somewhere to stay, even if the city's conflagrations in 1793 and 1802 meant that the barracks were constantly under repair.[33] British visitor William Woodis Harvey, who visited Haiti in 1827, attested to the good condition of the Grand Barracks: "[The garrison] at Cape François generally occupied the commodious barracks erected

zwei einflussreichsten Veröffentlichungen in den Kolonien waren Jean Mariettes dreibändige *Architecture Françoise* (1727–38) mit hunderten von Stichen von Palästen, Stadthäusern, Kirchen, Parks und öffentlichen Monumenten, und Jacques-François Blondels aktualisierte vierbändige Edition desselben Werkes (Paris, 1752–56).[38]

Die zweite Gruppe von Architekten waren weiße Baumeister, Steinmetze, Schreiner und Tischler aus dem Bereich der Zivilarchitektur. Obwohl es in Französisch-Westindien keine Gilden gab, lehrten und arbeiteten die Baumeister auf ähnliche Weise wie ihre Kollegen in der Metropole: Sie waren in Familienwerkstätten oder nichtfamiliären Partnerschaften organisiert, schickten ihre Kinder oder Sklaven in die Lehre und trugen Titel wie Meister (*maître*) oder Geselle (*compagnon*). Manche Baumeister wurden sehr reich, die reichsten von ihnen nannten sich *entrepreneurs des bâtiments*, Architekten, die große Werkstätten leiteten und Gebäude entwarfen, und manchmal für die königlichen Ingenieur-Architekten arbeiteten.[39] Im Saint-Domingue des achtzehnten Jahrhunderts waren Architekten und Handwerker oft zeitweilige Immigranten aus Frankreich, die vorübergehend auf der Insel wohnten, um schnellen Gewinn zu machen. Derart waren die fünf Architekturbildhauer, die 1766 in Cap-François eintrafen, um die vorletzte Fassade der Gemeindekirche fertig zu stellen, sowie die fünf Zimmerer namens Marsault, Marteau, Lacroix, Raimon und Rousseau, die ihre baldige Rückkehr nach Paris in den Jahren 1766, 1777 und 1784 in der lokalen Zeitung ankündigten.[40] Kürzlich konnte ich in einer Studie beinahe 40 weiße Architekten, Maurer, Schreiner, und Tischler identifizieren, die allein zwischen 1778 und 1788 in Cap-François arbeiteten.[41]

Diesen weißen Zivilisten waren freie *gens de couleur* hinsichtlich ihrer Fähigkeiten, Erfolge und Anzahl ebenbürtig, insbesondere in Cap-François und Port-au-Prince. Die freie, dun-

during the time of the French, it being one among the few buildings which escaped destruction when that town was burnt."[34]

Four kinds of architect and builder worked in Cap-François under the French. The most prestigious were the royal engineer architects from the *corps royal du Génie*, almost all of them French-born, who trained under the rigorous program of draughtsmanship, architectural design, stonecutting, perspective, carpentry, engineering, and mathematics conceived by the most famous engineer architect of all, Sébastien Le Prestre, *maréchal* de Vauban (1633–1707).[35] Since 1748 engineer architects trained in the *École royale du génie de Mézières* in the Ardennes, a formal liberal arts academy for engineer architects, the military equivalent to the Royal Academy of Architecture in Paris (1671).[36] Books constituted an essential part of the engineer architect's education: the most popular were the classical and Renaissance texts of Vitruvius, Serlio, Vignola, and Palladio; Louis XIV-era treatises by François Blondel, Augustin-Charles D'Aviler, Claude Perrault, and Pierre Bullet; and eighteenth-century volumes on stereotomy such as Amédée François Frézier's *La théorie de la pratique de la coupe des pierres et des bois...ou Traité de Stéréotomie* (Strasbourg and Paris, 1737), a popular book for preparing for guild masters' examinations.[37] In the colonies engineer architects relied much more on engravings and printed books than did their counterparts in France, resulting in a championing of the Baroque classicism of Paris and Versailles well after that style had gone out of fashion in the *métropole*—as we have just seen with the Grand Barracks and Place Royale. The two most influential publications in the colonies were Jean Mariette's three-volume *Architecture Françoise* (1727–38) with hundreds of engravings of the palaces, townhouses, churches, parks, and public monuments and Jacques-François Blondel's updated four-volume edition of the same work (Paris, 1752–56).[38]

kelhäutige Bevölkerung – sie erreichte um 1789 die Bevölkerungsgröße der Weißen – umfasste freigelassene Sklaven afrikanischer oder schwarz-kreolischer Herkunft (Erstere bekannt als *bossales*) und gemischtrassige Personen, normalerweise die Kinder oder Nachkommen weißer Sklavenbesitzer und afrikanischer Sklavinnen. Letztere wurden bezüglich der Vermischung der Ethnien obsessiv klassifiziert, als *mulâtres* (Mulatten), *méstis* (Halb-Weiß, Halb-Mulatte), *carterons* (Terzerone), und *câpres* oder *griffes* (Halb-Mulatte, Halb-Schwarz), in einer Rassentaxonomie, die auch in Hispanoamerika verbreitet war und dort sogar ein Genre der Figurenmalerei, bekannt als *pinturas de castas* (Kastenmalerei), hervorbrachte.[42] Obwohl sich ihr gesellschaftlicher Stand weit unterhalb dem der *grands blancs* (Plantagenbesitzer, Regierungsbeamte, reiche Geschäftsleute) befand, rivalisierten die freien *gens de couleur* als städtische Handwerker, Ladenbesitzer und kleine Grundeigentümer mit den *petits blancs*: Tatsächlich ging es ihnen ab den 1770er Jahren im Süden von Saint-Domingue wirtschaftlich besser als ihren weißen Nachbarn.[43] In ihrer statistischen Studie über notarielle Dokumente hat Dominique Rogers 36 Steinmetze, acht Schreiner, neun Dachdecker, 12 Tischler und drei *entrepreneurs de bâtiments* nicht-weißer Herkunft in Cap-François zwischen 1776 und 1789 identifiziert.[44] Ebenso wie Weiße besaßen sie und handelten mit Sklaven, von denen die meisten häusliche Tätigkeiten verrichteten, manche aber auch als Lehrlinge oder Spezialisten in ihren Werkstätten arbeiteten.

Einige der bedeutendsten farbigen Architekten und Baumeister waren wohlhabende, einflussreiche Mitglieder der Gesellschaft, die mittels Wohltätigkeit, Heirat und Anwaltsfunktionen ein Schutz- und Patronage-Netzwerk unterhielten. Der Tischler und »*carteron libre*« Joseph Pironneau (geb. 1748), der in den 1780ern eine von seinem Vater gegründete Familienwerkstatt führte, war in dieser Hinsicht besonders aktiv.[45] Einer seiner Nachkommen oder Verwandten, ein

The second group of architects were the white civilian architects, masons, carpenters, and joiners. Although there were no guilds in the French West Indies builders trained and ran their businesses in ways similar to those of their counterparts in the *métropole*: they organised into family workshops or non-familial partnerships, they sent their children or slaves into apprenticeship, they took on titles such as master (*maître*) and journeyman (*compagnon*), and some builders became very rich, the wealthiest calling themselves *entrepreneurs des bâtiments*, architects who ran large teams and designed buildings, sometimes working for the royal engineer architects.[39] In eighteenth-century Saint-Domingue architects and craftsmen were often temporary immigrants from France, sojourning on the island for a quick profit. Such were the five architectural sculptors who arrived in Cap-François in 1766 to finish the penultimate façade of the parish church and five carpenters named Marsault, Marteau, Lacroix, Raimon, and Rousseau, who announced their impending return to Paris in the local newspaper in 1766, 1777, and 1784.[40] In a recent study I have identified nearly 40 white architects, masons, carpenters, and joiners working in Cap-François between 1778 and 1788 alone.[41]

These white civilians were matched in skill, success, and numbers by their free *gens de couleur* counterparts, particularly in Cap-François and Port-au-Prince. Free people of colour—they equalled the whites in population by 1789—included emancipated slaves of African or black creole origin (the former known as *bossales*) and mixed-race people, usually the children or descendants of white male slave owners and African female slaves. These latter were classified obsessively by degrees of miscegenation as *mulâtres* (mulattos), *méstis* (half-white, half-mulatto), *carterons* (quadroons), and *câpres* or *griffes* (half-mulatto, half-black), in a taxonomy of race also prevalent in Hispanic America where it even inspired a genre

28-jähriger Tischler namens Julian Pironneau, lebte noch bis mindestens 1803 in Cap-François, obwohl er wie viele Menschen gemischter Abstammung bereits vor der französischen Evakuierung floh.[46] Auch der Tischler und »mulâtre libre« Jean-Pierre Pétigny spielte eine führende Rolle in seiner Gemeinde: Sein Name taucht in unzähligen sozialen und kommerziellen Zusammenhängen auf, wie zum Beispiel in den Jahren 1780 und 1782, als er die Testamente zweier freier schwarzer Frauen beglaubigte.[47] Anders als Julian Pironneau schlossen sich Mitglieder der Familie Petigny dem Regime Christophes an, und ein gewisser Célestin Pétigny wurde sogar zum Direktor von Henrys Théâtre Royal ernannt.[48] Manche Farbige machten durch Handelsbeziehungen mit Weißen ein Vermögen, wie etwa der freie schwarze Schreiner Charles Blaise, der 1785 und 1787 ein Haus und ein Büro an den französischen Händler Jean-Pons-Marc Roux und Allegret & Company vermietete. Ein weiterer bedeutender *entrepreneur* war Pierre-Guillaume Provoyeur, genannt Mirbalezia (geb. 1731), ein »mulâtre libre« aus Mirebalais, der zum Zeitpunkt seines Todes die fürstliche Summe von 70.000 *livres* wert war.[49] Provoyeur ist besser bekannt als Liebhaber von Cécile, der Frau von Toussaint Louverture (damals Toussaint, genannt Bréda).[50]

Bei der letzten Kategorie von Baumeistern – zahlenmäßig bei Weitem die größte, obwohl sie weniger häufig spezialisierte Arbeiter waren – handelte es sich um Sklaven. Diese stellten wahrscheinlich die Mehrzahl von Henry Christophes Arbeiterschaft und sind somit von besonderer Bedeutung für diese Studie. Saint-Domingue besaß eine höhere Dichte afrikanischer und eingeborener Sklaven als jede andere französische Kolonie, in einem Maßstab, der dem englischen Jamaika oder portugiesischen Brasilien gleichkam. Ihre Bevölkerung wuchs von 2.000 Individuen im Jahr 1681, zu 117.411 im Jahr 1720 bis hin zu 709.642 beim Ausbruch der Haitianischen Revolution 1791, mit bis zu 40.000 neu eingeschifften afrika-

of figure painting known as *pinturas de castas* (caste paintings).[42] Although they occupied a position in society well below that of the *grands blancs* (plantation owners, government officials, big businessmen), as urban artisans, shopkeepers, and small landowners free *gens de couleur* rivalled the *petits blancs* in status: indeed in the southern part of Saint-Domingue free people of colour were doing materially better than their white neighbours by the 1770s.[43] In her statistical study of notarised documents Dominique Rogers has identified 36 masons, eight carpenters, nine roofers, 12 joiners, and three *entrepreneurs de bâtiments* of colour in Cap-François between 1776 and 1789.[44] Like whites they owned and traded in slaves, most of them domestics but also including apprentices or specialised workers for their ateliers.

Some of the most important architects and builders of colour were rich and influential members of their community and maintained a network of patronage and protection through charitable acts, marriage, and as legal advocates. The "*carteron libre*" joiner Joseph Pironneau (b. 1748), who led a family workshop in the 1780s founded by his father, was particularly active in this regard.[45] One of his descendants or relatives, a 28-year-old joiner named Julian Pironneau, was still in Cap-François as late as 1803, although like many mixed-race people he fled before the French evacuation.[46] The "*mulâtre libre*" joiner Jean-Pierre Pétigny was also a civic leader: his name turns up in a myriad of contexts, social and commercial, as in 1780 and 1782 when he witnessed the wills of two free black women.[47] Unlike Julian Pironneau members of the Pétigny family threw in their lot with Christophe's regime, and a Célestin Pétigny was even made director of Henry's Théâtre Royal.[48] Some people of colour made their fortune trading with whites, such as the free black carpenter Charles Blaise, who let a house and an office in 1785 and 1787 to French merchant Jean-Pons-Marc Roux and Allegret & Company. An-

nischen »*captifs*« pro Jahr.[51] Im Jahr 1789 hatte die Zahl der Sklaven erstaunliche 90% der Gesamtbevölkerung erreicht. Sklaven waren die wichtigsten Arbeitskräfte bei Bauprojekten und leisteten auf vielen Ebenen ihren Beitrag. Die mühsamsten Aufgaben wie Landrodung, Bäumefällen, Steinbrechen, Lastenschleppen und schwere Bauarbeiten wurden entweder an Mannschaften vergeben, die Plantagenbesitzern und geistlichen Orden (genannt *nègres de corvée, nègres de louage* oder *nègres de journée*) unterstanden oder an Sklavenwerkstätten, die dem König gehörten und auf königlichen Plantagen untergebracht waren (*nègres du Roi*). Sklaven verrichteten aber nicht nur Arbeiten, die brachialer Kraft bedurften: Viele übten Gewerbe wie Schreiner-, Maurer-, Dachdecker-, und Tischlerhandwerk aus, meistens in Werkstätten, die Weiße oder *gens de couleur* betrieben, und oftmals Wandergewerbe waren. Plantagen unterhielten auch gelernte Sklaven, darunter Schreiner und Steinmetze: Als »*ouvrier*« oder »*nègre à talent*« kam ihnen ein besonderer Stellenwert zu, der ihnen unter anderem eigene Unterkünfte, bessere Kleidung und materielle Vorteile ermöglichte; auch wurden sie manchmal von benachbarten Plantagen für größere Bauprojekte angeheuert. Obwohl einige Werkstätten von weißen Zimmermännern geleitet wurden – wie im Falle der Royer Plantage in Belle-Rivière du Haut-Moustique in Saint-Domingue (1783), für die Vincent Suret als Hauptzimmerer arbeitete, zusammen mit seinem eigenen Sklaven, einem 20-jährigen Schreiner von der Goldküste namens l'Eveillé – wurden viele ausschließlich von Afrikanern betrieben.[52] Die in Saint-Domingue gelegene Plantage der Familie Fleuriau aus La Rochelle, Gegenstand jüngster Untersuchungen, stellte einen 50-jährigen Sklaven als »*maître mason*« an, der einen 27-jährigen Lehrling hatte und sowohl für neue Bauarbeiten als auch die Instandhaltung zuständig war, und darüber hinaus drei Schreiner, zu denen ein »*maître charpentier*« gehörte. Baumeis-

other important *entrepreneur* was Pierre-Guillaume Provoyeur *dit* Mirbalezia (born 1731), a *"mulâtre libre"* from Mirebalais who was worth the princely sum of 70,000 *livres* at his death.[49] Provoyeur is better known as the lover of Cécile, the wife of Toussaint Louverture (at the time called Toussaint *dit* Bréda).[50]

The final category of builders—by far the most numerous although they were less frequently specialised labourers—were slaves, and they probably comprised the majority of Henry Christophe's workforce so are of particular importance for this study. Saint-Domingue had the highest concentration of African or native-born slaves of any French colony, on a scale which rivalled British Jamaica or Portuguese Brazil, moving from a population of 2,000 in 1681 to 117,411 in 1720 to 709,642 at the outbreak of the Haitian Revolution in 1791, with as many as 40,000 African *"captifs"* arriving in its ports every year.[51] By 1789 slaves made up a staggering 90% of the entire population. Slaves were the principal labourers on building projects and contributed on many levels. The most punitive jobs such as land clearance, cutting down trees, quarrying rocks, carrying loads, and heavy unskilled construction labour were given to teams either commandeered from plantation owners and religious orders (called *nègres de corvée*, *nègres de louage*, or *nègres de journée*) or to slave workshops belonging to the King and housed on royal plantations (*nègres du Roi*). But slaves did not just provide brute force: many learned trades such as carpentry, masonry, roofing, and joinery, most frequently in ateliers run by whites or *gens de couleur*, often itinerant ones. Plantations also maintained skilled slaves on staff, including carpenters and masons: as an *"ouvrier"* or *"nègre à talent"* they acquired special status, including separate lodgings, better clothing, and other material advantages, and sometimes they were hired by neighbouring plantations for large building projects. Although some ateliers were overseen by a white carpenter—as in the Royer Planta-

ter-Sklaven kamen hauptsächlich aus Martinique oder Guadeloupe, einem führenden Ausbildungszentrum mit einer ungewöhnlich hohen Dichte an Baumeistern.[53]

Als Zeichen ihrer Wertschätzung erhielten die »Schreiner und Steinmetze der Plantage« auf der Fleuriau Plantage im Jahre 1780 eine Vergütung in Höhe von 24 *livres* 15 *sols* für ihre Arbeit an einem Dach.[54] Aber diese Wertschätzung hatte ihren Preis – wortwörtlich, denn Schreiner waren das vier- oder fünffache eines arbeitenden Kindes oder einer alten Person wert (jeweils zwischen 4.000 – 5.000 *livres* auf der Indigo-Plantage von Paul Belin Desmarais, und Steinmetze waren nur um ein Geringes preiswerter).[55] Plantagenbesitzer verliehen ihre Sklaven oft an andere Einwohner, beispielsweise als Georges Gregoire, *maréchal* de Balande aus Grande-Rivière, einen kongolesischen Steinmetz namens Hector (40 Jahre alt) für sechs Monate an den Cap-François-Bewohner Pierre Bardinet vermietete.[56] In Städten und Dörfern wurden Baumeister-Sklaven hausintern ausgebildet: Junge Sklaven wurden auf Kosten der Werkstätte trainiert, um die Arbeiterschaft der Werkstätte zu vergrößern oder um sie an andere Kunden zu verkaufen oder zu vermieten, und Handwerksmeister bildeten Sklaven fremder Besitzer gegen ein Honorar oder gegen unbezahlte Arbeit aus. Solche qualifizierten Arbeitskräfte waren für weiße oder *gens de couleur*-Baumeister, die ihre Geschäfte in der Stadt aufbauten, unentbehrlich, aber indem sie Sklaven mit einem Handwerk ausstatteten, ermöglichten sie diesen auch einen Lebensunterhalt, sollten sie ihre Freiheit erlangen.[57] Fast monatlich schaltete die Zeitung *Affiches Américaines* aus Saint-Domingue Anzeigen, die ausgebildete schwarze Schreiner oder Steinmetze zum Verkauf durch Plantagen oder Schreinerwerkstätten anboten, manche von ihnen erfahrene Handwerker, andere nur Lehrlinge. Gelegentlich wurden Sklaven sogar nach Frankreich geschickt, um ein »den Kolonien nützliches« Handwerk zu erlernen, allerdings blieben Baumeister

tion in Belle-Rivière du Haut-Moustique in Saint-Domingue (1783), where chief carpenter Vincent Suret worked with his own slave, a 20-year-old carpenter called l'Eveillé from the Gold Coast—many were staffed entirely by Africans.[52] The Saint-Domingue plantation of the Fleuriau family from La Rochelle, the subject of recent scholarship, employed a fifty year-old "*maître mason*" slave, who had a 27-year-old apprentice in charge of new construction and maintenance alike and kept three carpenters on staff, including a "*maître charpentier*"—slave master builders usually came from Martinique or Guadeloupe, a major training centre with an unusually high concentration of master builders.[53]

As a sign of their esteem the "carpenters and masons of the plantation" on the Fleuriau plantation were even given a gratuity of 24 *livres* 15 *sols* for their work on a roof in 1780.[54] But esteem came with a price—quite literally, as carpenters were worth four to five times as much as a working child or elderly person (between 4,000 – 5,000 *livres* each on the indigo plantation of Paul Belin Desmarais, and masons were worth only slightly less).[55] Plantation owners often rented their slaves out to other habitants, as when Georges Gregoire, *maréchal* de Balande, from Grande-Rivière let out a Congolese mason named Hector (40 years old) for six months to Pierre Bardinet, resident of Cap-François.[56] In cities and towns slave builders were apprenticed in-house: young slaves were trained at the workshop's expense to expand its own work force or to sell or rent to other clients, and master craftsmen trained slaves belonging to others for a fee or free labour. These skilled workers were essential to white or *gens de couleur* builders setting up businesses in the town but by providing a trade to slaves they also gave the latter a means to earn a living should they gain their own freedom.[57] Almost every month the Saint-Domingue newspaper *Affiches Américaines* ran advertisements offering skilled black carpenters or masons for sale from

immer eine kleine Minderheit angesichts der Kosten einer Ausbildung in Europa im Vergleich zu einer in den Kolonien.[58] Trotz alledem sollte man sich keine falschen Vorstellungen von einem ›bequemen‹ Leben der ausgebildeten Baumeister-Sklaven machen. Folglich liefen viele von ihnen einfach davon, so auch Jean-François und La Fortune (27 Jahre alt), zwei Schreiner von den Völkern der Nago und Kongo, die 1767 »mit allen Schreinerwerkzeugen« aus Cap-François flohen, oder der 55-jährige Steinmetz Spadille, ehemals von der Plantage des Monsieur Peyrac in Cul-de-Sac (Saint-Domingue), der sich 1783 den Maroons in den Bergen anschloss.[59]

Somit konnten Saint-Domingue im Allgemeinen und Cap-François im Besonderen zu Beginn der Unabhängigkeit florierende Gemeinschaften hochausgebildeter Baumeister jeder Art und Hautfarbe vorweisen. Sie alle wurden nach der Emanzipationsproklamation von Léger-Félicité Sonthonax am 29. August 1793 offiziell zu Freien.[60] Obwohl zahlreiche *gens de couleur* in den Süden oder andere französische Kolonien flohen und Dessalines den Großteil der weißen Bevölkerung von Cap-François im April 1804 abschlachten ließ – insbesondere untergetauchte französische Soldaten und ehemalige Plantagenbesitzer – verschonte er Spezialisten wie Ärzte und Priester. Und als Christophe 1806 die Macht ergriff, hieß er sowohl Weiße als auch *gens de couleur* in seiner Verwaltung willkommen und wertschätzte besonders diejenigen mit Fachberufen und kaufmännischen Beziehungen.[61] Es ist deshalb sehr wahrscheinlich, dass eine beträchtliche Anzahl gemischtrassiger Architekten und sogar einige Weiße immer noch ihr Gewerbe in Cap-François ausübten – die Tatsache, dass die Stadt so häufig wieder aufgebaut werden musste, bedeutete, dass es Baumeistern nicht an Arbeit mangelte – als Dessalines im Jahre 1804 mit dem Bau der Citadelle begann und Christophe 1806 die Arbeit an der Festung fortsetzte sowie den Sans-Souci-Komplex zu bauen begann.

plantations or carpenters' ateliers, some of them seasoned craftsmen and others mere apprentices. Occasionally slaves were even sent to France to learn a trade "useful to the colonies" however builders were always a small minority given the expense involved in sending an apprentice to Europe when he could be educated in the colonies.[58] Nevertheless we should not harbour any misconceptions that skilled slave builders lived comfortable lives. Consequently many of them simply ran away, as did Jean-François and La Fortune (27 years old), two carpenters of the Nago and Congo nations who fled Cap-François in 1767 "with all the tools of carpentry" and the 55-year old mason Spadille, formerly from the plantation of Monsieur Peyrac in Cul-de-Sac (Saint-Domingue), who joined the maroons in the mountains in 1783.[59]

Thus at the dawn of Independence Saint-Domingue in general and Cap-François in particular boasted thriving communities of highly-trained builders of every kind and of every skin colour, all of them officially freemen following the 29 August 1793 Emancipation Proclamation of Léger-Félicité Sonthonax.[60] Although many *gens de couleur* fled for the south or other French colonies and Dessalines massacred most of the white population of Cap-François in April 1804—notably French soldiers in hiding and former planters—he spared specialists such as doctors and priests and when Christophe took over in 1806 he welcomed whites and *gens de couleur* alike into his administration and also particularly esteemed those with specialty trades and mercantile connections.[61] It is therefore very likely that a significant number of mixed-race architects and even some whites were still plying their trade in Cap-François very fact that the city needed to be rebuilt so often meant that builders hardly lacked for employment—when Dessalines began construction of the Citadelle in 1804 and Christophe continued work on that fortress and began building the Sans-Souci complex in 1806.

Die Architekten und Baumeister der Citadelle und Sans-Soucis: Wahrheit und Legende

Seit der Zeit König Henrys wurden dramatisch voneinander abweichende Aussagen über die Identitäten der Architekten und Baumeister der Citadelle Laferrière, Sans-Soucis, und der Chapel Royal in Milot – heute die Kirche Unserer Lieben Frau der Unbefleckten Empfängnis [Abb. 29] – getroffen. Die Autoren setzten zudem den Baubeginn dieser Gebäude unterschiedlich an, insbesondere der Citadelle und der Kathedrale, die manche gar in die französische Ära datieren. Die Literatur ist zu solch einem Maße von diesen widersprüchlichen Darstellungen erfüllt, dass es sogar heute noch unmöglich ist, einen Konsens zu erzielen. Wenig hilfreich ist dabei die Tatsache, dass eine Vielzahl jüngster Forschungen dazu tendiert, Primärquellen aus zweiter Hand und oft ohne Quellenangabe zu zitieren, und dass seit den 1980ern nur wenig Archivforschung betrieben wurde. Vor dem Versuch einer Rekonstruktion der beteiligten Personen und einzelnen Ereignisse ist es also wichtig, die veröffentlichte Primärliteratur zu überprüfen und die Quellen ihrer Behauptungen ausfindig zu machen.

Über die Citadelle ist mehr geschrieben worden als über die anderen Gebäude. Als größtes Fort in der westlichen Hemisphäre beansprucht dieser gigantische Stein- und Ziegelbau, der in mehreren Phasen direkt auf den Fels gebaut wurde, ungefähr 15.000 Quadratmeter. Er konnte 3.000 Soldaten behausen – 5.000 im Falle einer Belagerung – und einen Jahresbedarf an Vorräten speichern [Abb. 2, 10].[62] In waghalsiger Lage errichtet, verbindet er gekrümmte und geradlinige Mauern miteinander, die um einen zentralen Innenhof angeordnet sind. Die Citadelle enthielt sechs Batterien, 365 Öffnungen für Kanonen, einen Gouverneurspalast, Offiziersschlafzimmer, Soldatenschlafsäle, Versammlungsräume, ein

The Architects and Builders of the Citadelle and Sans-Souci: Fact and Fiction

Since King Henry's day people have made dramatically disparate claims about the identities of the architects and builders of the Citadelle Laferrière, Sans-Souci, and the Chapel Royal—now the church of Our Lady of the Immaculate Conception [Fig. 29]—at Milot. Writers also disagree about when these buildings were begun, especially the Citadelle and Cathedral, both of which some have even traced back to the French era. These conflicting accounts have so plagued the literature that even today it is impossible to arrive at a basic consensus. It does not help that much of the more recent scholarship tends to quote primary accounts second-hand, often without providing their sources, and that little archival research has been undertaken since the 1980s. Before attempting a reconstruction of these people and events it is important to review the published primary literature and discover the source of these allegations.

More has been written about the Citadel. The largest fort in the Western Hemisphere, this gargantuan stone and brick structure, built in several phases directly onto the rock, occupies about 15,000 square metres and was capable of lodging 3,000 soldiers—5,000 in case of siege—as well as providing enough storage for a year's supply of provisions [Figs. 2, 10].[62] Dramatically sited and combining curving and rectilinear walls around a central courtyard it included six batteries, 365 openings for cannon, a governor's palace, bedrooms for officers, dormitories for soldiers, meeting rooms, a hospital, a billiards hall, a powder magazine, a munitions depot, prisons, and isolation chambers. The walls are between five and seven metres thick and average 45 meters in height and the roof was ingeniously designed to capture rainwater for storage in cisterns. The Citadelle combined the bastioned fortification tra-

Krankenhaus, eine Billardhalle, ein Pulvermagazin, ein Munitionsdepot, Gefängnisse und Isolationskammern. Ihre Mauern sind zwischen 5–7 m dick und im Durchschnitt 45 m hoch, und das Dach war auf geniale Weise konzipiert, um Regenwasser für die Einlagerung in Zisternen aufzufangen. Die Citadelle verband die bastionierte Befestigungstradition von Vauban mit dem »perpendikularen«, mehrstufigen Festungsstil des *Marquis* de Montalembert (1714–1800), der die Verteidigung durch größere Feuerkraft in turmartigen Mauern in den Mittelpunkt rückte.[63] Jean-Hérold Pérard greift die Ansichten früherer Autoren mit folgender Bemerkung auf: »Wenn man die Citadelle zum ersten Mal besucht, ist man versucht zu glauben, Christophes Projekt sei wahnsinnig«.[64] Andere, wie Victor-Emmanuel Roberto Wilson, nennen sie das »vergessene achte Weltwunder«, und tatsächlich bietet sie in ihrer gebirgigen Lage einen Anblick, der nicht weniger erstaunt als der Machu Picchus.[65]

Die meisten Quellen sind sich darin einig, dass die Citadelle irgendwann zwischen der Unabhängigkeitserklärung am 1. Januar 1804 und dem Jahr 1805 begonnen wurde, somit also während der Herrschaft Dessalines' und auf sein Drängen hin. Jedoch wird Christophe für gewöhnlich als ihr Erbauer angesehen, und sie erlangte ihre heutigen Ausmaße erst, nachdem eine Explosion des Pulvermagazins 1818 umfangreiche Restaurierungsmaßnahmen erforderlich machten.[66] Zwei Ausnahmen sind Harvey, der Haiti 1827 besuchte, und sein Landsmann John Candler, der 1840 dort war. Harvey schrieb, dass die Citadelle »ursprünglich von den Franzosen begonnen wurde, die, nachdem sie die Fundamente und Teile der Mauern errichtet hatten, gezwungen waren, entweder aus Materialmangel oder durch den Widerstand der Schwarzen, das Unternehmen abzubrechen«, während Candler schlicht behauptete, »[d]ie Zitadelle von La Ferriere [sic] [sei] von den Franzosen begonnen worden«.[67]

Abb. 10 Citadelle Laferrière, Detail
Fig. 10 Citadelle Laferrière, detail

dition of Vauban with the "perpendicular" multi-level fortress style of the *marquis* de Montalembert (1714–1800), a style focused more on defence which concentrated greater firepower within tower-like walls.[63] Jean-Hérold Pérard echoes earlier writers when he remarks: "[w]hen one visits the Citadelle for the first time, one is tempted to believe that Christophe's project was madness."[64] Others, like Victor-Emmanuel Roberto Wilson, call it the "forgotten eighth wonder of the world," and indeed in its mountainous setting it presents a spectacle every bit as astonishing as that of Machu Picchu.[65]

Most sources agree that the Citadelle was begun sometime between the Declaration of Independence on 1 January 1804 and 1805, therefore during Dessalines's rule and on his urging, although Christophe is usually credited as its creator, and it only gained its present dimensions after an explosion of its powder house in 1818 necessitated extensive restoration.[66] Two exceptions are Harvey, who visited Haiti in 1827, and his

Man hatte Harvey und Candler offensichtlich eine Lügengeschichte aufgetischt, gibt es doch in den französischen Archiven keinerlei Beweise für den Bau einer Inlandsfestung unter dem *ancien régime*. Im Gegenteil, einer der Gründe für den Erfolg des Sklavenaufstands und der anschließenden Revolution war, dass die Franzosen ihre Befestigungsanlagen nur entlang der Küste gebaut hatten, ohne damit zu rechnen, dass ihr Hauptgegner aus den Bergen und den Plantagen kommen würde. Nur eine einzige Inlandsfestung von vergleichbarer Größe war verspätet vorgeschlagen worden, eine riesige utopische Garnisonsstadt, für deren Standort ein Ort am Artibonitefluss im westlichen Distrikt namens Place de Guerre (ca. 1791–92) vorgesehen war. Sie wurde von M. Duportal, dem *maréchal de camp* und Generaldirektor der Befestigungen in Auftrag gegeben und »entsprach den Befehlen des Hofes« [Abb. 11].[68] Seltsamerweise stammen die einzigen erhaltenen Pläne dieses unverhohlen royalistischen Projektes – seine Straßen und Bastionen sind mit königlichen Namen gespickt – von 1793, dem Jahr der Enthauptung von Ludwig XVI. Das Projekt wurde von dem Chefingenieur des westlichen Distrikts, *capitaine du Génie* Charles-Marie Vincent (mit dem Christophe später an einem Programm für eine Landwirtschaftsreform kollaborierte) gründlich kritisiert, weil »es ein Objekt mit erschreckenden Kosten (*dépense effrayente*) und zu diesem Zeitpunkt unmöglicher denn je [wäre]«.[69] Französische Offizielle hatten eine Reihe von Standorten für eine Inlandszitadelle erwogen, darunter Hincha (das heutige Hinche, damals aber auf spanischem Territorium) und verschiedene Orte am Artibonitefluss, einschließlich Verettes' und Mirebalais'. An keiner Stelle in diesen Dokumenten wird ein Standort in der Nähe von Milot erwähnt, außer einer kleinen Batterie, die 1798 in Limonade gebaut wurde, 15 km entfernt und auf der anderen Seite des Grand Rivière du Nord.[70] Eine Zitadelle von der Größe und Höhe Laferrières überstieg die

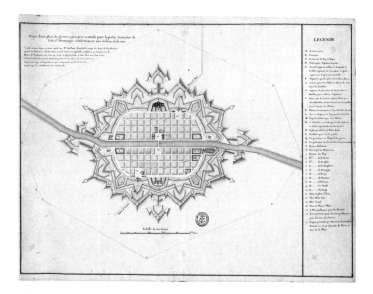

Abb. 11 Anonymes Projekt eines »place de guerre« nahe des Zentrums von Saint-Domingue, ca. 1791–92. In Auftrag gegeben von M. Duportal, Generaldirektor der Befestigungen von Saint-Domingue und der Inseln über dem Winde. Archives Nationales d'Outre-Mer, Aix-en-Provence, 15DFC564B

Fig. 11 Anonymous Project for a "place de guerre" near the centre of Saint-Domingue, ca. 1791–92. Commissioned by M. Duportal, Director-General of Fortifications for Saint-Domingue and the Windward Islands. Archives Nationales d'Outre-Mer, Aix-en-Provence, 15DFC564B

compatriot John Candler, who was there in 1840. Harvey wrote that the Citadelle "was originally begun by the French, who, after having laid the foundation and erected part of the walls, were obliged, from want of materials, or from the opposition of the negroes, to abandon the undertaking," while Candler claimed simply that "[t]he citadel of La Ferriere [sic] had been begun by the French."[67]

Harvey and Candler had been told a tall tale as there is no evidence in the French archives that any inland fort was constructed during the *ancien régime*. In fact one of the reasons

Mittel der zunehmend verzweifelten französischen Obrigkeit und wäre mit Sicherheit nicht unerwähnt geblieben.

Laut des haitianischen Präsidenten Charles Hérard *aîné* (1789–1850) und des Historikers Thomas Madiou (1814–84) wurde die Citadelle von Henry Christophe auf Befehl Dessalines' begonnen. Madiou schreibt ihren Entwurf dem Ingenieur gemischter Abstammung Henri Barré zu, und datiert den Bau auf Januar 1804.[71] Barré, ein »obskurer Offizier«, der 1803 Kommandeur der französischen Flotte in Saint-Domingue wurde und einer der Unterzeichner der französischen Kapitulation und Evakuierung Cap-François' am 30. November desselben Jahres war, blieb zurück, um für Christophe zu arbeiten, obwohl er den Titel des »*capitaine du génie*« erst 1805 erhielt.[72] Sein Name erscheint nicht in den Personalbögen des französischen Marineministeriums, und als Farbiger ist es ausgesprochen unwahrscheinlich, dass er in der Schule in Mézières eine formale Ausbildung als königlicher Ingenieur erhielt. Barré muss daher ein Verwalter anstelle eines ausgebildeten Architekten gewesen sein, der die Arbeit und Materialien koordinierte und dafür sorgte, dass die Arbeiter den Plänen des Architekten folgten. Diese Rolle entspricht der einzigen Erwähnung Barrés durch Christophe hinsichtlich der Citadelle, nämlich als er Jean-Louis Grandmaison ca. 1806 den Befehl gab, sicherzugehen, dass »[d]ie Schreiner das Holz gemäß den Maßen sägen, die ihnen der Battaillonschef des Génie, Henri Barré, gegeben hat«.[73]

Der ehemalige Tourismusminister Patrick Delatour trug noch mehr zur Verwirrung bei, als er 1980 behauptete, er habe ein Dokument in den französischen Militärarchiven in Vincennes entdeckt, aus dem hervorgehe, dass der führende Kopf hinter dem Bau der Citadelle nicht der *homme de couleur* Henri Barré, sondern ein weißer Architekt namens Jean-Etienne Barré sei. Das Dokument erklärt angeblich, dass Jean-Etienne in Orleans als Sohn von Jean Barré de Saint-Venant und Mar-

the slave revolt and subsequent revolution succeeded was that the French had only built fortifications on the coast, never considering that their principal enemy might in fact come from the mountains and plantations. Only a single inland fort of comparable size had belatedly been proposed, a giant utopian garrisoned city planned for a site on the Artibonite River in the Western District called the Place de Guerre (ca. 1791–93), commissioned by M. Duportal, *maréchal de camp* and Director-General of Fortifications, and "conforming to the orders of the Court" [Fig. 11].[68] Curiously, the only surviving plans of this blatantly royalist project—its streets and bastions bear a panoply of royal names—date from 1793, the year when Louis XVI lost his head. The project was soundly criticised by the Western District's chief engineer *capitaine du Génie* Charles-Marie Vincent (with whom Christophe would later collaborate in a programme of agricultural reform) because "it would be an object of frightening expense (*dépense effrayante*) and more impossible than ever at this moment."[69] French officials had considered a number of locations for an inland citadel, including Hincha (now Hinche, but then in Spanish territory), and various sites on the Artibonite River, including Verettes and Mirebalais. There is no mention in any of these documents of a site near Milot except for a small battery built in 1798 in Limonade, 15 kilometres away on the other side of the Grand Rivière du Nord.[70] A citadel of the size and elevation of Laferrière was beyond the means of the increasingly desperate French authorities and it would certainly not have gone unmentioned.

According to Haitian president Charles Hérard *aîné* (1789–1850) and historian Thomas Madiou (1814–84) the Citadelle was begun by Henry Christophe on Dessalines' direct orders. Madiou attributes the design to the mixed-race engineer Henri Barré, and dates the construction to January of 1804.[71] Barré, an "obscure officer" who became commander of French

guerite Pelletier geboren wurde, Teil einer Familie von Baumeistern, »die sich durch das Schreiben wissenschaftlicher
Werke über Architekturtechniken und die Qualität von Materialien hervorgetan hatte«, und dass Jean-Etienne in Saint-
Domingue als Hydraulikexperte gearbeitet hatte.[74] Doch
Tatsache ist, dass Jean-Etienne Barré de Saint-Venant (1768–
1845) jemand vollkommen anderes war. Er wurde in der Tat
bei Orleans (in Artenay) als Sohn von Jean-Etienne Barré
(einem Händler, nicht Architekten) und Marguerite Pelletier
geboren, diente im französischen Militär, einschließlich in
Westindien, und wurde Chevalier (1805), Offizier (1815) und
Kommandant (1821) der Ehrenlegion, Letzteres in seiner Zeit
als Kolonel und Gouverneur von Martinique.[75] Er starb nicht
irgendwann vor der Krönung König Henrys, wie Delatour
und Pérard behaupteten, sondern friedlich im Ruhestand in
Orleans, am 17. Mai 1845 im Alter von 77 Jahren. Es ist äußerst zweifelhaft, dass dieser hochdekorierte französische
Karrieresoldat ohne uns bekannte Architektenausbildung
über ein Jahrzehnt damit verbrachte, eine uneinnehmbare
Festung für einen Gegner Frankreichs zu bauen. Mit Sicherheit haben Delatour und Pérard den falschen Barré zu fassen
bekommen.

Drei weitere Figuren wurden mit der Konzeption der Citadelle in Verbindung gebracht. Wilson schreibt ihren Entwurf dem französischen Architekten La Ferrière zu, doch da
La Ferrière offensichtlich ein Ortsname und kein Familienname ist, können wir ihn getrost als Hirngespinst Wilsons
abtun.[76] Ein weiterer Architekt, der von Pérard genannt wird,
ist ein Ingenieur namens Martial Besse (1758–nach 1811) aus
Terrier Rouge, Sohn eines weißen Vaters und einer Sklavin,
der angeblich seine Unterschrift auf einen Konstruktionsplan
der Befestigungen von Léogâne setzte, bevor die Arbeit an
Sans-Souci begann, wenngleich Pérard uns nie mitteilt, wo
diese Karte ist.[77] Wir wissen, dass Besse ein General in der hai-

naval forces in Saint-Domingue in 1803 and was a signatory to the French capitulation and evacuation of Cap-François on 30 November of that year, stayed on to work for Christophe, although he did not hold the title of "*capitaine du génie*" until 1805.[72] His name does not appear in the personnel records of the French Ministry of the Marine and as a person of colour it is very unlikely that he received formal instruction as a royal engineer in the school at Mézières. Barré was therefore an administrator rather than a trained architect, coordinating labour and materials, and making sure work crews followed the architect's plans. This role correlates with the only mention Christophe himself made to Barré regarding the Citadelle, when he orders Jean-Louis Grandmaison in ca. 1806 to make sure that "[t]he carpenters saw the wood in the dimensions given them by the Chief of Battalion of the Génie Henri Barré."[73]

Former Tourism Minister Patrick Delatour added to the confusion when he claimed in 1980 to have discovered a document in the French military archives in Vincennes demonstrating that the mastermind behind the Citadelle's construction was not the *homme de couleur* Henri Barré but a white architect named Jean-Etienne Barré. The document allegedly states that Jean-Etienne was born in Orleans to Jean Barré de Saint-Venant and Marguerite Pelletier, part of a family of master builders, "who had distinguished themselves by the scholarly works they had written on architectural techniques and the quality of materials," and that Jean-Etienne worked in Saint-Domingue as a hydraulics expert.[74] But as it happens Jean-Etienne Barré de Saint-Venant (1768–1845) was someone else entirely. Born indeed just outside Orleans (in Artenay) of parents named Jean-Etienne Barré (a merchant, not an architect) and Marguerite Pelletier, he served in the French military, including in the West Indies, and became a Chevalier (1805), Officer (1815) and Commander (1821) of the

tianischen Armee und ein Unterzeichner der haitianischen Verfassungen von 1805, 1807 und 1811 war (die letzte davon unter Christophe), aber aus denselben Gründen wie Henri Barré ist es sehr unwahrscheinlich, dass er als königlicher Ingenieur ausgebildet wurde. Deshalb ist diese Behauptung meiner Ansicht nach unglaubwürdig.[78] Wilson lässt ihn einfach mit Henri Barré verschmelzen, und nennt ihn »Henri Barre [sic] (oder Besse)«.[79] Die letzte Figur, auf die ich in Kürze zurückkommen werde, ist Chéri Warloppe, den Vergniaud Leconte unzweideutig als den »Architekten des Palastes von Sans-Souci« bezeichnet, jedoch erneut ohne Quellenangabe, was verständlicherweise bei Michel-Rolphe Trouillot für Skepsis sorgt.[80]

Hubert Cole, Autor der zuletzt erschienenen Biografie Henry Christophes auf Englisch (1967), fügt der Mischung eine neue Zutat hinzu, indem er behauptet, deutsche Militäringenieure hätten die Zitadelle entworfen. Er wiederholt dabei eine verdächtig apokryph klingende Geschichte: »Die deutschen Militäringenieure, die die Zitadelle entwarfen und den Bau beaufsichtigten, mussten fortan innerhalb ihrer Mauern leben. Aus Angst, sie könnten die Geheimnisse der Zitadelle preisgeben, war es ihnen verboten worden, sie zu verlassen«.[81] Die Geschichte stammt wahrscheinlich von dem englischen Konsul und Spion Charles Mackenzie, der 1830 schrieb, dass »[Christophe] unter irgendeinem vagen Vorwand des Verrates einige deutsche Offiziere ermorden ließ, die von seinen Versprechen, Befestigungen zu erbauen, angelockt worden waren; sein wahres Motiv jedoch war es, die Bloßlegung seiner Verteidigung zu verhindern«.[82] Der Mythos der deutschen Ingenieure – er gehört heute zu dem festen Repertoire einheimischer Führer – ist wahrscheinlich eine Verschmelzung der Mär vom Palast als Kopie seines Namenspatrons in Potsdam (dazu später mehr) und der Tatsache, dass preußische Söldner kurzzeitig für König Henry arbeiteten.

Legion of Honour, the latter when he was a colonel and Governor of Martinique.[75] Instead of dying sometime before King Henry's coronation, as claimed by Delatour and Pérard, he died peacefully in retirement in Orleans at the age of 77 on 17 May 1845. It is extremely doubtful that this highly-decorated French career soldier with no known architectural training could have spent over a decade building an impregnable fortress for France's enemy. Clearly Delatour and Pérard have got hold of the wrong Barré.

Three more figures were credited with the conception of the Citadelle. Wilson attributes the design to the French architect La Ferrière, but as La Ferrière is obviously a place name and not a surname we can safely discard him as a figment of Wilson's imagination.[76] Another architect cited by Pérard is an engineer named Martial Besse (1758–after 1811) from Terrier Rouge, born of a white father and slave woman, who allegedly put his signature on a plan for the construction of the fortifications of Léogâne before work began on Sans-Souci, although Pérard never tells us where the map is.[77] We know that Besse was a general in the Haitian army and a signatory to the 1805, 1807, and 1811 Haitian Constitutions (the last of them under Christophe), but for the same reasons as Henri Barré he was very unlikely to have been trained as a royal engineer and therefore the claim is, to my mind, dubious.[78] Wilson simply conflates him with Henri Barré, calling him "Henri Barre [sic] (or Besse)."[79] The final figure, to whom I will return shortly, is Chéri Warloppe, whom Vergniaud Leconte unequivocally calls "the architect of the palace of Sans-Souci," but again without citing any sources, making Michel-Rolphe Trouillot understandably sceptical.[80]

Hubert Cole, author of the most recent biography of Henry Christophe in English (1967), introduces a new ingredient into the mix, claiming that German military engineers designed the citadel, repeating a suspiciously apocryphal-

Dies geschah jedoch viel später, nach dem Ende der Napoleonischen Kriege im Jahre 1815, als sie keine Anstellung mehr hatten, wie Harvey schreibt:

> Kurze Zeit nach dem Frieden von 1815 reiste eine Truppe preußischer Offiziere nach Hayti, vermutlich in der Hoffnung, ihre Lebensumstände aufzubessern; und nach ihrer Ankunft in Cap François boten sie Christophe ihre Dienste an [...]. Er akzeptierte ihr Angebot, und setzte sie in verschiedene Departements der Armee ein [...]. Doch kam es schließlich zu einem Missverständnis [...] welches Ärger und Verdruss auf beiden Seiten verursachte [...] und endlich in offenem Streit endete. Sie hatten, unter großen Anstrengungen und beträchtlichen Kosten, die notwendigen Vorbereitungen für die Herstellung von Kanonen getroffen; doch unglücklicherweise scheiterte der Versuch beim ersten Mal gänzlich.[83]

Harvey erwähnt keine Ingenieure oder Architekten unter den arbeitslosen preußischen Soldaten, die sich mit ihrem neuen Arbeitgeber offenbar nicht einmal gut verstanden. Coles Behauptung könnte vielleicht auch von dem Bericht eines frühen amerikanischen Besuchers herrühren, dem Arzt Jonathan Brown, der 1837 über die Citadelle schrieb, dass »[d]ieses stupende Bauwerk mit drei- oder vierhundert Kanonen bestückt war, und unter der Leitung und Aufsicht europäischer Ingenieure gebaut wurde, die für ihre ständige Gefangenschaft in dem Palast mit den Ehren und Vergütungen entschädigt wurden, die der schwarze König auf sie häufte«.[84] Hier haben wir den Topos der Arbeiter, die in ihrem eigenen Werk eingemauert werden, jedoch ohne ihre Identifizierung als Deutsche. Ihre Tätigkeit war, wie in Harveys Version, auf Kanonentechnologie beschränkt. Dennoch hat das Ganze einen falschen Klang und erinnert stark an Legenden über orientalische Herrscher, die ihre Architekten nach der Fertigstellung der

sounding story: "[t]he German military engineers who designed the citadel and supervised the construction lived on inside its walls, forbidden to leave for fear that they would betray its secrets."[81] The story probably came from British consul and spy Charles Mackenzie, who wrote in 1830 that "[Christophe] assassinated some German officers, who had been allured by his promises to erect fortifications, under some vague pretence of treason; but the real motive was to prevent the exposure of his defences."[82] The German engineers myth—it is a staple of local guides today—is likely a conflation of the fable that the palace was a copy of its namesake in Potsdam (about which more below) and the fact that Prussian mercenaries did work briefly for King Henry, but much later, after the end of the Napoleonic wars in 1815 when they were out of work, as Harvey notes:

> Shortly after the peace of 1815, a party of Prussian officers proceeded to Hayti, probably with the hope of improving their circumstances; and on their arrival at Cape François, tendered Christophe an offer of their services...he accepted their offer, and appointed them to different departments in the army...But a misunderstanding at length took place...which caused trouble and vexation on both sides...and eventually terminated in an open quarrel. They had, with great labour and at considerable expense, prepared the necessary works for constructing cannon; but unfortunately on the first trial the attempt utterly failed.[83]

Harvey does not mention any engineers or architects among the out-of-work Prussian soldiers, who clearly did not even get along with their new employer. Cole's claim might also derive from the report of an early American visitor, physician Jonathan Brown, who wrote about the Citadelle in 1837 that: "[t]his stupendous structure was mounted with three or four

größten Moschee oder des größten Tempels, den die Welt je gesehen hat, blenden. In der Tat erfreuen sich Führer seit Jahrzehnten daran, Besucher mit exakt solch einer Geschichte zu erschrecken (ich kann sie bis mindestens 1923 zurückverfolgen), in der Christophe seine Architekten auf dem Befestigungswall versammelte, um den Ausblick zu genießen, um sie sodann in den Abgrund schubsen zu lassen.[85] Diese Erzählung taucht sogar in Walcotts Theaterstück auf, in dem sich Brelle bei dem König beklagt: »Gott, was für eine Verschwendung von Blut bauten diese Kathedralen und Schlösser; Knochen im Mauerwerk, Schädel im Architrav, Müde Steinmetze, die von den kühlen Türmen fallen«.[86]

Soviel zur Urheberschaft des Citadelle-Entwurfs. Die Quellen erzählen ebenso fantastische Dinge über ihre Erbauer. Ähnlich wie die Geschichte von den deutschen Soldaten betonen diese Berichte, häufig verfasst von Christophes Gegnern, voreingenommenen Besuchern oder republikanischen Historikern, die an Sklavenhalterei erinnernden Arbeitsbedingungen, die Toten, und insbesondere die Grausamkeiten gegenüber jungen Frauen. Candler, der mit dem Hauptmann Agendeau sprach, einem mutmaßlichen ehemaligen Gefangenen, berichtete, dass jeder Stein im Gebäude ein Menschenleben gekostet habe (dasselbe sagen heutige Führer) und kam zu folgendem Schluss:

Diese berühmte Zitadelle wurde von Gruppen von Männern und Frauen errichtet, die dazu gezwungen wurden, mit sehr ungenügender Verpflegung zu schuften: Eine große Zahl starb in Folge von Erschöpfung, und viele weitere aufgrund von Wunden und Verletzungen, die sie während der grausamen Aufgabe erhalten hatten, Steine und andere schwere Materialien die steilen Berghänge hinauf zu schleppen. Gefangene wurden dazu eingesetzt. Hauptmann Agendeau wurde dorthin geschickt, zusammen mit 32 anderen farbigen Männern, aus

hundred cannon, and built under the direction and superintendence of European engineers, who were repaid for the captivity which confined them as fixtures in the place, by the honors and emoluments which were heaped upon them by the black king."[84] Here we have the topos about the labourers being walled up in their own creation, but without the specificity of their being German, and their work, as in Harvey's version, was limited to cannon technology. But it still rings false and recalls legends about Eastern Potentates blinding their architects upon completing the greatest mosque or temple the world has ever seen. In fact guides have enjoyed terrifying visitors for decades with precisely such a story (I can trace it at least to 1923) in which Christophe assembled his architects on the ramparts to enjoy the view before having them pushed off the precipice to their deaths.[85] This tale even appears in Walcott's play, when Brelle complains to the King: "God, what a waste of blood, these cathedrals, castles, built; Bones in the masonry, skulls in the architrave, Tired masons falling from the chilly turrets."[86]

So much for the authorship of the Citadelle's design. The sources have equally fantastic tales to tell about the people who built it. Like the story of the German soldiers these reports, often written by Christophe's enemies, unsympathetic visitors, and republican historians, emphasised the slave-like conditions of his work crews, the deaths, and particularly his cruelty to young women. Candler, who interviewed Captain Agendeau, an alleged former prisoner, reported that every stone in the building cost a human life (guides say the same thing today) and concluded that:

This famous citadel was reared by bands of men and women, who were compelled to labour on very insufficient rations of food: vast numbers died in consequence of exhaustion, and many more of wounds and bruises received in the cruel work

Rache für die Flucht zweier Mulatten, die sich Pétions Armee in Port-au-Prince angeschlossen hatten. Christophe hegte starke und unerschütterliche Vorurteile gegen die farbige Klasse, zu der Pétion gehörte«.[87]

Brown hielt sich auch mit Geschichten von Kerkern auf, obwohl er Baumeister unter den Sträflingen nicht direkt erwähnte: »Im Inneren dieser düsteren Festung gab es Kerker, die in weiser Voraussicht von Christophe errichtet wurden, um das Gefängnis, und womöglich das Grab derjenigen zu sein, die unter seinen Verdacht geraten waren [...] und innerhalb weniger Jahre dieser Epoche hausten darin zu jeder Zeit mehr als sechstausend Personen, die die Opfer von Christophes Eifersucht geworden waren«.[88] Mackenzie lieferte eine besonders grausame Darstellung der körperlichen Folter der Arbeiter an dem Gebäude, das er mit dem Turmbau zu Babel verglich: »Die Baustoffe und die Artillerie wurden alle von Menschenhand geschleppt; zusätzlich zu den Truppen wurde dafür regelmäßig die Bauernschaft eingesetzt [...]. Kein Alter und Geschlecht war von dieser Pflicht ausgenommen, und die königlichen Offiziere waren im Antreiben der Arbeit erbarmungslos. Ich sah eine junge Frau in Gonaives, deren Rücken mit tiefen Striemen übersät war, die ihr *der führende General* mit einer Kuhhaut zugefügt hatte, als sie mit dem Tragen von Steinen auf ihrem Kopf beschäftigt war. Die Sterblichkeit lag sehr hoch, und man sagt, dass die Härte dieses Dienstes eine der Hauptursachen der Revolution war«.[89]

Historiker des 19. Jahrhunderts wiederholten diese Geschichten. Madiou schrieb, dass »Christophe für den Bau dieser beachtlichen Konstruktion alle Einwohner unter seinem Befehl mit Rute und Knüppel zum Einsatz brachte. Mehrere hundert Männer waren bereits beim Transport von Materialien und schwerer Artillerie entlang eines Weges, der bis dato impraktikabel gewesen war, gestorben [...]. Die schlechte Be-

of forcing stones and other heavy materials up the steep sides of the mountain. Prisoners were employed upon it. Captain Agendeau was sent there, with thirty-two other coloured men, out of revenge for the escape of two mulattos who had gone to join Pétion's army at Port-au-Prince. Christophe had a strong and invincible prejudice against the coloured class, of whom Pétion was one."[87]

Brown also lingered over stories of dungeons, although he did not directly mention builders among the convicts: "Within the interior of this gloomy fortress were the dungeons prepared by the cautious foresight of Christophe, to be the prison, and perhaps tomb, of those who had fallen under his suspicions...and within a few years from this epoch they were habitually tenanted by more than six thousand persons who had become the victims of Christophe's jealousy."[88] Mackenzie provided a particularly gruesome account of the physical torture of the builders of a structure he compared to the Tower of Babel: "[t]he materials for building, and the artillery, were all dragged by human hands; for which, in addition to the troops employed, there were regular levies of the peasantry...Neither age nor sex was exempt from this duty, and the royal officers were unsparing in their exaction of labour. I saw a young woman at Gonaives, whose back was deeply whealed by a cow-skin applied to it *by the general in command*, when employed in carrying stones on her head. The mortality was very great, and it is said that the severity of this service was one of the principal causes of the revolution."[89]

Nineteenth century historians repeated these stories. Madiou wrote that "Christophe employed in the building of this formidable construction, under the rod and truncheon, all the populations subjected to his command. Already several hundred men had died transporting materials and heavy artillery up a path hitherto impracticable...The poor treatment which

handlung, der Männer und Frauen jeder Verfassung beim Bau der Befestigungen von Laferrière ausgesetzt waren, entfachte Gerüchte. Junge Bäuerinnen, sogar die schwächsten, wurden gezwungen, Steine und Kanonenkugeln auf ihren Köpfen zu tragen, und grobe Soldaten trieben sie mit Ruten- und Peitschenhieben an«.[90] Beaubrun Ardouin, der behauptete, die Citadelle sei von 20.000 Menschen gebaut worden, malte ein noch düstereres Bild: »Viele Arbeiter jeder Verfassung wurden hier beschäftigt; mehr und mehr Gefangene, an ihren Füßen angekettet, dienten als Handarbeiter, zusammen mit Männern und Frauen, die vom Bestellen der Felder fortgerissen wurden, von einem Ende des Königreichs bis zum anderen. Es wird angenommen, dass keine dieser Unglücklichen einen Lohn erhielten, da sie auf dem ›Boulevard de la Liberté Nationale‹ arbeiteten. Sie erhielten nur eine kleine Essensration vom Staat, unzureichend für die Wiedererlangung ihrer Kräfte: Infolgedessen starb eine unendliche Zahl durch diese unablässigen Mühen«.[91] Trouillot weist Ardouins republikanischen Sympathien die Schuld an seinen sensationssüchtigen Zahlen zu. Doch die Übertreibungen leben weiter fort: Ein Text von 2010 erhöht die Arbeiterschaft auf »22.000 Arbeiter jeden Alters«, sogar mit einer Anspielung auf Kinderarbeit, und ein anderer von 1992 nennt die Zahl 200.000, mit 20.000 Toten.[92]

Hénock Trouillot strebt eine ausgeglichenere Sichtweise an mittels unveröffentlichter Briefe des Königs – leider nennt auch er seine Quellen nicht – die belegen, dass die Baukampagne tatsächlich totalitär war, allerdings nicht in den dantesken Ausmaßen, die Madiou und Ardouin beschreiben. Zwischen 1804 und 1806 stellte Christophe die Arbeitskraft seines gesamten *départements* auf, tat dies jedoch auf rotierender Basis. So rekrutierte er jeden Samstag Handarbeiter von verschiedenen Plantagen für eine Woche, und tauschte sie danach mit anderen aus. Er suchte besonders nach »Steinmet-

men and women of all conditions suffered in building the for-tifications of Laferrière sparked rumours. Young female far-mers, even the most fragile, were forced to carry rocks and cannonballs on their heads, and coarse soldiers kept them working with blows from the rod and whip."[90] Beaubrun Ar-douin, who claimed that 20,000 people built the Citadelle painted an even darker picture: "[m]any workers of all condi-tions were employed there; More and more prisoners, chained to their feet, were serving as manual labourers, concurrently with men and women torn from the cultivation of the fields, from one end of the kingdom to the other. It is understood that none of these unfortunates received any salary, since they worked on the 'Boulevard de la Liberté Nationale'. They re-ceived only a small ration of food from the country, insuffi-cient to repair their strength: consequently an infinite num-ber died in these incessant labours."[91] Trouillot blames Ardouin's sensationalist numbers on the historian's republi-can sympathies. Yet the exaggerations continue: one source from 2010 increases the workforce to "22,000 workers of all ages," even hinting at child labour, and a 1992 source gives the number as 200,000 with 20,000 deaths.[92]

Hénock Trouillot seeks a more balanced perspective by using unpublished letters from the King—alas, he too does not provide their sources—which demonstrate that the build-ing campaign was indeed totalitarian but not quite to the Dantean extremes described by Madiou and Ardouin. Bet-ween 1804 and 1806 Christophe marshalled the labour of his entire *département* but he did so on a rotational basis, recruit-ing manual labourers from different plantations for a week each Saturday and then exchanging them for others. He par-ticularly sought out "masons, sawyers and carpenters" for work on the fortress, as noted in a letter of 19 April 1806, be-fore Dessalines's death, and he also recruited carpenters and tradesmen from the army.[93] In a letter of 20 August 1805 the

zen, Sägern und Schreinern« für die Arbeit an der Festung, wie es in einem Brief vom 19. April 1806 steht, vor dem Tod Dessalines', und rekrutierte auch Schreiner und Handwerker aus den Reihen der Armee.[93] In einem Brief vom 20. August 1805 befahl der damalige Generalissimus Christophe dem Oberst Fidèle, Landarbeiter vom gesamten Plaine du Nord einzuberufen, um Ziegel von verlassenen Plantagengebäuden zu zerlegen (*casser des briques*). Des Weiteren hatte jede Plantage eine Wagenladung zu der ein paar Leugen von dem Fort entfernten Robillard-Plantage zu bringen, von der aus Arbeiter im Laufe einer Woche 10.000 Ziegel zur Zitadelle schafften.[94] Am 16. Januar 1806 befahl er 19 Zuckerplantagen in der Region von Limonade, 16 im Quartier Morin, 10 in Plaine du Norde, und sieben in Petit Anse, jeweils täglich einen Ochsen- oder Mauleselkarren mit Ziegeln nach Milot zu befördern.[95] Da die Citadelle mehr Ziegel benötigte, als von alten Gebäuden gesammelt werden konnten, heuerte Christophe professionelle Ziegelbrenner an, die an einem Ort in der Nähe des Forts arbeiteten, beispielsweise einen gewissen Larose, einen »ehemaligen Ziegelbrenner der Mme Desforges«, der sich 1806 verpflichtete.[96] Von allen Reiseberichten war Harveys vermutlich der realistischste, ohne Erwähnung von Todesfällen, Grausamkeiten gegenüber Frauen, Knüppeln oder Peitschen: »Sobald er hinreichend Muße besaß, ein Unternehmen anzugehen, das so viel seiner Aufmerksamkeit und Zeit in Anspruch nehmen sollte, veranlasste er die Beschaffung der notwendigen Materialien für den Bau; schickte alle Handwerker und Soldaten, die der Mithilfe fähig waren, an die Arbeit; und, während er häufig selbst zugegen war, erlaubte er wenig oder keine Unterbrechung der Arbeit, bis diese endlich vollendet war«.[97]

then Generalissimo Christophe ordered Colonel Fidèle to enlist farm labourers from all over the Plaine du Nord to disassemble bricks (*casser des briques*) from abandoned plantation buildings and that each plantation was to bring a wagonload to the Robillard plantation, a few leagues from the fort, from which labourers carted 10,000 bricks up to the Citadelle over the course of a week.[94] On 16 January 1806 he ordered 19 sugar plantations in the region of Limonade, 16 in Quartier Morin, 10 in Plaine du Nord, and seven in Petit Anse each to convey daily an ox or mule cart full of bricks to Milot.[95] Since the Citadelle required more bricks than could be harvested from old buildings Christophe hired professional brickmakers to work on a site near the fort, such as a certain Larose, "former brickmaker to Mme Desforges," who was enlisted in 1806.[96] Of all the travellers' reports Harvey's was likely the most realistic, making no reference to deaths, cruelty to women, truncheons, or whips: "[a]s soon...as he found himself sufficiently at leisure to engage in an undertaking which would occupy so much of his attention and time, he caused the necessary materials for the building to be collected; set all the workmen, and the soldiers that were capable of rendering any assistance, to labour; and generally attending in person, allowed little or no intermission of the work, till it was at length completed."[97]

Construction and Descriptions of the Palace of Sans-Souci

In striking contrast to the web of speculation about the people who designed and built the Citadelle Laferrière, remarkably little has been written about the architects, builders, and prototypes of the Palace of Sans-Souci. Milot, spelled Millot in French times, was the site of a plantation owned by a family by that name, as confirmed by colonial-era maps: it

Konstruktion und Beschreibungen des Palastes von Sans-Souci

In auffälligem Gegensatz zum Geflecht aus Spekulationen über die Konstrukteure und Erbauer der Citadelle Laferrière ist erstaunlich wenig über die Architekten, Bauarbeiter und Prototypen des Palastes von Sans-Souci geschrieben worden. Milot, das zu französischen Zeiten Millot geschrieben wurde, war der Standort einer Plantage im Besitz einer Familie diesen Namens, wie von kolonialzeitlichen Karten bestätigt wird: Es handelt sich nicht um eine Verschmelzung von »Mille-eaux« – angeblich ein Verweis auf die starken Regenfälle in der Gegend, wie von heutigen Führern gerne behauptet wird. Tatsächlich bezeichnete Christophe den Bau immer schon als Sans-Souci.[98] Der Palast war Teil eines Netzwerks aus neun Stadtpalästen (der wichtigste am Place d'Armes in Cap-Henry) und fünfzehn königlichen Chateaus mit fantasievollen Namen wie Délices-de-la-Reine, Victoire, Embuscade, Bellevue-le-Roi, und dem Palais de la Belle-Rivière (1860–20) in Petite Rivière de l'Artibonite, dem einzig noch – wenngleich in schlechtem Zustand – erhaltenen. Dabei handelt es sich um einen eingeschossigen Bau aus Ziegeln und Schutt, mit einem markanten runden Salon, der aufgrund seiner großzügigen Ausstattung mit Türen und Fenstern als *Palais aux 365 portes* (Palast der 365 Türen) bekannt ist.[99] Sans-Soucis Erbauungsdatum ist auch ungewiss – Vergniaud Leconte gibt an, dass kurz nach der Ermordung Dessalines' 1806 damit begonnen wurde, während andere für den Zeitpunkt der Ausrufung der Monarchie im Jahr 1811 plädieren. Das Einzige, das wir mit Sicherheit wissen, ist, dass das Bauwerk im Jahr 1813 fertig gestellt wurde, da Pompée Valentin Baron de Vastey, der in Frankreich ausgebildete Privatsekretär und Hauptpropagandist Christophes', im selben Jahr schrieb, dass »wir der Vollendung des Palastes von Sans-Souci und der königlichen Kirche derselben Stadt

is not a conflation of "Mille-eaux"—supposedly a reference to the heavy rains in the region—as guides like to say today, and in fact Christophe always called it Sans-Souci.[98] The palace was part of a network of nine urban palaces (with the main one on the Place d'Armes in Cap-Henry) and fifteen royal chateaux with fanciful names such as Délices-de-la-Reine, Victoire, Embuscade, Bellevue-le-Roi, and the Palais de la Belle-Rivière (1860–20) at Petite Rivière de l'Artibonite, the only one to survive today, although in a poor state of repair. It is a one-storey brick and rubble building with a prominent circular salon and is fancifully called the *Palais aux 365 portes* (Palace of the 365 Doors) because of its generous fenestration.[99] Sans-Souci's date of construction is also uncertain—Vergniaud Leconte maintains that it was begun shortly after Dessaline's assassination in 1806 while others say it was begun with the monarchy in 1811. All we know for sure is that it was finished in 1813 since Pompée Valentin Baron de Vastey, Christophe's French-educated private secretary and main propagandist, wrote in that year that "we witnessed the completion of the palace of Sans-Souci, and the royal church of that town"—although this evidence does not stop some recent publications from placing the completion date as late as 1815.[100] Given the size and sophistication of the structure I suspect that Leconte is correct, and that Sans-Souci and the Citadelle were constructed simultaneously.

The palace's name has been the cause of considerable conjecture. The most popular theory, and the one which seems the most likely, is that Henry named it after the eponymous pleasure palace of Frederick the Great at Potsdam (1745–47) by Georg Wenzeslaus von Knobelsdorf. Republican Haitian writer and politician Hérard Dumesle (1824) was the first to compare the two palaces, although he did so only to contrast Henry's tyranny with Frederick's enlightened rulership: "That this palace was unjustly named Sans-souci!...Prussia's Sans-

75

beiwohnten« – auch wenn dieser Beleg einige jüngste Publikationen nicht davon abhält, das Abschlussdatum auf 1815 zu setzen.[100] Angesichts der Größe und Finesse des Gebäudes vermute ich, dass Leconte Recht hat, und dass Sans-Souci und die Citadelle gleichzeitig erbaut wurden.

Der Name des Palastes war seit jeher der Auslöser beträchtlicher Mutmaßungen. Die beliebteste und auch wahrscheinlichste Theorie ist, dass Henry ihn nach dem Lustschloss Friedrichs des Großen in Potsdam (1745–47), das von Georg Wenzeslaus von Knobelsdorf geplant wurde, benannte. Hérard Dumesle (1824), republikanischer Schriftsteller und Politiker Haitis, verglich als Erster die beiden Paläste, wenngleich er dies nur tat, um Henrys Tyrannei mit Friedrichs aufgeklärter Herrschaft zu vergleichen: »Dass dieser Palast unrechtmäßig den Namen Sans-souci erhielt! [...] Preußens Sans-souci ist anders als dieser; der eine gereicht zum kostbaren Andenken an bürgerliches Recht, der andere zeugt von den grausamen und ständigen Verletzungen aller göttlichen und menschlichen Rechte«.[101] Brown (1837) war der erste Autor, der ausdrücklich darauf hinwies, dass Henrys Palast nach demjenigen Friedrichs benannt war, und bezog dies auf Henrys gut dokumentierte Faszination für seinen preußischen Vorgänger: »Friedrich der Große von Preußen war eine Persönlichkeit, von der er mehr als von jeder anderen gefesselt war, weshalb er den Namen Sans-Soucis von Potsdam entlieh«.[102] Cole und Wilson bekräftigen die Verbindung zu Potsdam, Ersterer mit der Behauptung, Henry habe »den Namen aus Bewunderung für Friedrich den Großen gewählt«, Letzterer mit der vorsichtigeren Bemerkung, »der Legende nach« habe »Christophe [...] ihn [den Palast] auf eine Stufe mit seinem Namenspatron stellen wollen, der von Friedrich dem Großen von Preußen, den er sehr bewundert haben soll, errichtet wurde«.[103] Eines aber ist in Anbetracht des vollkommen unterschiedlichen Aussehens der beiden Gebäude gewiss: Henrys Sans-Souci be-

souci is different from this one; the one provides a precious memory of civil law, and the other attests to the cruel and permanent infractions made on all divine and human rights."[101] Brown (1837) was the first writer explicitly to state that Henry's palace was named after that of Frederick, relating it to Henry's well-documented fascination with his Prussian predecessor: "Frederick the Great of Prussia was a personage with whom above all others he was captivated, the name of Sans-Souci having been borrowed from Potsdam."[102] Cole and Wilson reiterate the Potsdam link, the former claiming that Henry "nam[ed] it out of admiration for Frederick the Great," and the latter more cautiously noting that "legend has it" that "Christophe...wanted it to be on a par with its namesake built by Frederick the Great of Prussia whom he was said to admire enormously."[103] One thing for sure—given that the two buildings look nothing like one another—is that Henry's Sans-Souci was not literally based on Knobelsdorf's palace as is dutifully reported by local guides, guidebooks, tourism authorities and some of the scholarship. Typical is the UNESCO website for this monument which also throws in the Schönbrunn Palace and Versailles for good measure: "[t]he Baroque staircase and the classical terraces, the stepped gardens reminiscent of Potsdam and Vienna, the canals and basins freely inspired by Versailles, impart an indefinable hallucinatory quality to the creation of the megalomaniac king."[104]

However there is another Sans-Souci, one which Cole and Hénock Trouillot mention in passing and which Michel-Rolph Trouillot takes more seriously as an alternative reason for Henry's choice.[105] One of Christophe's bitterest enemies during the Revolution was Jean-Baptiste Sans-Souci, a Congolese guerrilla fighter who refused to submit to Christophe's authority and whom Christophe assassinated in an ambush in 1802 not far from Milot. Michel-Rolph Trouillot, who does not discard the Potsdam theory, nevertheless suggests that

ruhte nicht buchstäblich auf dem Palast von Knobelsdorf, wie einheimische Führer, Handbücher, Tourismusbehörden und ein Teil der Forschung pflichtbewusst berichten. Ein typisches Beispiel ist die UNESCO-Webseite dieses Monuments, die obendrein noch Schloss Schönbrunn und Versailles dazugibt: »Der barocke Treppenaufgang und die klassischen Terrassen, die gestuften Gärten, die an Potsdam und Wien erinnern, die Kanäle und Bassine, die frei an Versailles angelehnt sind, verleihen der Schöpfung des megalomanen Königs eine undefinierbare, halluzinatorische Qualität«.[104]

Jedoch gibt es ein weiteres Sans-Souci, eines das Cole und Hénock Trouillot beiläufig erwähnen und das Michel-Rolph Trouillot als alternativen Grund für Henrys Wahl ernster nimmt.[105] Einer der erbittertsten Gegner Christophes während der Revolution war Jean-Baptiste Sans-Souci, ein kongolesischer Guerillakämpfer, der sich weigerte, sich Christophe zu ergeben und den dieser 1802 in einem Hinterhalt unweit von Milot tötete. Michel-Rolph Trouillot, der die Potsdam-Theorie nicht verwirft, schlägt dennoch vor, dass Henry den Namen Sans-Souci als eine Art Trophäe dieses toten Gegners auswählte: »Zufall und Versehen scheinen recht unwahrscheinlich [...]. [D]er König vollführte ein transformatives Ritual zur Absorption seines alten Widersachers«.[106] Trouillot führt dies auf eine ähnliche Praxis in Dahomey (dem heutigen Benin) zurück, bei der Paläste auf den Körpern besiegter Gegner errichtet wurden, so geschehen, als der Gründer Dahomeys, Tacoodonou, seinen Palast auf dem Leichnam von Da, dem Herrscher Abomeys, erbaute. Indes müssen wir daran denken, dass Christophe in der Karibik geboren wurde und dass seine Mutter höchstwahrscheinlich ebenfalls Kreolin war – jedenfalls von gemischter Abstammung – und dass, sollte er von dieser Tradition erfahren haben, dies mit größter Wahrscheinlichkeit vonseiten seiner dahomeyischen Gendarmen geschah, mit denen er sicher nur

Henry chose the name Sans-Souci in part as a kind of trophy for this dead warrior: "[c]oincidence and inadvertence seem quite improbable...the king was engaged in a transformative ritual to absorb his old enemy."[106] Trouillot traces it to a similar practice in Dahomey (modern Benin) of founding palaces on the bodies of defeated enemies, as when the founder of Dahomey, Tacoodonou, built his palace on the corpse of Da, ruler of Abomey. However we must recall that Christophe was born in the Caribbean and that his mother was most likely Creole as well—and of mixed-race—and that if he did learn of this tradition it was most likely from his Dahomeyan gendarmes with whom communication would have been rudimentary. Nevertheless the connection with the West African coast is compelling. I suspect that the urge to build the Citadelle and Sans-Souci Palace also came from a collective memory of the giant European slave castles which punctuate the Gold Coast and Bight of Benin, buildings such as the forts at Ouidah (Benin) or Elmina Castle (Ghana) [Fig. 12], some of which even had grand double staircases not unlike those of Henry Christophe's palace. A significant number of the people who designed and built Henry's buildings would have had first-hand experience of these horrific holding facilities for slave ships and the Citadelle and Sans-Souci palace might have built partly to confront that memory as castles built by freemen.[107]

Harvey (1827) offered one final explanation for the palace's name which had nothing to do with politics, ethnic traditions, or enlightenment leanings: "[o]ne of the most remarkable of Christophe's palaces was...called *Sans-Souci*, so named, probably, from the manner in which it was defended by nature."[108] In this case, as he is the only one to mention it, we might safely dismiss Harvey's claim that the name was a reflection of the building's bucolic setting as the product of the same kind of word play which gave us the Milot/*Mille-eaux* story.

rudimentär kommunizierte. Dennoch ist die Verbindung zu Westafrika naheliegend. Ich vermute, dass der Drang, die Citadelle und den Palast von Sans-Souci zu bauen, auch von einer kollektiven Erinnerung an die großen europäischen Sklavenburgen stammte, die entlang der Goldküste und der Bucht von Benin verteilt sind. Darunter sind Gebäude wie die Forts bei Ouidah (Benin) oder Elmina Castle (Ghana) [Abb. 12], von denen manche sogar große Treppenaufgänge besaßen, ähnlich denjenigen von Henry Christophes Palast. Eine beträchtliche Anzahl von Personen, die am Entwurf und Bau von Henrys Gebäude beteiligt waren, waren aus eigener Erfahrung mit diesen entsetzlichen Sammellagern für Sklavenschiffe vertraut. Somit könnten die Citadelle und Sans-Souci gebaut worden sein, um dieser Erinnerung gewissermaßen etwas gegenüberzustellen, nämlich von freien Männern errichtete Burgen.[107]

Harvey (1827) bot eine letzte Erklärung für den Palastnamen an, die nichts mit Politik, ethnischen Traditionen oder aufklärerischen Neigungen zu tun hatte: »Einer der bemerkenswertesten Paläste Christophes wurde [...] *Sans-Souci* genannt, wohl aufgrund der Art, in der er von der Natur verteidigt wurde«.[108] Da er sie als Einziger erwähnt, können wir Harveys Behauptung, der Name nehme auf die bukolische Lage des Gebäudes Bezug, getrost als das Produkt der Sorte Wortspiel vernachlässigen, die für die Milot/*Mille-eaux*-Geschichte verantwortlich ist.

In der Literatur gibt es nur wenige Anhaltspunkte zu den Architekten und Arbeitern von Sans-Souci. Es besteht kein Zweifel darüber, dass der König stark an dessen Konzeption beteiligt war und volle Anerkennung als Mit-Entwerfer erhalten sollte. Das Gebäude war eine entscheidende Komponente des königlichen Images – was man heute als seine »Marke« bezeichnen würde – und seine persönliche Beteiligung fügt sich in eine lange Reihe architekturbesessener Kö-

Abb. 12 Elmina Castle, Ghana, gegründet 1482, Treppe vor 1665
Fig. 12 Elmina Castle, Ghana, founded 1482, staircase before 1665

The literature provides few clues about Sans-Souci's architects and builders. There can be no doubt that the King was closely involved in its conception and should be given full credit as its co-designer. The building was a critical component of the King's image—what we might call his "brand" today—and his involvement would fall into a long tradition of architecture-besotted kings such as Louis XIV, who famously micro-managed the projects of his *Bâtiments du Roi* and corps of engineers.[109] Harvey confirmed that: "[t]his palace was planned and constructed under [Henry's] immediate superintendence."[110] However most sources focus on the armies of anonymous builders instead of the architect, peppering their accounts with the same references to forced labour and Orientalist legends which they used for the Citadelle. Brown wrote:

nige wie Ludwig XIV., der bekanntlich die Projekte der *Bâtiments du Roi* und des Ingenieurkorps bis ins kleinste Detail kontrollierte.[109] Harvey bestätigt, dass »[d]ieser Palast unter [Henrys] unmittelbarer Aufsicht geplant und konstruiert wurde«.[110] Viele Quellen konzentrieren sich jedoch auf die Heerscharen anonymer Arbeiter anstatt auf den Architekten, und würzen ihre Berichte mit denselben Anspielungen auf Zwangsarbeit und orientalistische Legenden, die sie bereits für die Citadelle verwendet hatten. Brown schrieb:

> Mit der despotischen Macht und einer Portion des weitsichtigen Ehrgeizes altägyptischer Könige ausgestattet, beschäftigte Christophe gewaltige Massen seiner Subjekte, versammelt aus jedem Distrikt seines Königreichs, um das gewaltige Unternehmen zu vollbringen, das er geplant hatte. Die felsige Gebirgsregion in der Umgebung seiner geplanten Residenz wurde von ihrem ursprünglichen Zustand verwandelt, um die Gärten seines Palastes zu formen. Hügel wurden eingeebnet, tiefe Schluchten aufgefüllt, und Straßen und Durchgänge geöffnet, die von seiner königlichen Behausung in alle Richtungen fortführten. Auf den Fundamenten, die er somit bereitet hatte, begann Christophe die Errichtung eines Gebäudes, das als eine Art Louvre intendiert war.[111]

Brown gab an, dass die Konstruktion des Palastes auf dieselbe Weise organisiert war wie die der Citadelle, mit *corvée*-Diensten von Männern und Frauen gleichermaßen. Er schrieb: »Wenn die Maßnahmen öffentlicher Notwendigkeit oder öffentlicher Zier es verlangten, wurde die gesamte arbeitende Bevölkerung eines Distrikts en masse zusammengerufen, und zur Fortsetzung ihrer Mühen gezwungen, bis die Arbeit erledigt war. Die Frauen mussten die Baustoffe tragen, während die Männer in der Errichtung des Werkes eingesetzt wurden: Und das Schwert und die Peitsche des Militärs verliehen den

With the despotic power and a portion of the prospective ambition of the ancient Egyptian kings, Christophe employed vast multitudes of his subjects, gathered from every district of his kingdom, to accomplish the stupendous undertaking which he had planned. The rugged mountainous region in the vicinity of his intended residence was changed from its original condition to form the gardens of his palace. Hills were levelled with the plain, deep ravines were filled up, and roads and passages were opened, leaving in all directions from the royal dwelling. Upon the foundations which he had thus prepared, Christophe began the erection of an edifice which was intended to be a sort of Louvre.[111]

Brown maintained that the construction of the palace was organised in the same way as that of the Citadelle, with corvée labour from men and women alike. He wrote: "[w]hen measures of public necessity or public embellishment required it, the whole labouring population of a district was called out en masse, and made to continue their toil until the work was finished. The females were required to carry the materials, while the men were employed in the construction of the work: and the sword and the lash of the military gave diligence and obedience to the laborers...In this manner were raised the immense structures of the Citadel Henry and the palace of Sans-Souci."[112] Vastey, who cannot be entirely trusted given his role as propaganda minister and his Afrocentrism *avant la lettre,* implied that Sans-Souci and the Citadelle were built entirely by black hands: "[t]hese two structures, erected by the descendants of Africans, shew that we have not lost the architectural taste and genius of our ancestors who covered Ethiopia, Egypt, Carthage, and Old Spain, with their superb monuments."[113] On the other hand, contemporary scholars such as Edward Crain and Wilson insist that the palace bears the unmistakable imprint of European (in Crain's case specifically French) architects.[114]

Arbeitern Eifer und Gehorsam [...]. Auf diese Weise wurden die gewaltigen Bauten der Zitadelle Henrys und des Palastes Sans-Souci emporgerichtet«.[112] Vastey, dem aufgrund seiner Tätigkeit als Propagandaminister und seines Afrozentrismus *avant la lettre* nicht ganz getraut werden kann, implizierte, Sans-Souci und die Citadelle seien vollständig von schwarzen Händen gebaut worden: »Diese beiden Gebäude, von den Nachkommen von Afrikanern errichtet, beweisen, dass wir den architektonischen Geschmack und das Genie unserer Vorfahren, die Äthiopien, Ägypten, Karthago und Alt-Spanien mit ihren herrlichen Monumenten bedeckten, nicht verloren haben«.[113] Andererseits beharren zeitgenössische Forscher wie Edward Crain und Wilson darauf, dass der Palast das unverkennbare Gepräge europäischer (im Falle Crains, speziell französischer) Architekten trägt.[114]

Gehen wir nun zum Erscheinungsbild des Palastes vor seiner Zerstörung durch das Erdbeben von 1842 über. Glücklicherweise sind mehrere Beschreibungen aus der Zeit König Henrys und der folgenden zwei Jahrzehnte erhalten. Die früheste stammt von Julien Prévost, *comte* de Limonade, in seiner hurrapatriotischen Chronik der Monarchie, die 1811 in Cap-Henry und 1814 in London veröffentlicht wurde. Er lobt den eben erst vollendeten Palast in höchsten Tönen als eine Verkörperung der *gloire* von Henrys Herrschaft:

Dieser großartige königliche Palast, der Ruhm Haitis, reichte bis zu den Wolken, und die Schönheit und Kühnheit seiner Konstruktion, seine prächtigen Gemächer, mit Parkettböden, getäfelt mit dem feinsten und seltensten Mahagoniholz, zusammengetragen unter großem Aufwand und mit peinlichster Sorgfalt, diese Möbel, diese eleganten Tapisserien, welche der gute Geschmack geschaffen hat, diese mit Symmetrie geschmückten Gärten [...] diese Wasserstrahlen, diese Obstbäume, diese europäischen Produkte, etc. haben den Rückzugs-

Let us now move to the appearance of the palace before its destruction in the 1842 earthquake; fortunately several descriptions exist dating back to King Henry's lifetime and the following two decades. The earliest is by Julien Prévost, *comte de Limonade*, in his jingoistic history of the monarchy published in Cap-Henry in 1811 and in London in 1814. He describes the just-finished palace in particularly glowing terms as an embodiment of the *gloire* of Henry's reign:

> This magnificent royal palace, the glory of Haiti, reached to the clouds, and the beauty and boldness of its construction, its sumptuous apartments, with parquet flooring, panelled with the finest and rarest mahogany, amassed at great expense and with scrupulous care, this furniture, these elegant tapestries which good taste has created, these gardens embellished with symmetry...these jets of water, these fruit trees, these European products, etc. have embellished the retreat of a hero, and made foreigners admire it, as well as a church, of which a daring cupola agreeably exhibits the riches of its architecture, and other public establishments, such as arsenals, barracks, shipyards, etc. were built in spite of the ravages of war...On the frontispiece of this monument should have been written the motto of Louis XIV: *Nec pluribus impar* ["Not unequal to many"].[115]

The earliest description by a foreigner—the only one from Henry's time since most non-Haitians were forbidden from visiting Milot—appears in a letter from two female teachers from Philadelphia whom Henry invited to Sans-Souci to educate his daughters but who soon found the court etiquette stifling. They have nothing to say about style or materials but mention a "saloon" and library and then another "spacious saloon, furnished with great magnificence and taste."[116] The first detailed account comes from the Austrian explorer Karl Ritter, who went to what he called the King's "summer pa-

ort eines Helden verschönert, und die Bewunderung von Fremden verdient, sowie eine Kirche, deren gewagte Kuppel die Reichtümer ihrer Architektur gefällig ausstellt, und andere öffentliche Einrichtungen, darunter Arsenale, Kasernen, Werften, etc., die trotz der Verheerung des Krieges gebaut wurden [...] Auf dem Frontispiz dieses Monuments sollte das Motto Ludwigs XIV. gestanden haben: *Nec pluribus impar* [»Auch nicht mehreren unterlegen«][115]

Die früheste Beschreibung durch einen Ausländer – die einzige aus Henrys Zeit, da es den meisten Nicht-Haitianern verboten war, Milot zu besuchen – taucht in einem Brief zweier Lehrerinnen aus Philadelphia auf, die Henry zur Erziehung seiner Töchter nach Sans-Souci eingeladen hatte, die jedoch bald die höfische Etikette als erdrückend empfanden. Über Stile oder Materialien verlieren sie kein Wort, doch erwähnen sie einen »Saloon« und eine Bibliothek, und einen weiteren »weiträumigen Saloon, eingerichtet mit großer Pracht und Geschmack«.[116] Der erste ausführliche Bericht wurde von dem österreichischen Forschungsreisenden Karl Ritter verfasst, der die »Sommerresidenz« des Königs, wie er sie nannte, mit der ersten Gruppe weißer Besucher am achten Tage nach Henrys Tod 1820 aufsuchte, und die früheste Zeichnung der Hoffassade anfertigte, welche 1836 in Stuttgart in Begleitung seines Reiseberichts veröffentlicht wurde [Abb. 13]. Auf »diese hervorragenden, ganz nach europäischem Geschmacke errichteten Gebäude« eingehend, schrieb er:

Das Schloß hat zwei Stockwerke und mehrere Seitengebäude, die zu Magazinen, Kanzleien u. dgl. bestimmt waren. Am Fuße des Berges liegt die Kapelle. Ein großer Thorweg mit eisernem Gitterwerk verschließt den äußern Hof des Schlosses; alsdann führt eine Haupttreppe in die erste Etage. Hier sahen wir eine große hölzerne, schwarz angestrichene Sonne, mit der Unter-

Abb. 13 Detail der Illustration der (nördlichen) Hoffassade des Palastes von Sans Souci von Karl Ritter, *Naturhistorische Reise nach der westindischen Insel Hayti* (Stuttgart, 1836). Bayerische Staatsbibliothek, It.sing. 883 m

Fig. 13 Detail of illustration of the court (north) façade of the Palace of Sans Souci from Karl Ritter, *Naturhistorische Reise nach der westindischen Insel Hayti* (Stuttgart, 1836). Bayerische Staatsbibliothek, It.sing. 883 m

lace" with the first group of white visitors on the eighth day after his death in 1820 and made the earliest drawing of the court façade, published to accompany his travelogue in Stuttgart in 1836 [Fig. 13]. Remarking upon "these splendid buildings, built entirely according to European taste" he wrote:

The palace has two floors and several side buildings, which were destined for storage rooms, offices and the like. At the foot of the mountain sits the chapel. A great gateway with an iron grille encloses the outer court of the palace; then a main staircase leads to the first floor. Here we saw a large wooden, black-streaked sun bearing the motto "*Je vois tout, et tout voit par moi dans l'univers*" [I see everything, and everything in the

schrift: »Je vois tout, et tout voit par moi dans l'univers.« Unter dieser Sonne sprudelt ein kleines Röhrwasser in einen steinernen Behälter herab [...]. Der ganze erste Stock enthielt sehr viele und reich nach europäischem Geschmacke decorirte Säle. Wir erstaunten über die hier angerichtete Verwüstung. Nicht selten mußten wir über schöne Draperien oder Trümmer von Spiegelgläsern hinwegsteigen. Die Meubels waren aus Mahagoniholz gearbeitet, die Fenster mit seidenen Vorhängen bedeckt und die Fußböden poliert. Glasfenster sah ich hier zum erstenmal in diesem Lande, selbst einige Glasmalereien traf ich in den Gemächern [...]. Im zweiten Stock, wo ebenfalls Alles verwüstet war, besichtigten wir Christophs Schlaf- und Badezimmer. Aus dem Letzteren begab man sich auf eine erhabene Terrasse, wo Christoph nach dem Bade spazieren zu gehen pflegte. Hier genießt man die entzückendste Aussicht und athmet die reinste Luft [...]. Im Vorhof nahmen wir zuförderst den Audienzsaal in Augenschein. Am Ende des Saales schwebte eine große, mit künstlichem Schnitzwerk versehene und aus Mahagoniholz gearbeitete Königskrone. Der Thron war ebenfalls äußerst kostbar.[117]

Ritters Bericht führt uns nur wenige Tage nach dem Tod des Königs die Schwere der Plünderungen und der Zerstörung vor Augen. Er erwähnt Mahagonimöbel, Seidenvorhänge, verglaste Fenster, und polierte Böden. Er nennt auch eine spezielle Form der Malerei auf der Rückseite eines Glasstückes (auch als Hinterglasmalerei bekannt), die sich seit dem Beginn der zweiten Hälfte des 16. Jahrhunderts in Tirol und Bayern besonderer Beliebtheit erfreute und auch in China für den englischen Markt gefertigt wurde.[118] Wir erfahren, dass das Schlafzimmer des Königs auf eine Terrasse hinausführte, und dass sich der Thronsaal unmittelbar hinter dem Vestibül befand. Ritter hat uns auch eine der längsten Beschreibungen der Chapel Royal hinterlassen, des »Haytianischen Pan-

universe is seen by me]. Beneath this sun a small spigot of water empties down into a stone basin...The whole first floor contained a great many halls, richly decorated according to European taste. We were astonished at the devastation here. Not infrequently, we had to step over beautiful draperies or debris from mirrors. The furniture was made of mahogany wood, the windows covered with silk curtains and the floors polished. I saw glass windows here for the first time in this country, I even encountered a few glass paintings [*Glasmalereien*] in the apartments...On the second floor, where everything was also devastated, we visited Christophe's bedroom and bathroom. From the latter one emerged onto a sublime terrace, where Christophe used to walk after bathing...In the vestibule we had our first glimpse of the audience hall. At the end of the hall was a large royal crown adorned with elaborate carving and made of mahogany. The throne was also extremely ornate.[117]

Ritter's description reveals the severity of the looting and destruction mere days after the King's death. He mentions mahogany furniture, silk curtains, glazed windows, and polished floors. He also mentions a specific kind of painting on the reverse side of a piece of glass (also known as *Hinterglasmalerei*) which were popular especially in Tyrol and Bavaria beginning in the second half of the 16th century and were also manufactured in China for the English market.[118] We learn that the King's bedroom gave onto a terrace and that the throne room was just behind the entrance vestibule. Ritter has also left us with one of the longest descriptions of the Chapel Royal, or "Haytian Pantheon" as it was sometimes called, to the northeast of the *cour d'honneur* [Fig. 29].[119] He writes: "[t]he church, in which everything was left unchanged, stood in strange contrast with the entire surroundings. Here you can see the earlier elegance; we counted three altars, which were adorned and richly ornamented. At the main altar I saw a well-pre-

theon«, wie sie manchmal genannt wurde, die sich nordöstlich der *Cour d'Honneur* befindet [Abb. 29].[119] Er schreibt: »Die Kirche, worin Alles unversehrt geblieben war, stand mit der ganzen Umgebung in sonderbarem Contraste. Hier sieht man noch die vorige Eleganz; wir zählten drei Altäre, die artig verziert und reich besetzt waren. Am Hauptaltar sah ich ein gut gehaltenes, braun gemaltes Marienbild, und einen Christuskopf; an den beiden Seitenaltären standen Heilige in Lebensgröße. Der Plafond war schön ausgemahlt, und der Fußboden mit geschliffenen Steinen belegt«.[120]

Dumesle liefert 1824 mehr Details zum Palast, auch wenn er seine gerechte Abscheu gegenüber seiner Extravaganz nicht verbirgt:

Der Palast [...] macht einen finsteren Eindruck. Eine Sonne schmückt das Pediment; von dem Rauch der Laternen verdunkelt, die dort in den Tagen großer Zeremonien aufgestellt wurden, strahlt diese Fassade nun eine Düsternis aus, die weder die Erhabenheit ihrer Tore noch ihre asiatische Architektur tilgen kann [...]. Im Erdgeschoss ankommend, ging ich zum Zwischengeschoß hinauf, wo ich ein Reservoir bemerkte, das sein Wasser aus dem Inneren erhält; nach Erreichen der großen Treppe zu unserer Linken kamen wir bald zu einem angrenzenden Gebäude, das einen Flügel des Bauwerkes bildete, welcher als Thronsaal diente. Beim Betreten dieses großräumigen Zimmers, das ehemals so pompös ornamentiert war und heute mit Schutt bedeckt ist, sage ich mir: Hier nahm der Tyrann in seiner Omnipotenz die Huldigungen der Höflinge entgegen.[121]

Es ist schwer zu sagen, was Dumesle mit »asiatisch« meinte. Entweder wollte er damit den Despotismus des Königs betonen, indem er das Dekor mit dem eines orientalischen Herrschers verglich, oder es handelt sich um eine rhetorische Kategorie, die in französischen Predigten seit der Zeit Lud-

served, brown-painted picture of the Virgin, and a head of Christ; on the two side altars there were life-sized saints. The ceiling was beautifully painted, and the floor was paved with cut stones."[120]

Dumesle, writing in 1824, provides more details about the palace, although he does not hide his righteous disgust at its extravagance:

> The Palace...presents something sinister. A sun decorates the pediment; obscured by the smoke of the lanterns placed there in the days of great ceremonies, this façade now radiates a lugubrious hue which neither the majesty of its gates nor its Asian architecture can efface...Arriving on the ground floor, I went up to the mezzanine, where I noticed a reservoir which receives its water from the interior; on reaching the great staircase on our left we soon reached an adjoining building, forming one of the wings of the edifice, which served as a throne-room. On entering this spacious apartment, formerly so pompously ornamented, and now covered with debris, I say to myself: it is here that the tyrant in his omnipotence received the homage of the courtiers.[121]

It is hard to say what Dumesle meant by "Asian." It is either meant to emphasise the King's despotism by relating the décor to that of an eastern potentate or it is a rhetorical category used in French preaching since the time of Louis XIV in which *asianisme* denotes something highly decorated compared to *atticisme*, something plain and sober.[122] Dumesle also seems to be suggesting that the throne room was in one of the wings of the building rather than in the centre where most scholars locate it today—an honest mistake given the extent of the looting by 1824.

Writing three years later Harvey is much more revealing about the layout and decoration of the interior and the func-

wigs XIV. eingesetzt wurde; darin bezeichnet *asianisme* etwas reich Dekoriertes, im Gegensatz zu *atticisme*, etwas Einfachem und Nüchternem.[122] Dumesle scheint demnach anzudeuten, dass sich der Thronsaal in einem der Flügel des Gebäudes befand anstatt im Zentrum, wo ihn die meisten Forscher heutzutage verorten – ein verständlicher Irrtum angesichts des Ausmaßes der Plünderungen im Jahr 1824.

Harveys Bericht drei Jahre später ist um Vieles aufschlussreicher, was den Grundriss und die Dekoration des Innenbereiches und die Funktionen der Räume anbelangt, doch sollten seine Beschreibungen des Dekors mit Vorsicht genossen werden, da er in der Vergangenheitsform spricht und die Ausstattung des Palastes wahrscheinlich vor langer Zeit entfernt worden war. Dies ist beispielsweise das erste Mal, dass wir von Mahagoniböden hören. Er schreibt:

Der Palast bestand aus zwei Stockwerken, mit Galerien entlang des ersten Stockes, die durch Flügelfenster auf den Hof hinabschauten; und außer dem großen *Salon*, der Audienzhalle, dem Esszimmer und der Bibliothek besaß er zahlreiche weitere Gemächer, die von verschiedenen Mitgliedern der königlichen Familie und des Haushaltes bewohnt wurden. All diese Zimmer waren geräumig, hoch, und prunkvoll eingerichtet: Ihre Böden waren aus Mahagoniholz gefertigt, dem Produkt der Insel; und ihre trefflichen Spiegel, ausgezeichneten Gemälde, und teuren Möbel, zusammen mit den anderen Ornamenten, mit denen sie ausgeschmückt waren, verliehen dem Ganzen ein vollkommen fürstliches Aussehen […]. Ein Wasserstrom wurde unter dem Gebäude befördert, in verschiedene Richtungen, und entleerte sich schließlich in ein großes Bassin, das für dessen Aufnahme an einem Ende des Palastes bereitet worden war. Auf diese Weise wurden alle Zimmer in einem Zustand erfrischender Kühle erhalten, sogar während der heißesten und drückendsten Stunden des Tages. Entweder aus Kalkül

tions of the rooms, but his descriptions of the décor should be interpreted with caution since he speaks in the past tense and it is likely that the palace's furnishings had long been removed. This is for example the first time we hear about mahogany floors. He writes:

> The palace consisted of two stories, having galleries along the first floor which looked, through glass casements, into the court below; and besides the grand *salon*, the audience-hall, the dining-room, and the library, it had numerous other apartments, occupied by different members of the royal family and household. All these rooms were spacious, lofty, and magnificently furnished: their floors were made of mahogany, the produce of the Island; and their splendid mirrors, superb paintings, and costly furniture, with the other ornaments with which they were decorated, gave to the whole an appearance altogether princely...a stream of water was conveyed under the building, in various directions, and at length emptied itself into a large basin, prepared for its reception at one extremity of the palace. By this means, all the rooms were kept in a state of refreshing coolness, even during the hottest and most oppressive hours of the day. Either from policy or from caprice, Christophe caused the windows of this palace to be disproportionately small...They were at the same time exceedingly numerous; and had they been placed in a more regular order, the exterior would, in this respect, have borne no slight resemblance to an English manufactory.[123]

I am confused by his reference to the smallness of the windows, since they seem quite proportionate today. By the time Mackenzie arrived (before 1830) there is no longer any doubt that the interior had been stripped bare. Mackenzie was the second Englishman to be struck by the building's resemblance to industrial architecture—it was not meant as a compli-

oder aus Willkür veranlasste Christophe, dass die Fenster dieses Palastes unverhältnismäßig klein seien [...]. Gleichzeitig waren sie überaus zahlreich; und wären sie in einer regelmäßigeren Anordnung platziert worden, hätte das Äußere in dieser Hinsicht keine geringe Ähnlichkeit mit einer englischen Manufaktur aufgewiesen.[123]

Sein Verweis auf die Kleinheit der Fenster leuchtet mir nicht ein, da sie heute recht proportional erscheinen. Es besteht kein Zweifel darüber, dass das Palastinnere bis zur Ankunft Mackenzies (vor 1830) komplett ausgeräumt worden war. Mackenzie war der zweite Engländer, der die Ähnlichkeit des Gebäudes mit industrieller Architektur bemerkte – was nicht als Kompliment gemeint war – und in der Tat schätzte er es im Allgemeinen besonders gering ein:

> Es ist ein großes, unförmiges Gebäude auf einem Berghang, das einer riesigen Baumwollfabrik gleicht [...]. Wir bestiegen durch das Eingangstor kommend einen breiten Treppenaufgang, den der Kupferstich recht gut einfängt, und passierten eine Folge geräumiger Gemächer, die inzwischen alle ausgeräumt waren, an deren Verwendung sich jedoch unser Führer wohl erinnerte. Manche waren für die Aufnahme von Schätzen bestimmt, manche waren private, andere öffentliche Gemächer; wieder andere waren von militärischen und zivilen Funktionären belegt. Die Böden, die aus Mahagoni bestanden hatten, waren alle herausgerissen worden.[124]

Mackenzies Kupferstich, wie derjenige von Ritter, stellte nur die Fassade des Hofes dar. Brown, der Sans-Souci 1833–34 besuchte, erwähnt als Erster Marmorböden, und in seiner Version befand sich das Mahagoni an den Wänden, als Verkleidung oder Täfelung: »Die Hallen und Salons waren mit Mahagoni ausgearbeitet, die Böden reich mit Marmor be-

ment—and indeed he had a particularly low opinion of it in general:

> It is a large clumsy building on the side of a mountain, resembling a huge cotton factory…We ascended through the gateway up a spacious flight of steps, which are pretty well expressed in the engraving, and then passed through a series of ample apartments, all now dismantled, but the uses of which were well remembered by our conductor. Some were destined for the reception of treasure, some were private, others public apartments; others were occupied by the military and civil functionaries. The floors, which had been of mahogany, had all been torn up.[124]

Mackenzie's engraving, like that by Ritter, depicted the court façade only. Visiting in 1833–1834 Brown is the first to mention marble floors and in his version the mahogany was on the walls, as panelling or wainscoting: "[t]he halls and saloons were wrought with mahogany, the floors were laid with rich marble, and numerous jets d'eau furnished coolness and a supply of pure water to the different apartments."[125] However since none of these features were still there we must again be cautious. Ritter's "polished" floors could have been either of marble or mahogany, but no source mentions marble before Mackenzie. Likely the "conductors" were already embellishing their stories.

Candler, who went to Sans-Souci in 1841, the year before the earthquake, shared his compatriot's distaste for the style of the building, and reported more or less what Mackenzie saw (including the comparison to industrial architecture). He notes that the mahogany was on the walls and floors alike, although it is unlikely that he saw any of it personally and he was probably just repeating what the guide told him, including a further embellishment: mosaic floors. He wrote:

deckt, und zahlreiche jets d'eau versorgten die verschiedenen Gemächer mit Kühle und reinem Wasser«.[125] Da allerdings keine dieser Ausstattungsmerkmale noch vorhanden waren, müssen wir erneut vorsichtig sein. Ritters »polierte« Böden könnten sowohl aus Marmor als auch aus Mahagoni gewesen sein, aber keine Quelle vor Mackenzie erwähnt Marmor. Es liegt nahe, dass die Führer bereits ihre Geschichten ausschmückten.

Candler, der 1841 nach Sans-Souci kam, dem Jahr vor dem Erdbeben, teilte die Abneigung seiner Landsleute gegen den Stil des Gebäudes, und berichtete mehr oder weniger das, was Mackenzie gesehen hatte (einschließlich des Vergleiches mit industrieller Architektur). Er vermerkt, dass sich das Mahagoni an Wänden wie an Böden befand, obwohl es unwahrscheinlich ist, dass er irgendetwas davon mit eigenen Augen sah. Vermutlich gab er nur das wieder, was der Führer ihm erzählte, inklusive einer weiteren Ausschmückung: Mosaikböden. Er schrieb:

Die Gebäude, obwohl einst prächtig, waren architektonisch nie von gutem Geschmack gewesen, und so entstellt wie sie heute durch Kanonen- und Musketenbeschuss sind, die Fenster zerborsten, die Wände zerbröckelnd, das Dach einstürzend, ähneln sie einer riesigen verlassenen Baumwollfabrik. Das gesamte Grundstück muss, als es zur Zeit Christophes noch ordentlich gepflegt wurde, eine fürstliche Angelegenheit gewesen sein, und liefert neben vielen anderen Beweisen einen weiteren dafür, dass er den Ehrgeiz besaß, mit jedem Zoll als König wahrgenommen zu werden. Die Zimmer waren geräumig und hoch, die Böden und Seitenpaneele aus poliertem Mahagoni, oder herrlich mit Mosaiken eingelegt: Die Gemächer sollen kostbar ausgestattet gewesen sein: Und die Gärten und Bäder für die jungen Prinzessinnen entsprachen alle der allgemeinen Pracht.[126]

The buildings, though once splendid, were never in good architectural taste, and defaced as they now are from the battering of cannon and musket balls, windows shattered, walls crumbling, and the roof falling in, they resemble a huge deserted cotton factory. The whole domain, when properly maintained in the days of Christophe, must have been a princely affair, and adds one to the many other proofs he gave, that it was his ambition to be thought every inch of him a King. The rooms were spacious and lofty, the floors and side panels of polished mahogany, or beautifully inlaid with mosaic: the apartments are said to have been sumptuously furnished: and the gardens and the baths for the young princesses were all in keeping with the general splendour.[126]

Although some contemporary scholars have taken his and Brown's descriptions at face value, maintaining in particular that the palace had marble and/or mosaic floors, there is not enough solid evidence for either and I suspect that they were either of mahogany or cut stone as in the Chapel Royal.[127] Candler's remark about Henry wanting to be "every inch of him a King" is precisely the sort of thinly-veiled mockery which characterised so many of these early visitors' reports.

The Real Architects of Sans-Souci

Two centuries of literature on the Citadelle Laferrière and Sans-Souci have left us with a perplexing list of alleged architects, including real people such as Henri Barré, Jean-Etienne Barré, Martial Besse, Chéri Warloppe, and the Prussian officers, and fictitious ones such as Henri Besse or La Ferrière. Of all of these only Henri Barré can definitively be associated with the construction team at the Citadelle, but as a coordinator of materials and manpower, as can Chéri Warloppe, but

Auch wenn einige zeitgenössische Forscher seine und Browns Ausführungen für bare Münze genommen haben und insbesondere beteuern, dass der Palast Marmor- und/oder Mosaikböden besaß, gibt es für beides keine handfesten Belege. Vermutlich waren sie entweder aus Mahagoni oder geschliffenem Stein, wie in der Chapel Royal.[127] Candlers Bemerkung, Henry habe »mit jedem Zentimeter […] König« sein wollen, ist genau die Sorte kaum verhüllten Spottes, die so viele dieser frühen Besucherberichte kennzeichnet.

Die wahren Architekten Sans-Soucis

Zwei Jahrhunderte der Fachliteratur über die Citadelle Laferrière und Sans-Souci haben eine verwirrende Liste angeblicher Architekten produziert, darunter echte Personen wie Henri Barré, Jean-Etienne Barré, Martial Besse, Chéri Warloppe und die preußischen Offiziere, sowie fiktive wie Henri Besse oder La Ferrière. Von all diesen kann allein Henri Barré definitiv mit der Konstruktion der Citadelle in Verbindung gebracht werden, wenn auch nur als Koordinator von Materialien und Arbeitskräften; genauso Chéri Warloppe, der allerdings ein noch schwierigerer Fall ist, wie wir bald sehen werden. Die in der Forschung herrschende Konfusion ist deshalb so verblüffend, weil die führenden Architekten des Königreichs seit der Zeit König Henrys in den Publikationen seiner drei Druckereien in Cap-Henry, Sans-Souci und der Citadelle zu finden waren, darunter Erlasse, Gesetze, die Königlichen Almanache und Propagandatraktate wie *Relation des Glorieux Evénements* des *comte de* Limonade (Cap-Henry, 1811). Diese gedruckten Texte, zusammen mit dem Manuskript *Armorial Général* (1812; 1814) und dem fragmentarischen «Béliard Armorial« (1811–20) lassen keine Zweifel an den Identitäten mancher der Personen, die diese Monumente entwarfen

much more circumstantially as we shall soon see. The confusion in the scholarship is particularly puzzling since the kingdom's leading architects have been hidden in plain view since King Henry's time in the publications of his three presses at Cap-Henry, Sans-Souci, and the Citadelle, including edicts, laws, the Royal Almanacs, and propaganda tracts such as the *comte de* Limonade's *Relation des Glorieux Evénements* (Cap-Henry, 1811). These printed texts, together with the manuscript *Armorial Général* (1812; 1814) and the fragmentary "Béliard Armorial" (1811–20) leave no doubt as to the identity of some of the people who designed and built these monuments, and more can be discovered about them in newspapers and archives.

The architects of the Citadelle and Sans-Souci, like those of the King's other palaces, worked for the Intendancy of the King's Buildings, which Henry established on the model of Louis XIV's *Surintendance des Bâtiments du Roi*.[128] From at least 1811 the Intendant, and therefore the most important architect in the Kingdom, was Monsieur *le baron* de Faraud, who served as the "*Intendant des Bâtimens de la Couronne*"—he was simultaneously the "*Directeur du Génie*" (Director of the Army Corps of Engineers)—and his bureau operated under the General Intendancy of the King's Household, led by *Intendant-général le comte de* Rosiers.[129] That same year Faraud was specifically called "Director of Fortifications."[130] A highly esteemed member of Henry's court, Faraud was a signatory to the *Loi pénale militaire* in the *Code Henry* in January 1812 and was listed among the "*Conseillers Privés du Roi*" in the 1819 *Extrait des registres du grand Conseil d'État*.[131] Faraud was created a baron in 8 April 1811, when King Henry first established a hereditary nobility, at which point he also held the rank of colonel. In the almanacs from 1815–1820 he is titled "*Directeur-général du Etat-major du Corps Royal du Génie*" (Director-General of the General Staff of the Royal Corps of Engineers) with the rank of

und erbauten, und über die in Zeitungen und Archiven mehr in Erfahrung gebracht werden kann.

Die Architekten der Citadelle und Sans-Soucis, wie diejenigen der anderen Paläste des Königs, arbeiteten für die Intendanz der Königlichen Gebäude, die Henry nach dem Vorbild der *Surintendance des Bâtiments du Roi* von Ludwig XIV. gründete.[128] Seit mindestens 1811 war der Intendant, und damit der wichtigste Architekt des Königreichs, Monsieur *le baron* de Faraud, der als »*Intendant des Bâtimens de la Couronne*« diente, gleichzeitig »*Directeur du Génie*« (Direktor des Armeekorps der Ingenieure) war und dessen Büro unter der Allgemeinen Intendanz des Königlichen Haushalts agierte, die von dem *Intendant-général le comte de* Rosiers geleitet wurde.[129] Im selben Jahr wurde Faraud ausdrücklich zum »Direktor der Befestigungen« ernannt.[130] Als hochgeschätztes Mitglied von Henrys Hof war Faraud ein Unterzeichner des *Loi pénale militaire* des *Code Henry* im Januar 1812 und wurde in dem *Extrait des registres du grand Conseil d'État* von 1819 als einer der »*Conseillers Privés du Roi*« aufgeführt.[131] Faraud wurde am 8. April 1811 zum Baron ernannt, als König Henry erstmals einen erblichen Adelsstand etablierte, zu welchem Zeitpunkt er auch den Rang eines Oberst bekleidete. In den Almanachen von 1815–20 wird er als »*Directeur-général du Etat-major du Corps Royal du Génie*« (Generaldirektor des Allgemeinen Stabs des Königlichen Ingenieurkorps) betitelt, mit dem Rang eines *maréchal de camp*, obwohl er 1820 nicht mehr Intendant war.[132] Faraud ersetzte womöglich Barré, der nach 1806 nicht mehr erwähnt wird und von dem Leconte glaubt, dass er vor 1811 starb, obwohl er auch Barrés Vorgesetzter gewesen sein könnte, da Barré nur *capitaine du Génie* war.[133]

Farauds führende Rolle hinsichtlich der Citadelle wird von seinem Wappen bestätigt, welches, anders als die eleganten französischen Mottos auf den meisten Wappen im *Armorial Général*, die einfachen Worte »CITADELLE HENRY« trug.

maréchal de camp, although by 1820 he is no longer the Intendant.[132] Faraud may have replaced Barré, who is not mentioned
after 1806 and who Leconte believes was dead before 1811, although he may also have been Barré's superior since Barré was
a mere *capitaine du Génie*.[133]

Faraud's leading role at the Citadelle is confirmed by the
device on his coat of arms which, unlike the elegant French
mottoes of most of the heraldry in the *Armorial Général*, bore
the simple words »CITADELLE HENRY«—and his shield
was adorned with an architect's divider, an explicit reference
to his métier [Fig. 4].[134] I have not been able to locate anyone
with the surname Faraud in any *ancien régime* notarial documents or other manuscript sources and neither does it appear
in Dominique Roger's exhaustive survey of notarial documents from Cap-François and Port-au-Prince from 1776–89.[135]
The only reference I have found is in the *Affiches Américaines*,
which reports in 1775 that a certain Joseph *dit* Faraud, a
25-year-old black creole slave from the Drouet Plantation in
Boucassin (just north of Port-au-Prince) escaped in 1775.[136]
He would have been in his mid-fifties when the Citadelle was
begun, so he could have been Henry's architect, but the advertisement gives no clue as to his métier. As for the *comte de*
Rosiers (Juste Chanlatte), he was a mixed-race notary born in
Jacmel in 1766 who studied at the Collège Louis-le-Grand in
Paris, spent time in the USA (1798–1803), returned to become
General Secretary to Dessalines, and was ennobled in 1811
along with Faraud. Although an accomplished man of letters
and poet (he became the King's Librarian in 1820), there is
nothing to suggest that Rosiers had any knowledge of the
building arts.[137]

According to the Almanacs for 1815 and 1816 (published
in 1814 and 1815) the Intendancy also included five *"Architectes des Palais"* working directly under Faraud, including (in
order of precedence) Messieurs André, Théophile Badaillac,

Sein Schild war außerdem mit einem Architektenzirkel verziert, ein eindeutiger Bezug auf sein Metier [Abb. 4].[134] Weder konnte ich jemanden mit dem Nachnamen Faraud in notariellen Dokumenten oder anderen schriftlichen Quellen des *ancien régime* finden, noch taucht er in Dominique Rogers erschöpfender Untersuchung notarieller Dokumente aus Cap-François und Port-au-Prince von 1776–89 auf.[135] Den einzig auffindbaren Verweis enthalten die *Affiches Américaines*, die 1775 berichten, dass 1775 ein gewisser Joseph *dit* Faraud, ein 25-jähriger schwarzer kreolischer Sklave von der Drouet Plantage in Boucassin (nördlich von Port-au-Prince) entfloh.[136] Er wäre Mitte fünfzig gewesen, als die Citadelle begonnen wurde, und hätte damit Henrys Architekt sein können, aber die Anzeige liefert keinen Hinweis auf sein Metier. Was den *comte de* Rosiers (Juste Chanlatte) betrifft, so war dieser ein Notar gemischter Abstammung, der 1766 in Jacmel geboren wurde und am Collège Louis-le-Grand in Paris studierte, einige Zeit in den USA verbrachte (1798–1803), nach seiner Rückkehr Generalsekretär Dessalines' wurde, und 1811 zusammen mit Faraud in den Adelsstand erhoben wurde. Zwar war er ein angesehener Gelehrter und Dichter (1820 wurde er Bibliothekar des Königs), doch deutet nichts darauf hin, dass er sich im Bauwesen auskannte.[137]

Laut den Almanachen der Jahre 1815 und 1816 (1814 und 1815 veröffentlicht), bestand die Intendanz auch aus fünf »*Architectes des Palais*«, die Faraud direkt unterstanden, darunter (nach ihrer Rangordnung) Messieurs André, Théophile Badaillac, Décourtil, Jean-Baptiste Badaillac, und François Poisson.[138] Bis 1820 war Théophile Badaillac durch Jean-Charles und Gervais ersetzt worden.[139] Diese Männer waren allesamt ausgebildete Baumeister, die entweder von Plantagen oder aus der Stadt kamen, und *gens de couleur* oder ehemalige Sklaven waren. Monsieur André könnte ein 36-jähriger Zimmerersklave namens André gewesen sein, womöglich aus dem

Décourtil, Jean-Baptiste Badaillac, and François Poisson.[138] By 1820 Théophile Badaillac had been replaced by Jean-Charles and Gervais.[139] All of these men would have been trained builders, either from plantations or the city, whether *gens de couleur* or ex-slaves. Monsieur André might have been a 36-year old carpenter slave named André, possibly from Congo, who in 1788 escaped a plantation belonging to the Dupont family in the Bas de Sainte-Anne (between Saint-Louis du Nord and Borgne in Northern Haiti) and would have been the same age as Faraud.[140] An Honoré André is also listed as a Chevalier of the Order of Saint-Henri and a lieutenant colonel in Henry's army in 1811.[141] Badaillac is a surname from the Southwest of France near Bordeaux, the epicentre the Saint-Domingue trade, and a Monsieur Badaillac was the administrator of a plantation belonging to the Monpertui family in Morne-Rouge, quite close to Milot, in 1768.[142] Perhaps Jean-Baptiste and Théophile Badaillac were the mixed-race issue of a member of this family or former slaves of the plantation who took on their administrator's surname. François Poisson may have had some connection—given the date and his métier—with a white master mason and carpenter named Julien Poisson who ran a large atelier for the French *Génie* building public fountains in Basse-Terre (Guadeloupe) in 1802–04: as noted earlier the Lesser Antilles was the French Atlantic's leading centre for architectural training and many master builders emigrated from there to Saint-Domingue under the *ancien régime*.[143] Décourtil's unusual surname brings to mind the famous botanist and historian of the Haitian Revolution Michel-Étienne Descourtilz (1777–1835) and his illustrator son Jean-Théodore (1796–1855), but the father was only in Haiti from 1798 to 1802 and the son between 1821 and 1826, and therefore both were absent during Henry's reign.[144] As for Gervais, he might have come from a plantation owned by a family of that name since the late 1760s in nearby Limonade.[145]

Kongo stammend, der 1788 von einer Plantage der Familie Dupont im Bas de Saint-Anne (zwischen Saint-Louis du Nord und Borgne im Norden Haitis) floh, und gleichaltrig mit Faraud gewesen wäre.[140] Ein Honoré André wird 1811 auch als Chevalier des Ordens von Saint-Henri und als Oberstleutnant in Henrys Armee aufgelistet.[141] Badaillac ist ein Familienname aus dem Südwesten Frankreichs nahe Bordeaux, dem Epizentrum des Handels mit Saint-Domingue, und ein Monsieur Badaillac war 1768 der Verwalter einer Plantage, die der Familie Monpertui in Morne-Rouge gehörte, recht nahe bei Milot gelegen.[142] Vielleicht waren Jean-Baptiste und Théophile Badaillac die Kinder gemischter Abstammung eines Mitgliedes dieser Familie oder ehemaliger Sklaven dieser Plantage, die den Namen des Verwalters annahmen. François Poisson mag – in Anbetracht des Datums und seines Metiers – in Verbindung zu einem weißen Steinmetz und Zimmerer namens Julien Poisson gestanden haben, der ein großes Atelier für das französische *Génie* leitete, das 1802–04 öffentliche Brunnen in Basse-Terre (Guadeloupe) baute: Wie zuvor bemerkt, waren die Kleinen Antillen das führende Zentrum der Architektenausbildung im französischen Atlantikraum, und viele Baumeister emigrierten unter dem *ancien régime* von dort nach Saint-Domingue.[143] Découtils ungewöhnlicher Nachname erinnert an den berühmten Botaniker und Historiker der Haitianischen Revolution, Michel-Étienne Descourtilz (1777–1835) und dessen Sohn, den Illustrator Jean-Théodore (1796–1855). Allerdings war der Vater nur von 1798 bis 1802 auf Haiti und der Sohn zwischen 1821 und 1826, sodass beide während der Herrschaft Henrys abwesend waren.[144] Was Gervais betrifft, so könnte er von einer Plantage stammen, die seit den späten 1760ern einer Familie dieses Namens im nahegelegenen Limonade gehörte.[145]

Neben Faraud ist André der einzige dieser Architekten aus den Almanachen, der die Bühne zweifelsfrei vor 1811 betritt:

Aside from Faraud André is the only one of these architects in the Almanacs who can unequivocally be placed on the scene before 1811: in an 1806 letter Christophe notes that André was chief mason at the Citadelle, assisted by another mason named Jasmin from the Nazères plantation.[146] Jasmin was likely a descendent of the free black mason Jean Jasmin (b. 1714), a prominent citizen of Cap-François who founded a hospital for people of colour there.[147] Born Aloon Kinton on the Gold Coast in present-day Ghana he was sold to a mason named Thoumazeau (or Thomasseau) who taught him his métier, was baptised as Jean Jasmin in 1736, and was sold in 1738 to building contractor Sieur Louis who freed him in 1741.[148] Jasmin built the hospital in 1756 and he owned a plantation four leagues from Cap-François. Another builder who turns up in Christophe's early correspondence is the master carpenter Castaing, who ran an atelier of carpenters and joiners at the Citadelle: he received lumber to build the royal apartments there in January of 1805 and in April of the same year his men were made to carry rocks up to the fortress.[149] Castaing likely came from the plantation owned by a family of that name in Grande-Rivière since it was less than 5 kilometres from Milot.[150]

Now we come to Chéri Warloppe, who appears not in the Intendancy of the King's Buildings but in the *Direction et Intendance des Jardins, Eaux et Forêts*, the government body under Thomas, *baron de* Béliard responsible for natural resources, forestry, roads, bridges, land reclamation, and civilian architecture (*ouvrages de maçonnerie et de charpente, pour la partie civile*). Warloppe's title was *chef pour le méchanique* (chief mechanic), suggesting that he had more to do with things like hydraulics and bridges than with architecture, and given that he was not one of the *Architectes des Palais* I find Leconte's claim that he was the sole architect of Sans-Souci hard to support. Nevertheless, some people from his bureau may have

In einem Brief von 1806 bemerkt Christophe, dass André Hauptsteinmetz der Citadelle war, assistiert von einem anderen Steinmetz namens Jasmin von der Nazères-Plantage.[146] Jasmin war vermutlich ein Nachfahre des freien schwarzen Steinmetzes Jean Jasmin (geb. 1714), einem prominenten Bürger von Cap-François, der dort ein Krankenhaus für Schwarze gründete.[147] Als Aloon Kinton an der Goldküste im heutigen Ghana geboren, wurde er an einen Steinmetz namens Thoumazeau (oder Thomasseau) verkauft, der ihm sein Metier beibrachte. 1736 wurde er Jean Jasmin getauft, und 1738 an den Bauunternehmer Sieur Louis verkauft, der ihm 1741 die Freiheit schenkte.[148] Jasmin baute 1756 das Krankenhaus und besaß vier Leugen von Cap-François eine Plantage. Ein weiterer Baumeister, der in Christophes frühen Korrespondenzen auftaucht, ist der Schreinermeister Castaing, der bei der Citadelle ein Atelier mit Schreinern und Tischlern unterhielt: Im Januar 1805 erhielt er Bauholz für die dortigen königlichen Gemächer und im April desselben Jahres wurden seine Männer damit beauftragt, Steine zur Festung zu tragen.[149] Castaing stammte wahrscheinlich von einer Plantage im Besitz einer Familie mit demselben Namen in Grande-Rivière, die sich weniger als 5 km von Milot befand.[150]

Kommen wir zu Chéri Warloppe, der nicht in der Intendanz der Königlichen Gebäude auftaucht, sondern in der *Direction et Intendance des Jardins, Eaux et Forêts*, der Regierungsbehörde unter Thomas, *baron de* Béliard, die für natürliche Ressourcen, Forstwirtschaft, Straßen, Brücken, Landgewinnung und zivile Architektur (*ouvrages de maçonnerie et de charpente, pour la partie civile*) zuständig war. Warloppes Titel war *chef pour le méchanique* (Chefmechaniker), was nahelegt, dass er mehr mit Dingen wie Hydraulik und Brücken als mit bewohnbaren Gebäuden zu tun hatte. Da er nicht unter den *Architectes des Palais* war, schätze ich Lecontes Behauptung, Warloppe sei der einzige Architekt Sans-Soucis gewesen, als

contributed to the design of the fountains, cisterns, and water-cooling systems in the Citadelle and palace, particularly Julien Dufresne, who was chief hydraulics engineer and his assistant Jacques Cézar (or César).[151] Dufresne may have come originally from Limbé as there was a plantation there belonging to the Dufresne de Pontbriant family.[152]

I will introduce one more name, even though evidence for his participation at Sans-Souci remains circumstantial and I am reluctant to add to a list which is already so plagued by conjecture. However Joseph-Antoine Dardan (1740–before 1814), a distinguished master mason and *architecte juré* from the City of Bordeaux resident in Cap-François, was handily the most highly-trained mason in the city at the end of the French occupation, particularly in the art of stereotomy (complex masonry vaults and stonecutting), which is one of the salient features of Sans-Souci's design.[153] In Bordeaux Dardan became an *architecte juré* after taking a test, a "*chef d'œuvre*" or "*pièce* [or *essai*] *de trait*" in stereotomy. His textbook would have been Frézier's *La théorie de la pratique de la coupe des pierres*, which was also available for sale in Saint-Domingue.[154] We first hear of Dardan when he paid his dues to Bordeaux's architecture guild (*Compagnie des maitres architectes*) in 1765 and for which he was elected bailiff in 1768.[155] Although he was scion of one of the city's leading families of masons—it included Étienne Dardan, *entrepreneur des ouvrages du Roi*—Joseph-Antoine left suddenly for Saint-Domingue in 1771.[156] No reason is given for his decision and he was still a paid-up member of the Company five months after his departure, but he remained estranged from his parents.[157] In 1774 Dardan placed an advertisement in the *Affiches Américaines* announcing that he is open for business on the rue Espagnole in Cap-François and that: "Furnished with a prodigious quantity of different materials & tools required for construction, [he] offers to undertake all contract work and site management with which one may wish

unhaltbar ein. Nichtsdestotrotz könnten manche Mitarbeiter seines Büros zu den Entwürfen der Brunnen, Zisternen und Wasserkühlsysteme in der Citadelle und dem Palast beigetragen haben, insbesondere der Chef-Hydraulikingenieur Julien Dufresne und sein Assistent Jacques Cézar (oder César).[151] Es ist möglich, dass Dufresne ursprünglich aus Limbé stammte, da sich die dortige Plantage im Besitz der Familie Dufresne de Pontbriant befand.[152]

Ein weiterer Name ist zu bedenken, auch wenn es nur wenige Indizien für dessen Beteiligung am Bau Sans-Soucis gibt und ich ungern eine Liste verlängern möchte, die bereits jetzt vor Mutmaßungen überquillt. Joseph-Antoine Dardan (1740–vor 1814) jedoch – ein hervorragender Steinmetzmeister, *architecte juré* aus Bordeaux und Einwohner Cap-François' – war passenderweise der am besten ausgebildete Steinmetz der Stadt am Ende der französischen Okkupation, besonders hinsichtlich der Kunst der Stereotomie (komplexe Mauergewölbe und Steinschnitt), die eine der Hauptmerkmale des Sans-Souci-Entwurfs darstellt.[153] In Bordeaux wurde Dardan zum *architecte juré*, nachdem er eine Prüfung abgelegt hatte, ein »*chef d'œuvre*« oder »*pièce* [oder *essai*] *de trait*« in der Stereotomie. Als Lehrbuch hätte er Frézier's *La théorie de la pratique de la coupe des pierres* verwendet, das auch in Saint-Domingue zu kaufen war.[154] Wir erfahren erstmals von Dardan, als er 1765 seine Gebühren an die Architektengilde Bordeaux' zahlte (*Compagnie des maitres architectes*), zu deren Verwalter er 1768 gewählt wurde.[155] Obwohl er Spross einer der führenden Steinmetzfamilien der Stadt war – zu der etwa Étienne Dardan, *entrepreneur des ouvrages du Roi*, zählte – brach Joseph-Antoine im Jahr 1771 unvermittelt nach Saint-Domingue auf.[156] Seine Entscheidung bleibt unbegründet und noch fünf Monate nach seiner Abreise war er ein voll bezahltes Mitglied der Kompanie, hatte jedoch den Kontakt zu seinen Eltern abgebrochen.[157] 1774 platzierte Dardan eine Anzeige in den *Af-*

to entrust him in Le Cap & the plain. He will provide people who will honour him with a visit Plans, Elevations, Quotes & Estimates of all the work they can offer him. He boasts of the excellent manner of working & the accuracy that he will achieve, to merit the confidence of the public."[158] Dardan possessed such extraordinary skills that the Governor and Intendant named him *Grand-Voyer* (chief of the roads administration) of the town and suburbs of Cap-François in 1777, making him one of only a handful of people in the entire history of the French Atlantic Empire to serve in the *Génie* without training with the corps of engineers in France.

Although Dardan's career with the Ministry of the Marine was cut short in 1781—he was a victim of jealousy from royal engineers who saw him as an outsider—he went on to run a prosperous architectural firm in the city which also did projects on the plantations.[159] Dardan remarked in 1781 that in Bordeaux his talents were not limited to "mere architecture," but that "he was also hired to measure the roads of the dependency, the alignments and levelling of the said City."[160] In 1793, after his parents died and the proceedings from a sale of the family land in the Gironde was divided among their successors, it was noted that Joseph-Antoine ("Joseph Dardan") had never returned from the colonies and that "his parents wrote many letters to him and they never acknowledged that they had received a response," and his inheritance was put into a trust.[161] There is no evidence in his family's dossier that he ever returned to France: indeed Dardan was still living in the *Petit Guinée* neighbourhood of Cap-François near Place de Clugny as late as July 1803, still styling himself "*ex-voyer de la commune du Cap.*"[162]

Significantly, no announcement of Dardan's departure appears in the regular *Déclarations de Départs* in the newspaper which included colleagues such as Charles Brown, a carpenter who fled to Jamaica in March; joiner Julien Pironneau and ar-

fiches Américaines, in der er verkündete, auf der rue Espagnole in Cap-François ein Geschäft eröffnet zu haben: »Mit einer außerordentlichen Menge verschiedener, für den Bau benötigter Materialien & Werkzeuge ausgestattet, bietet [er] an, jede Form der Auftragsarbeit und Bauleitung zu übernehmen, mit der man ihn in Le Cap & der Ebene zu betrauen wünscht. Er wird Personen, die ihn mit einem Besuch beehren, mit Plänen, Aufrissen, Angeboten & Schätzungen aller Aufträge versehen, die sie ihm anbieten können. Er brüstet sich mit der hervorragenden Arbeitsweise & der Genauigkeit, die er erreichen wird, um sich das Ansehen der Öffentlichkeit zu verdienen«.[158] Dardan verfügte über solch außergewöhnliche Fähigkeiten, dass der Gouverneur und Intendant ihn 1777 zum *Grand-Voyer* (Vorsteher der Straßenverwaltung) der Stadt und der Vororte von Cap-François ernannte. Damit gehörte er einer Handvoll von Personen in der gesamten Geschichte des französischen Atlantikreiches an, die in dem *Génie* dienten, ohne in Frankreich eine Ausbildung im Ingenieurkorps absolviert zu haben.

Obwohl Dardans Karriere im Marineministerium 1781 zu Ende ging – er wurde Opfer der Eifersucht königlicher Ingenieure, die ihn als Außenseiter betrachteten – leitete er später in der Stadt ein erfolgreiches Architekturbüro, das auch Projekte auf den Plantagen durchführte.[159] Dardan merkte 1781 an, dass seine Talente in Bordeaux nicht auf »reine Architektur« beschränkt waren, sondern dass »er auch angeheuert wurde, um die Straßen der Dependance, die Ausrichtungen und Nivellierungen in besagter Stadt zu messen«.[160] Im Jahr 1793, nachdem seine Eltern gestorben waren und der Erlös vom Verkauf des Familiengrundstücks in der Gironde unter den Erben aufgeteilt worden war, wurde vermerkt, dass Joseph-Antoine (»Joseph Dardan«) nie von den Kolonien zurückgekehrt war, und dass »seine Eltern ihm viele Briefe schrieben, auf die sie laut eigener Aussage keinerlei Antwort

chitect Jean Ducros, both of whom left for France in April; François-Guillaume Robard, who abandoned his big shop on rue Espagnole for the métropole sometime before April; carpenter Mathieu Mercier, who departed in May; Louis Carpentier, a joiner who sailed in June; and carpenter Jean Castede, who went back to France in July.[163] All evidence suggests that Dardan was still in Cap-François when Dessalines captured the city in November 1803.[164] Perhaps Dardan remained because he had a family with a woman of colour: the fact that his primary residence was in *Petit-Guinée*, the neighbourhood of the *gens de couleur*, would seem to corroborate this. If so, his ties to the mixed-race community might have given him protection against retaliation from the revolutionaries as Dessalines had allied himself with the *gens de couleur* by this time and architects were in short supply.[165] Indeed Dardan may have had sympathies for the cause thanks to his resentment toward a French military establishment which snubbed him.[166] Dardan would have been around 66 when Sans-Souci was begun, too old to be involved in manual labour but quite healthy enough to help draw up the plans and elevations for the building and serve in an advisory capacity. I suspect that he was dead by 1814 since he does not appear among the staff of the Intendancy of the King's Buildings.

In summary, *le baron* de Faraud, possibly ex-slave Joseph *dit* Faraud, was the chief architect of the Citadelle, at least from 1811, and likely from the time of its conception given that the Citadelle's name is his heraldic device. The only Citadelle builders whom we can definitively place on the scene before 1811 are Henri Barré, the masons André and Jasmin, and the carpenter Castaing. As the *Intendant des Bâtimens de la Couronne* in 1811 Faraud would also have been in charge of the project at Sans-Souci, already well underway. Sans-Souci was likely also built by at least some of the *Architectes des Palais* working under Faraud, although except for André they were

erhalten hatten«; sein Erbe wurde daher einer Stiftung übereignet.[161] In seinem Familiendossier gibt es keine Beweise dafür, dass er jemals nach Frankreich zurückkehrte: Vielmehr lebte Dardan mindestens bis zum Juli 1803 im Stadtteil *Petit Guinée* in Cap-François, in der Nähe des Place de Clugny, und bezeichnete sich selbst immer noch als »*ex-voyer de la commune du Cap*«.[162]

Bezeichnenderweise erscheint keine Mitteilung seiner Abreise in den regulären *Déclarations de Départs* der Zeitungen. Zu den Kollegen Dardans, die darin erwähnt wurden, gehörten Charles Brown, ein Zimmerer, der im Mai nach Jamaika floh; der Tischler Julien Pironneau und der Architekt Jean Ducros, die beide im April nach Frankreich abreisten; François-Guillaume Robard, der sein großes Geschäft an der rue Espagnole irgendwann vor April aufgab und in die *métropole* ging; der Zimmerer Mathieu Mercier, der im Mai abfuhr; Louis Carpentier, ein Tischler, der im Juni abreiste; und der Zimmerer Jean Castede, der im Juli nach Frankreich zurückkehrte.[163] Die Befunde lassen vermuten, dass Dardan sich noch in Cap-François aufhielt, als Dessalines die Stadt im November 1803 einnahm.[164] Möglicherweise verblieb Dardan auf Haiti, weil er eine Familie mit einer Farbigen gegründet hatte: Die Tatsache, dass sich sein Hauptwohnsitz in *Petit Guinée* befand, dem Stadtteil der *gens de couleur*, scheint dies zu bekräftigen. Sollte dies der Fall sein, hatten ihn seine Verbindungen zur Gemeinschaft der Menschen gemischter Abstammung womöglich vor Vergeltungsschlägen der Revolutionäre bewahrt. Dessalines hatte sich zu diesem Zeitpunkt mit den *gens de couleur* verbündet und es herrschte ein akuter Mangel an Architekten.[165] Tatsächlich mag Dardan aufgrund seiner Abneigung gegenüber dem französischen Militär, das ihn brüskiert hatte, mit der Revolution sympathisiert haben.[166] Dardan wäre beim Baubeginn Sans-Soucis 66-jährig und damit zu alt gewesen, um an körperlichen Arbeiten teilzunehmen, jedoch

first mentioned only in 1814, a year after the palace was completed. The palace's hydraulic works, including its grand staircase fountain, may have been designed by Julien Dufresne and Jacques Cézar—and possibly Chéri Warloppe—but again their names only appear after the palace was finished. I contend that Joseph-Antoine Dardan, as the most highly-trained architect in Haiti at the time and a possible partisan of the Revolution, also played a major role in Sans-Souci's design before 1811. Nevertheless, it must be stressed again that Dardan and Faraud must share their authorship with Henry Christophe, who likely chose the model for the palace and also closely supervised every step of its construction. Let us now turn to the possible prototypes for the palace.

The Models for the Sans-Souci Palace and Chapel Royal

The most interesting thing about the Palace of Sans-Souci—the one thing that is guaranteed not to be mentioned in travelogues and about which contemporary scholars have been equally silent—is how innovative it is as a work of architecture. Since King Henry's day everyone who has written about the building discusses it in terms of prototypes: whether Versailles, Saint-Cloud, the Louvre, Potsdam, and the Schönbrunn Palace and even British industrial architecture in the tradition of the cotton mills of New Lanark (begun 1786). To these writers Sans-Souci is by definition a copy—a sham château or miraculous palace in the jungle depending upon the writer's prejudices—and it is usually portrayed as being as slavish as the supposed ex-slave who built it. However, as we have seen, King Henry did not do things by half measures, particularly when it had to do with his monarchy's external image, whether his complex court costume, ceremonial, and heraldry or his Academy of Painting and Music with

gesund genug, um beim Zeichnen der Pläne und Aufrisse des Gebäudes mitzuhelfen und eine Beraterrolle zu übernehmen. Vermutlich starb er spätestens 1814, da er im Stab der Intendanz der Königlichen Gebäude nicht auftaucht.

Zusammenfassend lässt sich also sagen, dass *le baron* de Faraud, der mutmaßliche vormalige Sklave Joseph *dit* Faraud, spätestens ab 1811 Hauptarchitekt der Citadelle war, wahrscheinlich sogar bereits ab dem Zeitpunkt ihrer Konzeption, was sich aus seinem Gebrauch des Citadelle-Namens als Wappen schließen lässt. Die einzigen Citadelle-Erbauer, die definitiv vor 1811 in Erscheinung treten, sind Henri Barré, die Steinmetze André und Jasmin und der Zimmerer Castaing. Als *Intendant des Bâtimens de la Couronne* im Jahre 1811 wäre Faraud ebenfalls für das Projekt in Sans-Souci verantwortlich gewesen, das bereits in vollem Gange war. Vermutlich wurde Sans-Souci zumindest von manchen der *Architectes des Palais* erbaut, die für Faraud arbeiteten, auch wenn sie bis auf André erst 1814 erwähnt wurden, ein Jahr nach Vollendung des Palastes. Die Hydraulik des Palastes, einschließlich des Brunnens am großen Treppenaufgang, mag von Julien Dufresne und Jacques Cézar – und möglicherweise Chéri Warloppe – entworfen worden sein, doch deren Namen tauchen wie gesagt erst nach Fertigstellung des Palastes auf. Ich vermute, dass Joseph-Antoine Dardan, der am besten ausgebildetste Architekt Haitis zu dieser Zeit und ein möglicher Partisane der Revolution, ebenfalls eine große Rolle beim Entwurf Sans-Soucis vor 1811 spielte. Gleichwohl muss aufs Neue betont werden, dass Dardan und Faraud ihre Urheberschaft mit Henry Christophe teilen, der höchstwahrscheinlich das Palast-Modell auswählte und jeden Schritt seiner Konstruktion überwachte. Wenden wir uns nun den möglichen Prototypen des Palastes zu.

Abb. 14 Palast von Sans-Souci, (südliche) Gartenfassade
Fig. 14 Palace of Sans-Souci, garden (south) façade

its seven full-time *peintres du Roi*.[167] Instead of commissioning a literal copy of a European palace—and even a cursory glance at any of the palaces just mentioned will show that this building looks nothing like them—he sought something unique which would stand up to the monuments of the enemies he despised and the allies he courted. Sans-Souci was his showpiece. His other palaces (if the Palais de la Belle-Rivière is any indication) were poorly built and generic in design, modest buildings which could be built speedily and cheaply to imprint a visual reminder of his rule throughout his realm. Even the French colonial government buildings of *ancien régime* Saint-Domingue did not approach King Henry's palace in quality or sophistication of design: the grand designs of the French were too often truncated by limited funds, and many were never realised. Sans-Souci was an entirely different class of building from anything built by Europeans on Saint-Domingue or indeed in their American possessions in general.

Die Vorbilder des Sans-Souci Palastes und der Chapel Royal

Die interessanteste Eigenschaft des Palastes von Sans-Souci – die eine Eigenschaft, die garantiert nicht in Reiseberichten erwähnt wird und zu der zeitgenössische Forscher gleichermaßen schweigen – ist der innovative Charakter der Architektur. Seit der Zeit König Henrys hat jeder, der über das Gebäude geschrieben hat, es hinsichtlich seiner Prototypen besprochen: sei es Versailles, Saint-Cloud, der Louvre, Potsdam, Schloss Schönbrunn, und sogar britische Industriearchitektur in der Tradition der Baumwollspinnereien von New Lanark (1786 begonnen). Für diese Autoren ist Sans-Souci per definitionem eine Kopie – ein nachgemachtes Chateau oder ein fantastischer Palast im Dschungel, je nach den Vorurteilen des Autors – ein ›sklavisches Werk‹ entsprechend dem vermeintlichen Ex-Sklaven, der es erbauen ließ. Doch wie wir gesehen haben, machte König Henry keine halben Sachen, insbesondere was die Fremdwahrnehmung seiner Monarchie betraf. Das beweist die Komplexität der Tracht, des Zeremoniells und der Heraldik seines Hofes, oder aber seine Akademie für Malerei und Musik mit ihren sieben hauptamtlichen *peintres du Roi*.[167] Anstatt buchstäblich eine Kopie eines europäischen Palastes in Auftrag zu geben – sogar ein oberflächlicher Blick auf jeden der eben erwähnten Paläste zeigt, dass dieses Gebäude keinem von ihnen ähnelt – trachtete er nach etwas Einzigartigem, das neben den Monumenten seiner verhassten Gegner und seiner umworbenen Verbündeten bestehen konnte. Sans-Souci war sein Vorzeigeobjekt. Seine anderen Paläste (falls das Palais de la Belle-Rivière als Anhaltspunkt dienen kann) waren schlecht gebaut und gewöhnlich im Entwurf, bescheidene Gebäude, die schnell und billig errichtet werden konnten, um dem Land eine visuelle Mahnung an seine Herrschaft aufzuprägen. Sogar die französischen Kolonialregierungsbauten im Saint-Domingue des *ancien régime* reichten an König Henrys Palast

This being said, the building, like Henry's court culture, official language, and legal system, is unmistakably French. In fact the Palace of Sans-Souci is built quite precisely in the early style of Louis XV. A rectangular two-storey-plus-attic *corps de logis* with a long horizontal profile it makes minimal use of columns or pilasters and features understated entablatures, prominent central ressauts on both façades, and a sectional roofline comprised of low pitched roofs over the wings, a rectangular dome over the central pavilion, and two hip-roofed terminal pavilions [Figs. 1, 14, 15]. It recalls in particular the work of Robert de Cotte (1656/57–1735), since 1708 *premier architecte du roi* under the *Bâtiments du Roi*, and Germain Boffrand (1667–1754), two of the new style's main protagonists in the first quarter of the eighteenth century.[168] The preference for the restrained Baroque Classicism of the Regency and Louis XV's reign is not surprising since it had also been the favoured style of French colonial architects throughout the Atlantic Empire and was therefore the one Henry would have known best. To give one example: on the Island of Guadeloupe a cluster of official buildings planned for Basse-Terre and Pointe-à-Pitre as late as the 1770s and 1780s still closely emulated the Paris *hôtel particulier* of the second quarter of the eighteenth century.[169]

One model is close enough that it can be confirmed as the main inspiration for Sans-Souci, but Henry's architects still took generous liberties with it: Boffrand's project for the Palace of Malgrange (first version, 1712–15), built for the Duke of Lorrain as a *maison de plaisance* outside the ducal capital of Nancy but never completed, is strikingly close to the Milot palace [Figs. 16–18].[170] Illustrations of the building would have been readily accessible as a full set of plans and elevations were published in Boffrand's *Livre d'architecture* (Paris, 1745)—this detail is important since even in French colonial times the vast majority of public buildings were based on en-

bezüglich seiner Qualität oder der Raffinesse seines Entwurfs nicht heran: Die grandiosen Pläne der Franzosen wurden allzu oft durch beschränkte Geldmittel gestutzt, und viele niemals ausgeführt. Sans-Souci gehörte einer vollkommen anderen Gebäudeklasse an, die sich von Allem unterschied, was Europäer auf Saint-Domingue, ja in ihren amerikanischen Besitzungen überhaupt, gebaut hatten.

Gleichwohl ist das Gebäude, ebenso wie Henrys höfische Kultur, die offizielle Sprache und das Rechtssystem, unverkennbar französisch. Der Palast von Sans-Souci ist im frühen Stil Ludwigs XV. errichtet. Das rechteckige, mit zwei Stockwerken plus Dachgeschoss ausgestattete *Corps de Logis* mit einem langen horizontalen Profil macht nur minimalen Gebrauch von Säulen und Pilastern. Es weist ein dezentes Gebälk, hervorstehende zentrale Risalite auf beiden Fassaden und eine eingeteilte Dachlinie auf, die aus geringfügig geneigten Dächern über den Flügeln, einer rechteckigen Kuppel über dem zentralen Pavillon und zwei mit Walmdächern versehenen, abschließenden Pavillons besteht [Abb. 1, 14, 15]. Es ruft insbesondere das Werk von Robert de Cotte (1656/57–1735) in Erinnerung, der seit 1708 *premier architecte du roi* der *Bâtiments du Roi* war, und von Germain Boffrand (1667–1754), zwei Hauptprotagonisten des neuen Stils im ersten Viertel des achtzehnten Jahrhunderts.[168] Die Vorliebe für den zurückgenommenen Barock-Klassizismus der *Régence* und der Herrschaft Ludwigs XV. überrascht nicht, da dies auch der bevorzugte Stil der französischen Architekten der Kolonialzeit im gesamten Atlantikreich war, und damit derjenige, mit dem Henry am meisten vertraut gewesen wäre. Um nur ein Beispiel anzuführen: Auf der Insel Guadeloupe ahmte eine Ansammlung offizieller Bauten, die erst in den 1770ern und 1780ern für Basse-Terre und Pointe-à-Pitre geplant wurden, das Pariser *hôtel particulier* des zweiten Viertels des achtzehnten Jahrhunderts aufs Genaueste nach.[169]

Abb. 15 Palast von Sans-Souci, (nördliche) Hoffassade und großer Treppen-aufgang

Fig. 15 Palace of Sans-Souci, court (north) façade and great staircase

gravings. Both are long rectangular structures with a projecting pavilion on the garden façade and a colonnade on the court façade, two long, unadorned wings of two storeys each with an arcade on the ground floor, high rectangular windows above, and a low pitched roof, although Sans-Souci lacked dormer windows and its garden façade had an attic so high that it served as a third full storey and it also had second storey end towers on the court facade. Both Malgrange and Sans-Souci have a heavy entablature under the roofline uniting the wings with the pavilions and three-bay pavilions at the ends with attics and pitched roofs, although at Malgrange they form true ressauts whereas at Sans-Souci they are flush with the rest of the façade. At Sans-Souci a second cornice separates the two lower storeys which is absent in Boffrand's model

Abb. 16 Germain Boffrand: Palais de La Malgrange (Lorrain), Gartenfassade. Aus dem *Livre d'architecture* (1745), Tafel XVI. Zentralinstitut für
Kunstgeschichte, München. BZI: 4° CA 242/725 R (Rara-Magazin)

Fig. 16 Germain Boffrand: Palais de La Malgrange (Lorrain), garden façade.
From *Livre d'architecture* (1745), pl. XVI. Zentralinstitut für Kunstgeschichte,
Munich. BZI: 4° CA 242/725 R (Rara-Magazin)

Eines der Vorbilder ist ähnlich genug, um als größte Inspi-
rationsquelle Sans-Soucis bestätigt zu werden, auch wenn
sich Henrys Architekten großzügige Freiheiten herausnah-
men: Boffrands nie abgeschlossenes Projekt für den Palast
von Malgrange (erste Version, 1712–15), gebaut für den Her-
zog von Lorrain als *maison de plaisance* außerhalb der herzog-
lichen Hauptstadt Nancy, besitzt auffallende Ähnlichkeit mit
dem Palast von Milot [Abb. 16–18].[170] Illustrationen des Gebäudes wären leicht zugänglich gewesen, da ein vollständiger
Satz von Plänen und Aufrissen in Boffrands *Livre d'architecture* (Paris, 1745) veröffentlicht wurde – dieses Detail ist be-
deutsam, da sogar während der französischen Kolonialzeit die
große Mehrheit öffentlicher Gebäude auf Kupferstichen be-
ruhte. Beide sind lange, rechteckige Bauten mit einem proji-
zierenden Pavillon auf der Gartenfassade und einer Kolonnade auf der Hoffassade, zwei langen, ungeschmückten
Flügeln mit jeweils zwei Stockwerken, mit einer Arkade im
Erdgeschoss, hohen rechteckigen Fenstern darüber, und
einem Dach mit geringer Neigung; allerdings verfügte Sans-
Souci über keine Dachfenster und das Dachgeschoss seiner

Abb. 17 Germain Boffrand: Palais de La Malgrange (Lorrain), Vorhof-
fassade. Aus dem *Livre d'architecture* (1745), Tafel XV. Zentralinstitut für
Kunstgeschichte, München. BZI: 4° CA 242/725 R (Rara-Magazin)

Fig. 17 Germain Boffrand: Palais de La Malgrange (Lorrain), forecourt
façade. From *Livre d'architecture* (1745): pl. XV. Zentralinstitut für Kunstgeschichte, Munich. BZI: 4° CA 242/725 R (Rara-Magazin)

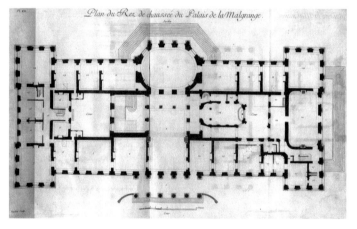

Abb. 18 Germain Boffrand: Palais de La Malgrange (Lorrain), Grundriss des
Erdgeschosses. Aus dem *Livre d'architecture* (1745), Tafel XII. Zentralinstitut
für Kunstgeschichte, München. BZI: 4° CA 242/725 R (Rara-Magazin).

Fig. 18 Germain Boffrand: Palais de La Malgrange (Lorrain), ground floor
plan. From *Livre d'architecture* (1745): pl. XII. Zentralinstitut für Kunstgeschichte, Munich. BZI: 4° CA 242/725 R (Rara-Magazin)

Gartenfassade war so hoch, dass es als ganzer dritter Stock diente. Außerdem hatte die Hoffassade im zweiten Stock abschließende Türme. Sowohl Malgrange als auch Sans-Souci besitzen ein schweres Gebälk unterhalb der Dachlinie, das die Flügel mit den Pavillons verbindet, und dreijochige Pavillons an den Enden mit Dachgeschossen und Satteldächern, obwohl sie bei Malgrange echte Risalite bilden, wohingegen sie bei Sans-Souci mit dem Rest der Fassade bündig sind. Bei Sans-Souci trennt ein zweites Gesims die beiden unteren Stockwerke voneinander, was in Boffrands Vorbild fehlt, aber in mehreren Werken von Robert de Cotte auftaucht, insbesondere am Ostflügel der Abtei von Saint-Denis (1700–12) oder dem bischöflichen Palast in Verdun (1724–51).[171]

Das hervorstechende Motiv der Gartenfassade von Malgrange [Abb. 16] ist ein zentraler Risalit mit zwei Stockwerken und einem Dachgeschoss, der die Gestalt eines dreijochigen korinthischen Portikus annimmt. Er wird von einem dreieckigen Pediment bedeckt, auf beiden Seiten von einem einzelnen Joch auf einem schrägen Winkel flankiert, und trägt ein hohes Dachgeschoss, das der Kuppel als Sockel dient. Im jetzigen Zustand Sans-Soucis ist es schwierig festzustellen, wie häufig dort die klassischen Säulenordnungen verwendet wurden, wenngleich im Erdgeschoss immer noch ein Paar dorischer Pilaster jedes der flankierenden Joche einrahmt und es scheint, als ob vormals drei weitere die bogenförmigen Öffnungen des Portikus voneinander trennten [Abb. 19, 20]. Anders als bei Malgrange waren diese keine Kolossalordnungen: Tatsächlich war das obere Geschoss Sans-Soucis wahrscheinlich glatt. Wie Louis Le Vaus Chateau in Vaux-le-Vicomte (1657–61) [Abb. 21] und spätere Gebäude wie Robert de Cottes Projekt für die Residenz in Würzburg (1723), umschließt der Pavillon bei Malgrange einen schräg-ovalen Salon, der die Ausmaße des Risalits bestimmt.[172] Allerdings hat Boffrand dessen Krümmung hinter geradlinigen Wänden verborgen,

Abb. 19 Palast von Sans-Souci, Portikus der Gartenfassade
Fig. 19 Palace of Sans-Souci, portico of garden façade

but appears in several works by Robert de Cotte, notably the east wing of the Abbey of Saint-Denis (1700–12) or the Episcopal Palace at Verdun (1724–51).[171]

The salient motif of Malgrange's garden façade [Fig. 16] is a two-storey-plus-attic central ressaut taking the form of a pavilion with a three-bay Corinthian portico capped with a triangular pediment, flanked on each side by a single bay on a diagonal angle, and supporting a high attic which serves as a plinth for the dome. It is difficult in its current condition to tell how much Sans-Souci used the classical orders, however

Abb. 20 Palast von Sans-Souci, Portikus der Gartenfassade, Seitenansicht
Fig. 20 Palace of Sans-Souci, portico of garden façade, side view

a pair of Doric pilasters still frames each of the flanking bays on the ground floor and it looks as if three more once separated the arched openings of the portico [Figs. 19, 20]. Unlike at Malgrange these were not giant orders: indeed the upper storey at Sans-Souci was probably smooth. Like Louis Le Vau's château at Vaux-le-Vicomte (1657–61) [Fig. 21] and later buildings such as Robert de Cotte's project for the Residenz in Würzburg (1723) the pavilion at Malgrange encloses a transverse oval salon which determines the dimensions of the ressaut.[172] However Boffrand has concealed its curvature behind rectilinear walls unlike at Vaux where the convex walls are exposed and become the main motif of the facade. Sans-Souci also does not hide its curves, but here—in a dramatic reversal—they are concave, in fact pronouncedly so, recalling the façades of Francesco Borromini or Guarino Guarini more than anything in the French canon. Sans-Souci's pavilion replaces the oval with a rectangle with deeply scooped-out outer corners so that the flanking bays are much wider than those of the main portico and serve as the garden façade's two principal entrances [Fig. 22]. The arched door and upper two windows accommodate to the curvature of the wall [Fig. 20], a particularly difficult task requiring a sophisticated knowledge of stereotomy. In fact Frézier's manual has much to say about cutting arched openings such as niches through convex corners (Vol III, Book IV, Part II, pl. 88, 95). Curvilinear forms are rare and understated in French architecture of the time except in some of the work of Jacques Hardouin-Mansart de Sagonne—an undeservedly understudied master of the late Baroque—who makes a playful foray into curves and countercurves with Saint-Louis Cathedral in Versailles (1743–54), although they are subtler than those at Sans-Souci.[173]

Another departure from Malgrange is Sans-Souci's semicircular pediment [Fig. 19]: curving pediments are relatively rare on French porticoes and when they do appear, as at Las-

anders als in Vaux, wo die konvexen Wände freigelegt sind und zum Hauptmotiv der Fassade werden. Auch Sans-Souci versteckt seine Kurven nicht, hier sind sie jedoch – in einer dramatischen Umkehrung – konkav, und zwar auf explizite Weise, sodass sie eher auf die Fassaden Francesco Borrominis oder Guarino Guarinis verweisen als auf irgendetwas im französischen Kanon. Der Pavillon von Sans-Souci ersetzt das Oval durch ein Rechteck mit tief ausgehöhlten Außenecken, woraufhin die flankierenden Joche viel weiter als diejenigen des zentralen Portikus ausfallen und somit als die beiden Haupteingänge der Gartenfassade fungieren [Abb. 22]. Die Bogentür und oberen zwei Fenster passen sich der Wandkrümmung an [Abb. 20], ein besonders schwieriges Unterfangen, das ein tiefes Verständnis der Stereotomie voraussetzt. In der Tat enthält Fréziers Handbuch viel über das Schneiden gewölbter Öffnungen, wie etwa Nischen, durch konvexe Ecken (Band III, Buch IV, Teil II, Tafel 88, 95). Gekrümmte Formen sind in der französischen Architektur dieser Zeit selten und dezent, außer in einem Teil des Werkes von Jacques Hardouin-Mansart de Sagonne – ein unverdientermaßen vernachlässigter Meister des Spätbarock – der mit der Kathedrale von Saint-Louis in Versailles (1743–54) ein spielerisches Experiment mit Kurven und Gegenkurven wagte, allerdings subtiler als in Sans-Souci.[173]

Eine weitere Abkehr von Malgrange ist Sans-Soucis halbrundes Pediment [Abb. 19]: Gekrümmte Pedimente sind auf französischen Portiken verhältnismäßig rar und wenn sie doch auftreten, wie beim Hotel de Bragelonne (1707) von Lassurance in Paris oder dem Hotel de Réauville (1714–17; später Caumont) von de Cotte in Aix en Provence, neigen sie dazu, sich auf Gebäuden mit drei ganzen Stockwerken zu befinden – in einer Ausnahme, Paul Grivels Hotel de Beauffremond in Paris (1718–36), ist der gesamte dreijochige Pavillon konvex.[174] Die Treppen an der Gartenfassade von Sans-Souci weichen

Abb. 21 Louis Le Vau, Chateau bei Vaux-le-Vicomte (1657–61)
Fig. 21 Louis Le Vau, château at Vaux-le-Vicomte (1657–61)

Abb. 22 Palast von Sans-Souci. Inneres des Portikus der Gartenfassade
Fig. 22 Palace of Sans-Souci, interior of portico of garden façade

ebenfalls von Boffrands Vorbild ab, zumindest teilweise aufgrund der Herausforderungen des hügeligen Standortes. Der hexagonale Treppenaufgang von Malgrange wird durch ein Paar gekrümmter Treppen ersetzt, die auf beiden Seiten von den konkaven Jochen hinabstürzen; vor dem Portikus stand einst jedoch auch eine rechteckige Terrasse, die Ausblicke auf den Garten erlaubte. Der Palast sitzt auf einem gewölbten Keller, der als Lager diente und am Ostende zugänglich ist.

Die Hoffassade von Sans-Souci stimmt stärker mit dem Geist von Malgrange überein, allerdings wiederum ohne die Kolossalordnungen [Abb. 15, 17, 23]. Der Pavillon ist fünf Joche weit und hat zwei Stockwerke und ein Dachgeschoss. Wie sein Vorbild macht er Gebrauch von eingebundenen Säulen, jedoch nur im Erdgeschoss. Ritters Druck zeigt, dass die Säulen im ersten Stock durch ein Eisengitter und eine Holzüberdachung ersetzt wurden, die von eisernen Stützarmen

surance's Hotel de Bragelonne (1707) in Paris or de Cotte's Hotel de Réauville (1714–17; later Caumont) in Aix en Provence, they tend to be on buildings with three full storeys—in an exception, Paul Grivel's Hotel de Beauffremond in Paris (1718–36), the entire three-bay pavilion is convex.[174] The stairs on the garden façade at Sans-Souci also depart from Boffrand's model, at least partly because of the challenges of the hilly site, replacing the former's hexagonal staircase with a pair of curving flights which sweep down each side from the concave bays, although there was once also a rectangular terrace in front of the portico to afford views of the garden. The palace sits atop a vaulted cellar which served as a storeroom which is accessed on the east end.

The court façade at Sans-Souci adheres more closely to the spirit of Malgrange, but again subtracting the giant orders [Figs. 15, 17, 23]. The pavilion is five bays wide and has two storeys and an attic and like its model it uses engaged columns, although just on the ground floor. Ritter's engraving shows that on the first storey the columns were replaced by an iron grille and a wood canopy held up with iron support arms [Fig. 13]. As with the garden façade the end pavilions, each three bays wide, do not project and they also support iron grilles and canopies on the *étage*. The Sans-Souci portico has also eliminated the Malgrange pavilion's porch, although it subtly projects forward by means of diagonal wall sections on each flank, and it replaces Malgrange's entablature and balustrade at the top with a triangular pediment (once bearing the royal arms).[175] As in the garden façade the Sans-Souci palace has also opted for the Doric order and although the portico still has six columns as at Malgrange it has only three openings. It is a sign of the academic rigour of Sans-Souci's architect that the entablature over the colonnade features prominent triglyphs and metopes, correct usage for a Doric building.

aufrechtgehalten wurde [Abb. 13]. Wie bei der Gartenfassade ragen die Endpavillons, beide drei Joche weit, nicht heraus und stützen ebenfalls eiserne Gitter und Überdachungen auf der *étage*. Der Portikus von Sans-Souci verzichtet auch auf die Veranda des Malgrange-Pavillons, obwohl er mittels diagonaler Wandabschnitte auf beiden Flanken leicht hervorsteht. Außerdem ersetzt er das Gebälk und die obere Balustrade von Malgrange durch ein dreieckiges Pediment (das vormals das königliche Wappen trug).[175] Wie die Gartenfassade verwendet Sans-Souci die dorische Ordnung, und obwohl der Portikus wie bei Malgrange auch sechs Säulen aufweist, befinden sich in ihm nur drei Öffnungen. Es ist ein Zeichen der architektonischen Sorgfalt des Architekten von Sans-Souci, dass das Gebälk über der Kolonnade markante Triglyphen und Metopen aufweist, was einem korrekten Gebrauch bei einem dorischen Gebäude entspricht.

Die Ähnlichkeiten zwischen den beiden Palästen enden jedoch bei dem riesigen *escalier à double rampe* (doppelten Treppenaufgang), der Sans-Souci auf der Hofseite stützt, wo das Erdgeschoss wesentlich tiefer liegt als auf der Rückseite [Abb. 15]. Es gibt in der französischen Architektur nichts Vergleichbares: Das nächstliegende Vorbild ist der obere Teil von Jacopo Barozzo da Vignolas großem Treppenaufgang der Villa Farnese in Caprarola (1559 begonnen), der durch mehrere Stiche bekannt war, insbesondere durch einen von Giovanni Battista Falda (ca. 1655).[176] Wie die Villa Farnese verfügt Sans-Souci über paarweise angeordnete, mit zwei Rampen ausgestattete diagonale Treppenaufgänge auf jeder Seite, mit einer Grotte in der Mitte (in Caprarola befindet sich die Grotte im unteren Treppenaufgang; der obere konzentriert sich stattdessen auf ein rustiziertes Portal). Die Grotte des Palastes von Milot ist ein geräumiges, hemisphärisches Gewölbe (5 m hoch), mit riesigen rustizierten Scheitelsteinen, einer Balustrade davor, und einer einzigen Wasserquelle im Zentrum (ur-

Abb. 23 Palast von Sans-Souci. Hoffassade, Detail
Fig. 23 Palace of Sans-Souci, Court Façade, detail

However the similarity between the two palaces ends with the huge *escalier à double rampe* (double staircase) which supports Sans-Souci on the court side where the ground level is substantially lower than at the back [Fig. 15]. There is nothing comparable in French architecture: in fact the closest model is the upper part of Jacopo Barozzo da Vignola's great staircase at the Villa Farnese at Caprarola (begun 1559), known through several engravings, notably one by Giovanni Battista Falda (ca. 1655).[176] As at Caprarola, Sans-Souci features a matching double-ramped diagonal stairway on each side with a grotto in the middle (at Caprarola the grotto is located in the lower staircase; the upper one focuses instead on a rusticated portal). The grotto at the Milot palace is a spacious hemispherical vault (it is five metres high) with giant rusticated

131

sprünglich hing eine vergoldete hölzerne Sonne über den Scheitelsteinen, und ein Paar bronzener Löwen saß auf den Sockeln zu beiden Seiten des Bassins darunter).[177] Die Grotte beweist abermals eine Vertrautheit mit der Komplexität der Stereotomie: In der Tat widmet Frézier den »voutes sphériques« ein ganzes Kapitel (Band I, Kapitel VII).

Henrys Architekten verschmelzen Vignolas italienische Treppe mit einer sehr berühmten französischen: Dem *Escalier des Ambassadeurs* von Louis Le Vau und Charles Le Brun in Versailles (1671 begonnen). Diese Treppe wurde zwar 1752 abgerissen, war aber durch Stiche bekannt, etwa durch den Entwurf und Aufriss, die beide 1721 von Jean-Michel Chevotet und Louis Surugue in Paris veröffentlicht wurden.[178] Obwohl es sich um einen Innenraum handelt, war die Treppe von Außentreppen wie derjenigen in Caprarola inspiriert. Die Gesandtentreppe besitzt nur ein einziges Paar divergierender diagonaler Rampen, von Balustraden bekrönt, aber sie platziert die Grotte und den Brunnen im Zentrum, ebenso wie die Treppe von Sans-Souci, und – was wichtiger ist – sie enthält auch den breiten, einzelnen Aufgang am Boden, der sich in den Hof auffächert (diese Form erscheint auch in Buch drei von Sebastiano Serlios *I Sette libri dell'architettura* von 1537).[179] Wenn der *Escalier des Ambassadeurs* wirklich eines der Vorbilder war, hätte es Henry sicher behagt, dass die imposanteste Treppe Versailles' verdoppelt werden musste, um seinem Palast in Sans-Souci zu genügen.

Der grundlegende rechteckige Entwurf Sans-Soucis – das zentrale *Corps de Logis* misst 51 × 25 m und ist 25 m hoch – ist eine Abänderung desjenigen von Malgrange oder unzähliger französischer Prototypen des frühen achtzehnten Jahrhunderts, trotz des eben erwähnten Fehlens eines ovalen Salons.[180] Die drei längsverlaufenden Flügel bilden Raumfluchten in der traditionellen französischen Zeremonialfolge von Prunksälen [Abb. 24]. Ihre Hallen sind durch acht Meter hohe Tür-

Abb. 24 Palast von Sans-Souci. Nördliche Enfilade, vom Ende des West-flügels aus gesehen
Fig. 24 Palace of Sans-Souci, northern enfilade viewed from the end of the west wing

keystones at the top, a balustrade in front, and a single source of water in the centre (originally a gilt wooden sun hung above the keystones, and a pair of bronze lions once sat on plinths to either side of the basin below).[177] The grotto again

bögen voneinander getrennt. Die nordlichen und südlichen Flügel enthielten jeweils fünf Räume, ein zentrales Vestibül mit einer Länge von fünf Jochen (13,5 m breit, dieselbe Breite wie die beiden Portiken), zwei flankierende Säle mit sechs Jochen, und zwei abschließende Räume mit drei Jochen, während der mittlere Flügel in acht Räume aufgeteilt war: Ein zentraler Thronsaal mit den Maßen 13,5 × 7,5 m, ein Treppenhaus auf beiden Seiten, drei kleinere Gemächer im Osten und zwei größere im Westen. Es existiert auch eine klare seitliche Blickachse vom Haupteingang zum Garteneingang, wie bei Malgrange (oder Vaux-le-Vicomte). Die zentralen und südlichen Flügel besaßen jeweils drei ganze Stockwerke, wohingegen der nördliche Flügel nur zwei hatte, plus einen beschränkten *grenier*, der, bis auf die beiden Turmpavillons an den Enden, von einem Schrägdach verborgen wurde [Abb. 13, 24]. Die Aufteilung des *rez-de-chaussée* wurde im ersten und zweiten Stockwerk wiederholt, die – gemäß Leconte, der allerdings seine Quellen nicht preisgibt – vier Bankettsäle über dem südlichen Flügel und, über dem Zentrum und dem nördlichen Flügel, die Audienzräume des Königs und der Königin enthielten, sowie die Bibliothek, das Studierzimmer des Königs, Badezimmer, die Gemächer des Königs (im Nordwesten) und der Königin (im Nordosten), die beide auf die Schlussbalkone hinausgingen.[181] Die Gemächer der zwei Prinzessinnen befanden sich im Obergeschoss der Turmpavillons an der Hoffassade. Das *Corps de Logis* konnte im Erdgeschoss auch von beiden Enden durch breite, einmal gewölbte Eingänge in den nördlichen und südlichen Flügeln, und durch ein Paar engerer Öffnungen im zentralen Flügel betreten werden.

Eine der herausragenden Eigenschaften Sans-Soucis ist seine ungewöhnlich vielfältige Steinmetzarbeit, die zu großen Teilen von der Antike übernommen wurde [Abb. 23]. Der Palast verbindet *opus incertum* im römischen Stil (grobe Steine, die unregelmäßig in Mörtel gesetzt werden) – wie beim Brun-

demonstrates familiarity with the complexities of stereotomy: in fact Frézier devotes an entire chapter to "voutes sphériques" (Vol. I, Chapter VII).

Henry's architects merge Vignola's Italian staircase with a very famous French one: Louis Le Vau and Charles Le Brun's *Escalier des Ambassadeurs* at Versailles (begun 1671), demolished in 1752 but known through engravings such as the plan and elevation published by Jean-Michel Chevotet and Louis Surugue in Paris in 1721.[178] Although an interior space, it was inspired by exterior staircases like that at Caprarola. The Ambassadors' Staircase only has a single pair of diverging diagonal ramps, crowned with balustrades, but it locates the grotto and fountain in the centre as in the Sans-Souci staircase and—more importantly—it includes the broad single stairway at the bottom which fans out into the courtyard (this form also appears in Book Three of Sebastiano Serlio's *I Sette libri dell'architettura* of 1537).[179] If the *Escalier des Ambassadeurs* was indeed one of the models it may have pleased Henry that Versailles' most imposing staircase had to be doubled to serve his palace at Sans-Souci.

The basic rectangular plan of Sans-Souci—the main *corps de logis* measures 51 by 25 metres and is 25 metres high—is a redaction of that of Malgrange or any number of early eighteenth-century French prototypes, although it lacks the oval salon as just noted.[180] The three longitudinal ranges create enfilades in the traditional French ceremonial sequence of state rooms [Fig. 24], their halls separated by high arched doorways with ceilings eight metres high. The northern and southern ranges contained five rooms each, a central vestibule five bays long (13.5 metres wide, the same width as the two porticos), two flanking halls of six bays, and two end rooms of three bays, while the middle range was divided into eight: a central throne room measuring 13.5 by 7.5 metres, a stair hall on either side, three smaller chambers to the east and

nen, dem Treppenaufgang, den Fundamenten der Gartenfassade, und manchen Wänden des *Corps de Logis* – mit *opus mixtum* (abwechselnde Lagen aus Ziegeln und Schutt) im Großteil des *Corps de Logis*, während die eingebundenen Säulen und Pilaster, Gebälke, Brunnen-Bogensteine, Balustraden, hintere Treppe, Wachhäuschen, und manche der Fenster- und Türumgebungen vollständig aus Ziegelsteinen gemacht sind.[182] Quadermauerwerk wird auch im Pediment der Gartenfassade und im rechteckigen Panel darüber verwendet. Das Gebäude enthält sogar Doppelbögen aus Ziegeln, wie die in römischen Bädern, mit einer Steinlage dazwischen, so beispielsweise die Stützbögen der nördlichen Raumflucht im *Corps de Logis*.

Obwohl diese Komplexität hinter ockerfarbenem Putz verborgen blieb, ist die Kombination so vieler klassischer Techniken bemerkenswert und originell: Keine davon wurde für die größten französischen Festungen der Karibik verwendet, weder für das Fort Saint-Charles auf Guadeloupe (heute Fort Delgrès, 1702–80) [Abb. 25], das Fort Saint-Louis auf Martinique (1672–1710), noch, auf Saint-Domingue, das Fort Vallières bei Môle Saint-Nicolas (1764 begonnen) oder das Fort-Dauphin (heute Fort-Liberté, 1731 begonnen).[183] Französisches Mauerwerk der Kolonialzeit bestand normalerweise vollkommen aus Stein, meistens eine Kombination aus behauenen Quadern und einer Spachtelung aus Kalkstein-, Korallen-, oder Tuffstein-Schutt, fixiert in einem Mörtel aus Sand und Kalk – der feinste Werkstein auf Saint-Domingue stammte aus Môle Saint-Nicolas oder wurde aus Frankreich importiert – wenngleich wie in Sans-Souci die dekorativen Details, seien es Fenster- und Türrahmen, Pilaster, Säulen oder Gesimse, aus Ziegeln gemacht waren.[184] Eine ähnliche Kombination aus *opus incertum* und *opus mixtum* tritt auch bei der Citadelle auf [Abb. 2, 10], auch wenn dort, wie es einer Festung gebührt, viel mehr Stein verwendet wurde; außerdem

two larger ones to the west. There is also a clear lateral line of vision from the front entrance through to the garden entrance as at Malgrange (or Vaux-le-Vicomte). The central and southern ranges had three full storeys each whereas the northern range had only two plus a constricted *grenier* hidden by a sloping roof [Figs 13, 24], except for the two tower pavilions at the ends. The divisions of the *rez-de-chaussée* were repeated on the first and second storeys which included—according to Leconte, who however does not reveal his sources—four banquet halls over the south range, and, over the centre and northern range, the audience chambers of the King and Queen, library, King's study, bathrooms, the King's apartments (to the northwest) and those of the Queen (to the northeast), the latter two giving onto the end balconies.[181] The two princesses' apartments occupied the top storey of the tower pavilions on the court facade. The *corps de logis* could also be entered on both ends on the ground floor through wide single arched entrances in the northern and southern ranges and a pair of narrower openings in the central range.

One of the most outstanding qualities of Sans-Souci is the unusually varied nature of its masonry, much of it taken from Antiquity [Fig. 23]. The palace combines Roman-style *opus incertum* (rough stones set irregularly in mortar)—as in the fountain, staircase, foundations of the garden façade, and some of the walls of the *corps de logis*—with *opus mixtum* (alternating courses of brick and rubble) in most of the *corps de logis*, while the engaged columns and pilasters, entablatures, fountain voussoirs, balustrades, rear staircase, sentry boxes, and some of the window and door surrounds are made entirely of brick.[182] Ashlar masonry is also used inside the pediment of the garden façade and on the rectangular panel above it. The building even includes double brick arches like those in a Roman baths with a stone course in between, as with the supporting arches of the northern enfilade in the *corps de logis*.

Abb. 25 Baracken, Fort Saint-Charles (heute Fort Delgrès), Basse-Terre, Guadeloupe, 1766–80

Fig. 25 Barracks, Fort Saint-Charles (now Fort Delgrès), Basse-Terre, Guadeloupe, 1766–80

weist die Citadelle Ecksteine aus Ziegeln und Steinen auf, die am Palast nicht vorkommen. Die Ähnlichkeiten zwischen den zwei Gebäuden verleihen der Theorie, dass beide von denselben Arbeiterschaften unter der Aufsicht Farauds errichtet wurden, mehr Glaubwürdigkeit. Es sähe König Henry nicht unähnlich, sich eines an das römische Imperium gemahnenden Stils zu bedienen, um Eindruck zu schinden; was überrascht, ist, dass solch eine akademische Methode in einer Region eingesetzt wurde, in der sie zuvor noch nie benutzt worden war.

Einige Details des Palastes beziehen sich auf die Architektur von Cap-François, das unter dem französischen Regime einen eigenständigen Stil entwickelte. Besonders charakteristisch ist die zentrale Kuppel des Palastes, deren Dachlinie in einem Paar *Pignons* oder Bekrönungen endet, ein in Cap verbreitetes Profil, das immer noch auf manchen der älteren Häuser der Stadt zu sehen ist, wobei die Dachziegel heute oft

Although these complexities would have been hidden behind ochre-coloured plaster the combination of so many classical techniques is striking and original: none of them were used in the major French fortresses in the Caribbean, whether at Fort Saint-Charles in Guadeloupe (now Fort Delgrès, 1702–80) [Fig. 25], Fort Saint-Louis in Martinique (1672–1710), or, in Saint-Domingue, Fort Vallières at Môle Saint-Nicolas (begun 1764) or Fort-Dauphin (now Fort-Liberté, begun 1731).[183] French colonial masonry was usually entirely of stone, usually a combination of hewn ashlar and a filling made of limestone, coral, or tufa rubble fixed in a mortar of sand and lime—in Saint-Domingue the finest ashlar came from Môle Saint-Nicolas or was imported from France—although as at Sans-Souci the decorative details such as window and door frames, pilasters, columns, and cornices were brick.[184] A similar combination of *opus incertum* and *opus mixtum* also appears at the Citadelle [Figs. 2, 10], although it uses much more stone as befits a fortress and features a kind of brick-and-stone quoining at the corners which does not appear in the palace. These similarities lend more credence to the theory that the two buildings were constructed by the same work crews, probably under Faraud's supervision. It is not out of character that King Henry would employ a style redolent of the Roman Empire since he built to impress; what is unexpected is that such an academic method would be employed in a region where it had never been used before.

Some details of the palace relate to the architecture of Cap-François, which developed a distinct vernacular style under the French regime. Particularly characteristic is the palace's central dome, the roofline of which ends in a pair of *pignons*, or finials, a common profile in Cap-François which can still be seen on some of the older houses in the city, the original tiles often now replaced by corrugated iron [Figs. 13, 26]. Another motif which derives from the architecture of colo-

durch Wellblech ersetzt worden sind [Abb. 13, 26]. Ein weiteres Motiv, das der kolonialen Architektur Cap-François'
entstammt, ist die einfache Pfeilerarkade im Erdgeschoss mit
einem einfachen Gurtgesims auf Höhe der Kämpferlinie der
Bögen: Diese Form findet sich an den verbleibenden Flügeln
der Großen Kaserne, die im Unterschied zu Sans-Souci außerdem über Sockel verfügt [Abb. 8]. Schließlich zeigt der Druck
Ritters, wie bereits erwähnt, dass die beiden Seitenrisalite und
der zentrale Portikus der Hoffassade einmal im ersten Stock
Balkone mit Eisengittern und überhängenden Holzbaldachi-
nen besaßen. Diese Art von Balkon war im kolonialzeitlichen
Cap-François und bis ins neunzehnte Jahrhundert hinein be-
liebt, auch wenn sie in den letzten Jahrzehnten so gut wie verschwunden sind. Ähnliche aus dem späteren neunzehnten
Jahrhundert haben in Orten wie Pointe-à-Pitre (Guadeloupe)
überlebt [Abb. 27].[185] Eisengitter tauchten in Cap-François
spätestens in den 1730ern auf, wie zum Beispiel in dem Entwurf von Louis-Joseph Delalance für das Magasin Royal
(1737), das gegenüber dem Quay Saint-Louis (heute rue B) gebaut wurde [Abb. 28].[186] Diese Details deuten an, dass zumindest manche der Architekten von Sans-Souci in den Werkstätten von Cap-François ausgebildet wurden oder mit dem
capois Stil vertraut waren.

Die Chapel Royal ist ein ebenso beachtenswertes Bauwerk:
Sie verfügt über den ersten runden Kirchengrundriss (20 m
im Durchmesser) und die erste Kuppel, die jemals auf dem Gebiet des ehemaligen französischen Atlantikreiches errichtet
wurden [Abb. 29].[187] Der Bau runder Kirchen war unpraktisch
und schwierig zugleich, da er Steinmetze voraussetzte, die der
Stereotomie kundig waren, um die gekrümmten Wände her-
zustellen und sie mit Fenstern und Türen zu durchstoßen.
Nur zwei solcher Kirchen wurden überhaupt in den französischen Atlantikkolonien zum Bau vorgeschlagen, eine in
Pointe-à-Pitre im Jahr 1806 und die andere – tatsächlich ein

Abb. 26 Haus aus dem achtzehnten Jahrhundert an der ehemaligen Rue du Morne des Capucins & Rue Saint-Michel, Cap-Haitien

Fig. 26 Eighteenth-century house on former Rue du Morne des Capucins & Rue Saint-Michel, Cap-Haitien

nial Cap-François is the plain ground floor arcade on piers with a basic string course at the springing of the arches: this form is used on the surviving wings of the Great Barracks, although with plinths which are lacking at Sans-Souci [Fig. 8]. Finally, as noted, Ritter's print shows that the two end ressauts and the central portico of the court façade once had first floor balconies with iron grilles and overhanging wooden canopies. This kind of balcony was popular in colonial Cap-François and remained so well into the nineteenth century, although they have all but vanished in recent decades; similar ones survive in places like Pointe-à-Pitre (Guadeloupe) from later in the century [Fig. 27].[185] Iron grilles appeared in Cap-François as early as the 1730s, as in Louis-Joseph Delalance's design for the Magasin Royal (1737), built facing onto the

141

Abb. 27 Pointe-à-Pitre, 13 rue Delgrès. Haus aus dem neunzehnten Jahrhundert mit Eisengitter und hängender Überdachung
Fig. 27 Pointe-à-Pitre, 13 rue Delgrès. Nineteenth-century house with iron grille and hanging canopies

Dodekagon – in Saint-Louis, Senegal, im Jahr 1820. Keine der beiden wurde gebaut; im Falle des anonymen Guadeloupe-Entwurfs merkte das Komitee der Kirchenvorsteher durchaus spezifisch an, dass »die Kosten für die Errichtung der Kirche nach dem runden Plan (*en rotonde*) zu hoch waren für die gegenwärtigen Umstände [...] [und] dass es keine Arbeiter gäbe, die der Ausführung eines solchen Projektes fähig wären«.[188] Die senegalesische Kirche des königlichen Ingenieur-Architekten Nicolas-Georges Courtois wurde aus ähnlichen Gründen abgelehnt, obgleich sie eigentlich keine gekrümmten Wände hatte.[189] Des Weiteren sahen weder das Kirchenprojekt von Guadeloupe noch das aus dem Senegal eine Kuppel vor: Diese waren noch teurer als gekrümmte Wände und bedurften spezialisierter Steinmetz- oder Zimmererfertigkeiten,

Quay Saint-Louis (now rue B) [Fig. 28].[186] These details indicate that at least some of the architects of Sans-Souci were
trained in the workshops of Cap-François or had become
accustomed to working in the *capois* style.

The Chapel Royal is an equally remarkable structure, as it
has the first circular church plan (20 metres in diameter) and
first dome ever constructed in the lands of the former French
Atlantic Empire [Fig. 29].[187] Round churches were both im-
practical and difficult to build, as they required masons skilled
in stereotomy to create the curving walls and pierce them
with windows and doors. Only two such churches were ever
proposed in the French Atlantic colonies, one in Pointe-à-
Pitre in 1806 and the other—in fact a dodecagon—in Saint-
Louis, Senegal, in 1820. Neither of them were built; in the case

Abb. 28 Louis-Joseph Delalance, Projekt für das Magasin Royal,
Cap-François, Saint-Domingue, 1738. Archives Nationales d'Outre-Mer,
Aix-en-Provence 15DFC335A
Fig. 28 Louis-Joseph Delalance, Project for the Magasin Royal,
Cap-François, Saint-Domingue, 1738. Archives Nationales d'Outre-Mer,
Aix-en-Provence 15DFC335A

Abb. 29 Chapel Royal, Palast von Sans-Souci
Fig. 29 Chapel Royal, Palace of Sans-Souci

die für die meisten kolonialen Architekten unerreichbar
waren. Somit übertraf die Chapel Royal, ebenso wie der Palast
von Sans-Souci, alles von den gehassten französischen Vorgängern Henrys Unternommene.

Die Kapelle ist ein rundes Steingebäude mit einem ganzen
Vorbau, der von vier dorischen Säulen und vier korrespondie-
renden Pilastern an der Mauer gestützt wird, mit einem dreieckigen Pediment, niedrigem Dachgeschoss und einer zentralen Rundbogentür, die von zwei Statuennischen flankiert
wird. Dieses Motiv wiederholt sich an den beiden Seitenpor-
talen, die jedoch auf die Säulen und den Vorbau verzichten.
Ein schweres Gebälk verläuft entlang des oberen Teils der
Mauer bis auf Höhe des Dachgeschosses. Das Gebäude sitzt
auf der Nordseite, wo die Bodenhöhe viel niedriger ist, auf
einem erhöhten Sockel (nur das Nordportal und die Nordseite
des Hauptportals benötigen eine Zugangstreppe). Eine

of the anonymous Guadeloupe design the committee of churchwardens noted quite specifically that "the price of building the church on the circular plan (*en rotonde*) was too high for the present circumstances...[and] that there would be no workmen capable of carrying out such a project."[188] The Senegal church, by royal engineer architect Nicolas-Georges Courtois, was rejected for similar reasons, even though it did not actually have any curving walls.[189] Furthermore, neither the Guadeloupe nor Senegal church projects included a dome: cupolas were even more expensive than curved walls and required specialist masonry or carpentry skills that were beyond most colonial architects. Thus, as with the Sans-Souci palace, the Chapel Royal exceeded anything attempted by Henry's hated French predecessors.

The chapel is a round stone building with a full porch supported by four Doric columns and four corresponding pilasters on the wall, with a triangular pediment and low attic and a central arched doorway flanked by a pair of statue niches. This motif is repeated on the two side portals which however dispense with the columns and porch. A heavy entablature runs around the top of the wall to the attic level and the building sits on an elevated plinth on the northern side where the ground level is much lower (only the northern portal and north side of the main portal require a staircase for access). A shallow rectangular sacristy is attached to the east end behind the high altar, lit by five windows. The interior is lined by a blind arcade on wide pilasters, each arch enclosing either one of the three portals, the high altar, or pairings of windows with blind arches (or in the case of the two flanking the altar a window and door to the sacristy). The wooden dome, which culminated in an ogival *pignon*, was destroyed in the 1842 earthquake (the current one was rebuilt in 1933 based on Ritter's engraving).[190] The church sits on a crypt which can be seen only at the rear (eastern) wall where the ground level is

schmale, rechteckige Sakristei ist an das Ostende hinter dem Hochaltar angebaut und wird von fünf Fenstern erleuchtet. Das Innere ist von einer Blendarkade auf breiten Pilastern ausgekleidet; jeder Bogen umschließt dabei entweder eines der drei Portale, den Hochaltar, oder Fensterpaare mit Blendarkaden (oder, im Falle der zwei, die den Altar flankieren, ein Fenster und eine Tür zur Sakristei). Die hölzerne Kuppel, die in einem spitzbogigen *pignon* kulminierte, wurde im Erdbeben von 1842 zerstört (die jetzige wurde 1933 nach dem Ritter-Stich neu gebaut).[190] Die Kirche sitzt auf einer Krypta, die nur an der rückseitigen (östlichen) Wand gesehen werden kann, wo die Bodenhöhe niedriger ist, und die durch die Tür hinter dem Hochaltar zugänglich ist. Trotz ihrer Rolle als Pantheon des Königreichs wurde nur ein einziger National-held, der Finanzminister General André Vernet (gest. 1813), jemals dort beerdigt.[191] Wie es in den erdbebengefährdeten Französischen Antillen Tradition war, verfügt die Kirche über einen separaten Glockenturm, der heutige jedoch ist eine krude Rekonstruktion.

Wie der Palast ist die Chapel Royal im französischen Stil gehalten, wobei sie zeitgenössischere Architekturströmungen widerspiegelt. Eine Mode für zentralisierte Bauten kam in Frankreich während und nach dem Jahrzehnt der Revolution auf, mit Gebäuden, die einen Enthusiasmus für Prototypen Griechenlands und der italienischen Spätrenaissance mitein-ander verbanden.[192] Die berühmtesten Beispiele sind die Pa-riser *barrières* (1784–91) von Claude-Nicolas Ledoux, vor allem die Rotonde de la Villette und die Barrière de Chartres, die auf Rundtempeln der Antike und italienische Villen wie An-drea Palladios Villa Rotonda (1567 begonnen) basierten. Ein weiteres mögliches Vorbild ist ein Prototyp für eine dorische Rundkirche von François de Neufforge, veröffentlicht in seinem populären *Recueil élémentaire d'architecture* (Paris, 1757–68), die dasselbe dorische Pediment aus vier Säulen auf-

lower and it is accessible through a door behind the high altar. Despite its role as the kingdom's Pantheon, only a single national hero, Finance Minister General André Vernet (d. 1813), was ever buried there.[191] The church has a separate bell-tower, as was traditional in the earthquake-prone French Antilles, although today's is a crude reconstruction.

Like the palace, the Chapel Royal is French in style, this time reflecting more contemporary architectural trends. A fashion for centralised structures emerged in France in the decade of the Revolution and afterward, buildings which combined an enthusiasm for Greek and late Renaissance Italian prototypes.[192] The most celebrated examples are Claude-Nicolas Ledoux's Paris *barrières* (1784–91), notably the Rotonde de la Villette and Barrière de Chartres, which were based on circular temples from Antiquity and Italian villas such as Andrea Palladio's Villa Rotonda (begun 1567). Another possible model is a prototype for a Doric circular church by François de Neufforge published in his popular *Recueil élémentaire d'architecture* (Paris, 1757–68), which has the same Doric pediment of four columns (with two more on the sides and one at the back where the Milot chapel has the sacristy), but the dome is much more modest.[193] The closest parallel to the Milot Chapel Royal—in fact at first glance they seem to be twins—is the church of Saint-Pierre Saint-Paul at Courbevoie (1790–93) in Paris' western suburbs [Fig. 30]. By Ledoux's pupil Louis Le Masson (1743–1826), it is built on an oval plan inspired by Gianlorenzo Bernini's S Andrea al Quirinale in Rome (1658–72), and its profile echoes Bernini's S Maria dell'Assunzione in Ariccia (begun 1662), itself a simulacrum of the Roman Pantheon.[194] By contrast the Chapel Royal is nothing like Jacques-Germain Soufflot's Paris Panthéon (1757–90) with its high, boxy profile and tall, narrow dome. Henry clearly chose the Pantheon form because one of this building's main roles was to serve as the "Haytian Pantheon" as we have

weist (mit zwei weiteren an den Seiten und einer auf der Rückseite, wo sich die Sakristei der Kapelle von Milot befindet); die Kuppel ist allerdings viel bescheidener.[193] Die größte Übereinstimmung mit der Chapel Royal von Milot – auf den ersten Blick hält man sie gar für Zwillinge – besitzt die Kirche Saint-Pierre Saint-Paul in Courbevoie (1790–93), in den westlichen Vororten von Paris [Abb. 30]. Von einem Schüler Ledoux', Louis Le Masson (1743–1826), entworfen, steht sie auf einem ovalen Grundriss, der von Gianlorenzo Berninis S. Andrea al Quirinale in Rom (1658–72) inspiriert ist. Ihr Profil beruft sich auf Berninis S. Maria dell'Assunzione in Ariccia (1662 begonnen), selbst ein Simulacrum des römischen Pantheons.[194] Dagegen erinnert die Chapel Royal nicht im Geringsten an Jacques-Germain Soufflots Pariser Panthéon (1757–90), mit seinem hohen, kastenförmigen Profil und seiner hohen, schmalen Kuppel. Offensichtlich wählte Henry die Pantheon-Form, weil das Gebäude, wie wir gesehen haben, hauptsächlich als »haitianisches Pantheon« dienen sollte. Der Architekt bemühte sich um einen Entwurf, der das römische Vorbild heraufbeschwor, wenn auch in einer Inkarnation der französischen Revolution. Wieder einmal spielt Henrys Patronage auf die Antike an.

Die Kirchen von Courbevoie und Milot sehen sich bei frontaler Betrachtung frappierend ähnlich – von der Straße aus wirkt die Erstere eher rund als oval – mit demselben dorischen Vorbau (Courbevoie hat kein Dachgeschoss) und einem ähnlichen Kuppelprofil, wenngleich die französische Kirche keine Fenster im Oval hat. Beide Kirchen verfügen darüber hinaus über einen rechteckigen Flügel an der Rückseite der Cupola, derjenige von Courbevoie ist jedoch länger und beherbergt die Apsis und die Seitenkapellen. Henrys Vorliebe für Kuppelkirchen trat auch im Rahmen seiner Krönungszeremonie in Cap-Henry im Juni 1811 auf. Da er einen Schauplatz für die Feierlichkeiten benötigte – René-Gabriel Rabiés

Abb. 30 Saint-Pierre Saint-Paul, Courbevoie (1790–93) von Louis Le Masson
Fig. 30 Saint-Pierre Saint-Paul, Courbevoie (1790–93) by Louis Le Masson

seen, and the architect sought a design which more closely evoked the Roman prototype, albeit in a French revolutionary incarnation. Once again King Henry's patronage hints at Antiquity.

The Courbevoie and Milot churches are uncannily similar when viewed head on—from the street the former looks round rather than oval—with the same Doric porch (Courbevoie lacks the attic) and similar dome profile, although the French church has no windows in the oval. Both churches also have a rectangular wing attached to the back of the cupola, although at Courbevoie it is longer and houses the apse and side chapels. Henry's predilection for domed churches also emerged during his coronation in Cap-Henry in June of 1811. Needing a venue for the celebrations—René-Gabriel Rabié's Church of Notre-Dame-de-l'Assomption (1772–1774) was still

Kirche von Notre-Dame-de-l'Assomption (1772–74) war noch ohne Dach [Abb. 5, 6] – gab er eine hastig errichtete »Kathedrale« auf dem Champs de Mars (nördlich der Großen Kaserne) in Auftrag, die 250 Fuß lang war und beinahe ebenso weit, mit einer 80 Fuß hohen Kuppel direkt über dem königlichen Thron. Obwohl sie in einem Großteil der Literatur als permanenter Bau behandelt wird, war sie in Wahrheit ein kurzlebiges Gebäude und wie jede Festarchitektur aus Holz und anderen leichten Baumaterialien konstruiert. Sie wurde nur fünf Tage nach ihrer Verwendung wieder abgerissen.[195] Die »Kathedrale« des Champ de Mars beweist, dass Henry auch flüchtige Architektur beauftragte, wenn er unter Zeitdruck stand, aber solche Bauten standen umso mehr im Gegensatz zu den soliden, hochmodernen und dauerhaften Monumenten von Milot und La Ferrière, Bauwerke, die, wie sich herausstellen sollte, für die Ewigkeit bestimmt waren.

Die letzten Tage des Patriarchen

Wie sein Vorgänger Dessalines unterlag König Henry am Ende einer Rebellion und mit ihm löste sich auch sein Königreich in Luft auf. Am 15. August 1820 erlitt der 53-jährige Monarch einen Schlaganfall, während er die Messe in der Kirche von Limonade besuchte. Inzwischen hatte seine Popularität bereits einen Tiefpunkt erreicht und im frühen Oktober lehnte sich die Bevölkerung in Saint-Marc und Cap-Henry gegen den angeschlagenen Monarchen auf.[196] In seinem Palast verbarrikadiert, erschoss er sich am 8. Oktober – so erzählt man – mit einer silbernen Kugel, anstatt sich dem Aufstand zu stellen, zu einer Zeit, in der er kaum auf die Terrasse vor seinem Schlafgemach hinauszukriechen im Stande war. Plünderer griffen bald den Palast an, bajonettierten brutal seinen Sohn Jacques-Victor-Henry und warfen seinen Leichnam auf einen Mist-

missing its roof [Figs. 5, 6]—he commissioned a hastily-built "cathedral" on the Champs de Mars (north of the Great Barracks) which was 250 feet long and almost as wide with an 80-foot cupola directly over the royal throne. Although discussed in most of the literature as if it had been a permanent building it was in fact an ephemeral structure, built like all festival architecture of wood and other lightweight materials, and it was dismantled only five days after it was used.[195] The Champ de Mars "Cathedral" shows that Henry did commission flimsy architecture when he was pressed for time, but such structures contrasted all the more with the solidly-built, state-of-the-art permanent monuments of Milot and La Ferrière, buildings which were, as it turned out, for the ages.

The Patriarch's Last Stand

Like his predecessor Dessalines King Henry ultimately succumbed to rebellion, and with him his kingdom vanished like smoke. On 15 August 1820 the 53-year-old monarch was felled by a stroke while attending mass at the church in Limonade. By then his popularity was already at a low ebb and by early October the people openly revolted against the crippled monarch in Saint-Marc and Cap-Henry.[196] On 8 October, barricaded in his palace, he shot himself with a silver bullet—or so the tale goes—rather than face insurrection at a time when he could barely crawl out to the terrace in front of his bed chamber. Looters swiftly attacked the palace and brutally bayoneted his son Jacques-Victor-Henry, throwing his body onto a dung heap. Although the Queen and princesses Améthyste-Henry and Anne-Athénaïre-Henry managed to escape (they lived for a time in England and finally in Pisa, where they are buried) their palace and all of its trappings were looted over the course of eight days. Henry's body was secreted

haufen. Die Königin und die Prinzessinnen Améthyste-Henry und Anne-Athénaïre-Henry konnten zwar fliehen (sie lebten eine Zeitlang in England und schließlich in Pisa, wo sie begraben sind), ihr Palast und all sein Schmuck wurden jedoch im Verlauf von acht Tagen geplündert. Henrys Körper wurde heimlich in die Citadelle geschafft und angeblich dort begraben, sein gegenwärtiger Verbleib ist jedoch ein Rätsel.

Henrys verheerter Palast wurde zu einem bleibenden Symbol des Despotismus in der Karibik und Lateinamerika, ein Prototyp der Sorte »vermoderte[r] Größe«, die Gabriel García Marquez zu Beginn seines Romans *Der Herbst des Patriarchen* (1975) schildert, in einer Passage, die, bis auf die Kühe, den Beschreibungen der frühen Besuche Sans-Soucis durch Ritter, Dumesle und Harvey auf unheimliche Weise ähnelt:

Während des Wochenendes fielen die Aasgeier über die Balkone des Präsidentenpalastes her, zerrissen mit Schnabelhieben die Drahtmaschen der Fenster und rührten mit ihren Flügeln die innen erstarrte Zeit auf [...]. Es war, als traumwandle man durch den Bereich einer anderen Zeit, denn die Luft war dünner in den Trümmergruben der weiten Höhle der Macht, und die Stille war älter [...]. Das Mittelportal schien sich durch die bloße Stoßkraft der Stimme von selbst zu öffnen, und so stiegen wir zum Hauptstock auf einer steinernen Freitreppe hinauf, deren Opernteppichbelag von den Hufen der Kühe zerstampft worden war, und vom ersten Vestibül bis zu den privaten Schlafgemächern sahen wir die zerfallenen Kanzleiräume und Empfangssalons, in denen die dreisten Kühe sich tummelten und die Samtvorhänge fraßen und an den Sesselquasten knabberten, wir sahen die Heldengemälde von Heiligen und Militärs auf dem Fußboden zwischen zerbrochenen Möbelstücken und frischen Kuhfladen, wir sahen einen von den Kühen verspeisten Speisesaal, sahen den von Kuhdung geschändeten Musiksalon, die zertrümmerten Dominotischchen

away to the Citadelle and allegedly buried there, although its current whereabouts remain a mystery.

Henry's despoiled palace became an enduring symbol of despotism throughout the Caribbean and Latin America, a prototype for the sort of "rotting grandeur" depicted in the opening of Gabriel García Marquez's *The Autumn of the Patriarch* (1975), a passage which is, except for the cows, eerily similar to the descriptions by Ritter, Dumesle, and Harvey of their early visits to Sans-Souci:

> Over the weekend the vultures got into the presidential palace by pecking through the screens on the balcony windows and the flapping of their wings stirred up the stagnant time inside... It was like entering the atmosphere of another age, because the air was thinner in the rubble pits of the vast lair of power, and the silence was more ancient...the main door seemed to open by itself with just the push of a voice, so we went up to the main floor along a bare stone stairway where the opera-house carpeting had been torn by the hoofs of the cows, and from the first vestibule on down to the private bedrooms we saw the ruined offices and protocol salons through which the brazen cows wandered, eating the velvet curtains and nibbling at the trip of the chairs, we saw heroic portraits of saints and soldiers thrown to the floor among broken furniture and fresh cow flops, we saw a dining room that had been eaten up by the cows, the music room profaned by the cows' breakage, the domino tables destroyed and the felt on the billiard tables cropped by the cows...In that forbidden corner which only a few people of privilege had ever come to know, we smelled the vultures' carnage for the first time...[197]

As Sibylle Fischer bluntly remarked about the regime of King Henry I Christophe: "The experiment in monarchy in Haiti had failed."[198]

und den von den Kühen zerfetzten Filzbelag der Billardtische
[...]. In jenem verbotenen Gebiet, das zu kennen das Vorrecht
sehr weniger gewesen war, rochen wir zum erstenmal den Ge-
ruch des Aasgeiergemetzels [...].[197]

In aller Deutlichkeit äußerte sich Sibylle Fischer zu dem Regime des Henry I Christophe: »Das Experiment der Monarchie auf Haiti war gescheitert«.[198]

Was sollen wir mit Henrys Scheitern anfangen und, was
noch wichtiger ist, mit seinem Vermächtnis? Manche vertre-
ten den Standpunkt, er sei ein Verräter an seiner eigenen
Rasse gewesen, da er das Hofzeremoniell, die Architektur und
Kultur Europas wählte anstatt die der westafrikanischen
Küste, oder, näher an seiner Heimat gelegen, diejenigen der
Maroon- oder Quilombo-Gemeinschaften auf Haiti, in den
Guayanas und Brasilien, welche afrikanische und indianische
Technologien und Stile miteinander vermischten. Sie fügen
hinzu, dass seine Entscheidung für den Katholizismus und
gegen den Vodun ebenfalls zu seinem Niedergang beitrug. Gewiss sind seine republikanischen Gegner und einige der Lite-
raten, die von seiner Geschichte fasziniert sind, dieser Mei-
nung, beispielsweise Césaire, dessen Stückprolog die Zeilen
enthält: »Klar war Christophe der König. Ein König wie Ludwig XIII., Ludwig XIV., Ludwig XV. und einige andere. Und
wie alle Könige, alle echten Könige, *ich meine alle weißen Könige*, schuf er einen Hof und umgab sich mit einem Adel«.[199]
Andere würden sagen, dass er als schwarzer kreolischer König
dieser Ära keine andere Wahl hatte, dass er innerhalb der Kultur arbeitete, in die er hineingeboren worden war, und dass
seine an die westliche Welt gerichtete architektonische Herausforderung ihn zu einem Helden seines Volkes machte
(tatsächlich wird er im heutigen Haiti als Held verehrt, in
einem Triumvirat mit Toussaint Louverture und Dessalines,
und sein Gesicht und seine Zitadelle zieren den 100-Haitia-

What should we make of Henry's failure, and more importantly of his legacy? Some would maintain that he was a traitor to his race by choosing European-style court ceremonial, architecture, and culture over those of the West African coast or, closer to home, the maroon or quilombo communities in Haiti, the Guianas, and Brazil, which mixed African with Native American technologies and styles. They would add that his choice of Catholicism over Vodun also contributed heavily to his downfall. These are certainly the opinions of his republican enemies and some of the literary figures fascinated by his story such as Césaire, the prologue of whose play includes the line: "Sure Christophe was the King. King like Louis XIII, Louis XIV, Louis XV and some others. And like all kings, all real kings, *I mean to say all white kings*, he created a court and surrounded himself with a nobility."[199] Others would say that as a black creole king in that era he had no choice, that he was working within the culture into which he was born, and that his architectural challenges to the Western World made him a hero to his people (indeed today he remains a hero in Haiti, one of the triumvirate including Toussaint Louverture and Dessalines, and his face and citadel adorn the 100 Haitian Gourdes banknote). Henry would have insisted that only the trappings of a European-style monarchy could impress Europeans, as did his mouthpiece Prévost as we have seen above. As it happens the King was only able to answer these charges in a work of fiction. Here is Césaire again:

This people must pursue, want, attain something impossible! Against Fate, against History, against Nature...I say the Citadelle, the liberty of a whole people. Built by all the people, men and women, children and the elderly. Built by the whole people! Look, its head is in the clouds, its feet dig into the abyss, its mouths spit grape-shot across the sea, to the bottom of the valleys, it is a city, a fortress, a heavy cuirass of stone...

nische-Gourden-Schein). Henry hätte darauf bestanden, dass nur die Insignien einer Monarchie im europäischen Stil bei Europäern Eindruck schinden könnten, wie es sein Sprachrohr Prévost tat. Es fügt sich, dass der König nur in einem fiktiven Werk Antwort auf diese Anschuldigungen geben konnte. Hier noch einmal Césaire:

>Dieses Volk muss etwas Unmögliches verfolgen, wollen, erlangen! Wider das Schicksal, wider die Geschichte, wider die Natur [...]. Ich sage die Citadelle, die Freiheit eines ganzen Volkes. Gebaut von allen Menschen, Männern und Frauen, Kindern und Greisen. Gebaut vom ganzen Volk! Siehe, ihr Kopf ist in den Wolken, ihre Füße graben sich in den Abgrund, ihre Münder spucken Traubenhagel über das Meer, bis in die Böden der Täler hinein, sie ist eine Stadt, eine Festung, ein schwerer Kürass aus Stein [...] unauslöschbar! [...] Für dieses Volk, das gemacht wurde um zu knien, bedurfte es eines Monuments, es auf seine Beine zu heben. Hier ist es! [...] Die Nullifikation des Sklavenschiffes!«[200]

Henry hätte sein architektonisches Programm gerade deshalb verteidigt, weil es als Zeichen haitianischer Erneuerung vom Volk für das Volk gebaut wurde, um die Missetaten der Vergangenheit aufzuheben. Viele der corvée-Arbeiter jedoch, die zur Errichtung seiner Gebäude gezwungen wurden, hätten kaum daran geglaubt, dass es irgendetwas mit *liberté* zu tun hatte.

Der Zweck dieses Buches besteht allerdings nicht darin, Henrys Herrschaft zu verurteilen oder zu bewerten, ob sie effektiver war als diejenigen seines Rivalen Pétion und seines Nachfolgers Präsident Jean-Pierre Boyer (1776–1850), der Haiti nach dem Tod Henrys als Demokratie, die von Port-au-Prince aus regiert wurde, vereinte. Boyers Einwilligung im Jahre 1825, eine Abfindung von 150 Millionen Francs als

inexpungable!...For this people, who were made to kneel, a monument was needed to raise them to their feet. Here it is!...The nullification of the slave ship!"[200]

Henry would have defended his architectural programme precisely because it was built by and for the people as a sign of Haitian resurgence, to cancel out the misdeeds of the past, but many of the corvée labourers who were forced to build his structures would have found it hard to believe that it had anything to do with *liberté*.

However the purpose of this book is not to cast judgment on Henry's reign or to say whether it was more effective than that of his rival Pétion and successor President Jean-Pierre Boyer (1776–1850), who reunited Haiti after Henry's death as a democracy ruled from Port-au-Prince. Boyer's acquiescence in 1825 to a ransom of 150 million francs to France to compensate for French losses, putting his nation into crippling debt for decades, was at least as controversial as Christophe's buildings and penchant for colourful uniforms.[201] I will leave such speculation to the historians. What is of interest here is the intrinsic value of Sans-Souci as a work of architecture. Fortunately as architectural historians we are not obliged to vilify buildings built by tyrants: if so we would not have much to study. We would have to denounce (among many hundreds more) Versailles, Caserta, Poggio a Caiano or the Pitti Palace, not to mention the Forbidden City in Beijing or the Taj Mahal, most of them built by tyrants who were far out of Henry's league in the extent of their power and despotism. My goal here has been to set the record straight about Sans-Souci's designers, builders, models, and motives, even if the sources will not allow a full reconstruction and some of the builders must remain conjectural. It has also been to introduce into the canon of mainstream architectural history a monument of extraordinary importance to Caribbean and Latin

Kompensation für französische Verluste zu zahlen, wodurch seine Nation jahrzehntelang von Schulden gelähmt wurde, war mindestens ebenso kontrovers wie Christophes Bauten und sein Faible für farbenprächtige Uniformen.[201] Ich überlasse solcherlei Spekulationen den Historikern. Was hier interessiert, ist der Eigenwert Sans-Soucis als Architektur. Glücklicherweise sind wir als Architekturhistoriker nicht dazu verpflichtet, Gebäude zu verdammen, weil sie von Tyrannen errichtet wurden: Ansonsten blieben uns nur wenige Forschungsgegenstände. Neben hunderten von anderen Gebäuden müssten wir Versailles, Caserta, Poggio a Caiano oder den Palazzo Pitti verurteilen, ganz zu schweigen von der Verbotenen Stadt in Beijing oder dem Taj Mahal, deren Bauherren größtenteils Tyrannen waren, die Henry hinsichtlich Macht und Despotismus bei Weitem übertrafen. Mein Ziel ist es gewesen, unsere Vorstellungen von Sans-Soucis Architekten, Erbauern, Vorbildern und Motiven richtigzustellen, auch wenn die Quellenlage uns eine volle Rekonstruktion nicht erlaubt und manche der Erbauernamen nur auf Vermutungen beruhen. Darüber hinaus habe ich auch ein lange von unserem Fach vernachlässigtes Monument in den ›Mainstream‹ des architekturhistorischen Kanons einführen wollen, ein Monument, das eine außerordentliche Bedeutung für die karibische und lateinamerikanische Literatur und Kunst, das Nationalbewusstsein Haitis, und den Globalismus der napoleonischen Ära überhaupt besitzt. Der Erfolg dieses Buches wird daran zu messen sein, ob es ein ernsthaftes Interesse am Palast von Milot wiederentfacht. Sans-Souci war keineswegs ein wackeliger Bau für einen Scheinkönig, sondern ein durchdachtes, hochmodernes Monument, das im Laufe zweier Jahrhunderte voller extravaganter, regierungsfinanzierter Pläne für die Errichtung von Utopien und El Dorados in der Karibik, Guyana, Nordamerika und Westafrika, nie von Henrys französischen Vorgängern erreicht wurde.

American literature and art, Haitian national identity, and Napoleonic-era globalism more widely which has been strangely neglected by our own field. This book will have succeeded if it rekindles serious interest in Sans-Souci of Milot, which far from being a flimsy piece of festival architecture made for a sham king was an erudite, state-of-the-art monument never equalled by Henry's French predecessors over two centuries of extravagant government-sponsored schemes to build utopias and El Dorados in the Caribbean, Guiana, North America, and West Africa.

1 Aimé Césaire, *La tragédie du Roi Christophe* (Paris, 1963): 118.

2 Alejo Carpentier, *The Kingdom of this World* (Harriet de Onís übers., London, 1967): 90.

3 Richard A. Loederer, »A Voodoo Castle in Haiti: The Jungle Stronghold of King Christophe and the Black Magic He Used to Build It,« *The New York Times* (27. Mai 1923): 4.

4 Über die Bedeutung des Bauwerks für die Entwicklung des Magischen Realismus: Sibylle Fischer, *Modernity Disavowed: Haiti and the Cultures of Slavery in the Age of Revolution* (Durham NC, 2004): 247. Christophe und seine architektonischen Schöpfungen waren Gegenstand zweier Theaterstücke (Walcotts *Henri Christophe: A Chronicle in Seven Scenes* von 1949 und Césaires *Die Tragödie von König Christoph* von 1963) und eines Romans (Carpentiers *El reino de este mundo*, 1949) und die Citadelle und Sans-Souci sind ein wiederkehrendes Thema in Edwidge Danticats *The Farming of Bones* (1998). Zur Bedeutung der Citadelle und Sans-Soucis für die haitianische Malerei siehe Gérard Alexis, »The Caribbean in the Hour of Haiti,« und Sergio Ramírez Mercado, »A Dark Animal Dressed in Sequins,« beide in Margarita J. Aguilar et al., Hrsg., *Caribbean: Art at the Crossroads of the World* (New York, 2012): 117; 281–83.

5 Eine Ausnahme ist John F. Scott, der die Citadelle Laferrière und Sans-Souci in seiner Studie *Latin American Art Ancient to Modern* erwähnt (Gainesville, 1999): 187.

6 Michel-Rolph Trouillot, *Silencing the Past: Power and the Production of History* (2. Ausg., Boston, 2015): 32.

7 Giscard Bouchotte, »Henry Ier: Un roi soleil sous les tropiques,« *Africultures* 64 3 (2005): 92–93; Fischer, *Modernity Disavowed*, 247; Hubert Cole, *Christophe: King of Haiti* (New York, 1967): 30–31; Earl Leslie Griggs und Clifford H. Prator, Hrsg., *Henry Christophe & Thomas Clarkson: A Correspondence* (Berkeley und Los Angeles, 1952): 38; CLR James, *The Black Jacobins: Toussaint Louverture and the San Domingo Revolution* (Nachdruck London, 2001): 19; Vergniaud Leconte, *Henri Christophe dans l'histoire d'Haïti* (Paris, 1932): 1–3.

1 Aimé Césaire, *La tragédie du Roi Christophe* (Paris, 1963): 118.

2 Alejo Carpentier, *The Kingdom of this World* (Harriet de Onís trans., London, 1967): 90.

3 Richard A. Loederer, "A Voodoo Castle in Haiti: The Jungle Stronghold of King Christophe and the Black Magic He Used to Build It," *The New York Times* (27 May 1923): 4.

4 On the buildings' role in the development of Magic Realism see: Sibylle Fischer, *Modernity Disavowed: Haiti and the Cultures of Slavery in the Age of Revolution* (Durham NC, 2004): 247. Christophe and his architectural creations have been the subject of two plays (Walcott's *Henri Christophe: A Chronicle in Seven Scenes* of 1949 and Césaire's *The Tragedy of King Christophe* of 1963) and a novel (Carpentier's *El reino de este mundo*, 1949) and the Citadelle and Sans-Souci are a recurrent theme in Edwidge Danticat's *The Farming of Bones* (1998). On the importance of the Citadelle and Sans-Souci in Haitian painting see Gérard Alexis, "The Caribbean in the Hour of Haiti," and Sergio Ramírez Mercado, "A Dark Animal Dressed in Sequins," both in Margarita J. Aguilar et al., eds., *Caribbean: Art at the Crossroads of the World* (New York, 2012): 117; 281–83.

5 One exception is John F. Scott, who mentions the Citadelle Laferrière and Sans-Souci in his survey *Latin American Art Ancient to Modern* (Gainesville, 1999): 187.

6 Michel-Rolph Trouillot, *Silencing the Past: Power and the Production of History* (2nd ed., Boston, 2015): 32.

7 Giscard Bouchotte, "Henry Ier: Un roi soleil sous les tropiques," *Africultures* 64 3 (2005): 92–93; Fischer, *Modernity Disavowed*, 247; Hubert Cole, *Christophe: King of Haiti* (New York, 1967): 30–31; Earl Leslie Griggs and Clifford H. Prator, eds., *Henry Christophe & Thomas Clarkson: A Correspondence* (Berkeley and Los Angeles, 1952): 38; CLR James, *The Black Jacobins: Toussaint Louverture and the San Domingo Revolution* (reprint London, 2001): 19; Vergniaud Leconte, *Henri Christophe dans l'histoire d'Haïti* (Paris, 1932): 1–3.

8   Jean-Hérold Pérard, *La Citadelle restaurée* (Port-au-Prince, 2010): 58; Leconte, *Henri Christophe*, 246–47.

9   Victor-Emmanuel Roberto Wilson, »The Forgotten Eighth Wonder of the World,« *Callaloo* 15, 3 (1992): 850; Cole, *Christophe King of Haiti*, 191–92, 204; Leconte, *Henri Christophe*, 249–53. Clive Cheesman hat kürzlich der Behauptung einiger Forscher widersprochen, Henrys Hof habe mehr auf dem englischen basiert, indem er zeigte, dass die höfischen, kirchlichen und militärischen Titel seines Regimes französischen Vorbildern nachempfunden waren. Siehe Clive Cheesman, *The Armorial of Haiti: Symbols of Nobility in the Reign of Henry Christophe* (London, 2007): 8.

10 Ein Faksimile dieses außergewöhnlichen Buches wurde vor Kurzem veröffentlicht: Cheesman, *The Armorial of Haiti*, 18–199.

11 Der Begriff »*gloire*«, den Ludwig als wahres Zeichen gottgegebenen Königtums betrachtete, wurde 1663 von Colbert verwendet, speziell um die Rolle der Architektur in der Darstellung königlicher Autorität zu bezeichnen [Robert W. Berger, *A Royal Passion: Louis XIV as Patron of Architecture* (Cambridge, 1997): 5]. Evans malte auch ein Porträt des Prince Royal, Prinz Victor Henry; beide wurden später in der Royal Academy in London ausgestellt.

12 Cheesman, *The Armorial of Haiti*, 6; Frédérick Mangones, »The Citadel as Site of Haitian Memory,« *Callaloo* 15, 3 (Sommer 1992): 858.

13 Doris L. Garraway, »Empire of Freedom, Kingdom of Civilization: Henry Christophe, the Baron de Vastey, and the Paradoxes of Universalism in Postrevolutionary Haiti,« *Small Axe* 16, 3, 39 (November 2012): 9; Bouchotte, »Henry Ier,« 93; Fischer, *Modernity Disavowed*, 250–51.

14 Doris L. Garraway, »Print, Publics, and the Scene of Universal Equality in the Kingdom of Henry Christophe,« *L'Esprit Créateur* 56, 1 (Frühjahr 2016): 82.

15 Cole, *Christophe King of Haiti*, 192; Leconte, *Henri Christophe*, 250. Die Übersetzung ist von Cole.

16 Bouchotte, »Henry Ier,« 93; Cole, *Christophe King of*

8   Jean-Hérold Pérard, *La Citadelle restaurée* (Port-au-Prince, 2010): 58; Leconte, *Henri Christophe*, 246–47.

9   Victor-Emmanuel Roberto Wilson, "The Forgotten Eighth Wonder of the World," *Callaloo* 15, 3 (1992): 850; Cole, *Christophe King of Haiti*, 191–92, 204; Leconte, *Henri Christophe*, 249–53. Clive Cheesman has recently countered some scholars' contention that Henry's court was based more on that of Britain by showing that the court, religious, and military titles of his regime were directly modelled on French prototypes. See Clive Cheesman, *The Armorial of Haiti: Symbols of Nobility in the Reign of Henry Christophe* (London, 2007): 8.

10 A facsimile of this extraordinary book has recently been published: Cheesman, *The Armorial of Haiti*, 18–199.

11 The term "*gloire*", one which Louis openly aspired as the true sign of divinely-appointed kingship, was used specifically by Colbert to denote architecture's role in representing royal authority in 1663 [Robert W. Berger, *A Royal Passion: Louis XIV as Patron of Architecture* (Cambridge, 1997): 5]. Evans also painted a portrait of the Prince Royal, Prince Victor Henry, and the two were later exhibited at the Royal Academy in London.

12 Cheesman, *The Armorial of Haiti*, 6; Frédérick Mangones, "The Citadel as Site of Haitian Memory," *Callaloo* 15, 3 (Summer 1992): 858.

13 Doris L. Garraway, "Empire of Freedom, Kingdom of Civilization: Henry Christophe, the Baron de Vastey, and the Paradoxes of Universalism in Postrevolutionary Haiti," *Small Axe* 16, 3, 39 (November 2012): 9; Bouchotte, "Henry Ier," 93; Fischer, *Modernity Disavowed*, 250–51.

14 Doris L. Garraway, "Print, Publics, and the Scene of Universal Equality in the Kingdom of Henry Christophe," *L'Esprit Créateur* 56, 1 (Spring 2016): 82.

15 Cole, *Christophe King of Haiti*, 192; Leconte, *Henri Christophe*, 250. The translation is Cole's.

16 Bouchotte, "Henry Ier," 93; Cole, *Christophe King of Haiti*, 192; Ralph Korngold, *Citizen Toussaint* (Boston: 1944): 255.

17 Alexis, "The Caribbean in the Hour of Haiti," 107;

Haiti, 192; Ralph Korngold, *Citizen Toussaint* (Boston: 1944): 255.

17 Alexis, »The Caribbean in the Hour of Haiti,« 107; Cheesman, *The Armorial of Haiti*, 7; Michel Philippe Lerebours, *Haïti et ses peintres de 1804 à 1980* I (Port-au-Prince, 1989): 92–94; Griggs und Prator, *Henry Christophe and Thomas Clarkson*, 64, 98. Üblicherweise wird behauptet, Evans sei als Direktor der Akademie nach Haiti gebracht worden, jedoch wird er, wie Lerebours aufzeigt, im Almanach nie als mehr als »*professeur*« aufgeführt.

18 Lieutenant-Général Baron Pamphile de Lacroix, *Mémoires pour servir à l'histoire de la révolution de Saint-Domingue* II (Paris, 1819): 286–87. Siehe auch Cole, *Christophe, King of Haiti*, 211; Griggs und Prator, *Henry Christophe & Thomas Clarkson*, 49–50; und Jonathan Brown, *History and Present Condition of St Domingo* II (Philadelphia, 1837): 204.

19 Zitiert in Griggs und Prator, *Henry Christophe and Thomas Clarkson*, 45. Siehe auch Leconte, *Henri Christophe*, 286–301.

20 Bouchotte, »Henry Ier,« 94; Cole, *Christophe King of Haiti*, 241–42; Leconte, *Henri Christophe*, 312–14.

21 Cheesman, *The Armorial of Haiti*, 194.

22 Griggs und Prator, *Henry Christophe and Thomas Clarkson*, i.

23 Zitiert in Cole, *Christophe, King of Haiti*, 250.

24 Darüber, wie weiße Historiker Christophe als »verrückten, grausamen Megalomanen« und die Citadelle als »nutzloses Monument« darstellten, siehe Mangones, »The Citadel as Site of Haitian Memory,« 858.

25 Ich werde das kolonialzeitliche Architekturerbe von Cap-François ausführlich in meinem in Kürze erscheinenden Buch Gauvin Alexander Bailey, *Architecture and Urbanism in the French Atlantic Empire: State, Church, and Society, 1604–1830* (Montreal and Kingston, 2018) besprechen. Siehe auch: James E. McClellan, *Colonialism & Science: Saint Domingue in the Old Regime* (Chicago, 2010): 75–76; Pierre Pinon, »Saint-Domingue: L'île à villes,« in Laurent Vidal and Émilie D'Orgeix, eds., *Les villes françaises du Nouveau Monde* (Paris, 1999): 109, 11–12.

Cheesman, *The Armorial of Haiti*, 7; Michel Philippe Lerebours, *Haïti et ses peintres de 1804 à 1980* I (Port-au-Prince, 1989): 92–94; Griggs and Prator, *Henry Christophe and Thomas Clarkson*, 64, 98. It is usually claimed that Evans was brought to Haiti as director of the academy, but as Lerebours points out he is never listed as anything more than "*professeur*" in the Almanac.

18 Lieutenant-Général Baron Pamphile de Lacroix, *Mémoires pour servir à l'histoire de la révolution de Saint-Domingue* II (Paris, 1819): 286–87. See also Cole, *Christophe, King of Haiti*, 211; Griggs and Prator, *Henry Christophe & Thomas Clarkson*, 49–50; and Jonathan Brown, *History and Present Condition of St Domingo* II (Philadelphia, 1837): 204.

19 Quoted in Griggs and Prator, *Henry Christophe and Thomas Clarkson*, 45. See also Leconte, *Henri Christophe*, 286–301.

20 Bouchotte, "Henry Ier," 94; Cole, *Christophe King of Haiti*, 241–42; Leconte, *Henri Christophe*, 312–14.

21 Cheesman, *The Armorial of Haiti*, 194.

22 Griggs and Prator, *Henry Christophe and Thomas Clarkson*, i.

23 Quoted in Cole, *Christophe, King of Haiti*, 250.

24 On how white historians depicted Christophe as an "insane, cruel megalomaniac" and the Citadel as a "useless monument", see Mangones, "The Citadel as Site of Haitian Memory," 858.

25 I discuss the colonial architectural heritage of Cap-François at length in my forthcoming book Gauvin Alexander Bailey, *Architecture and Urbanism in the French Atlantic Empire: State, Church, and Society, 1604–1830* (Montreal and Kingston, 2018). See also: James E. McClellan, *Colonialism & Science: Saint Domingue in the Old Regime* (Chicago, 2010): 75–76; Pierre Pinon, "Saint-Domingue: L'île à villes," in Laurent Vidal and Émilie D'Orgeix, eds., *Les villes françaises du Nouveau Monde* (Paris, 1999): 109, 11–12.

26 On the history of the Place-Royale see Moreau de Médéric Louis Moreau de Saint-Méry, *Description...de l'isle Saint-Domingue* I (Philadelphia, 1797): 445–47. The ori-

26 Zur Geschichte des Place-Royale siehe Médéric Louis Moreau de Saint-Méry, *Description...de l'isle Saint-Domingue* I (Philadelphia, 1797): 445–47. Der Originalentwurf befindet sich in den Archives Nationales d'Outre-Mer in Aix-en-Provence [ANOM F/3/296/E11, »Plan de la Place Royale et des façades des islets formant la dite Place à l'Entrée de la Ville...,« unterzeichnet von Calon de Felcourt (8. November 1780)]. Moreau erwähnt Artaus Vornamen nicht, er erscheint jedoch in einigen notariellen Dokumenten, z. B. ANOM *DPPC NOT SDOM//371*, »Accord entre M Artaud et C Angard« (8. September 1786). 1777 vermerkt eine Zeitungsannonce, dass »sieben Tischler-Neger« für den Architekten arbeiteten [*Affiches Américains* (7. Juni 1777): 276]. Artaud wird in derselben Zeitung zum letzten Mal am 29. Juni 1803 genannt (S. 212).

27 Moreau de Saint-Méry, *Description*, I, 446–47. Siehe auch: Pinot, »Saint-Domingue,« 119.

28 Eine Zeichnung des Brunnens ist erhalten [ANOM *F3 296 E69*, »Fontaine nouvellement construite. Place Royale 1789«]

29 ANOM *15DFC360A*, »Plan et élévation du projet d'un corps de caserne à faire au Cap« (1752); ANOM *F3 296 E2*, »Perspective des Cazernes du Cap en 1783«; Médéric Louis Élie Moreau de Saint-Méry, *Recueil de vues des lieux principaux de la colonie françoise de Saint-Domingue* (Paris, 1791): Tafel 3.

30 Weil die Truppen in gesundheitsschädlichen, niedrig gelegenen Mietshäusern in der Nähe des Hafens untergebracht waren, wurde die Kaserne schnell errichtet. Bereits 1755 wurde sie als »sehr weit fortgeschritten» bezeichnet und war im Juni 1756 gebrauchsfertig: »Par le compte qui vous sera remis de ce plan l'ouvrage vous paraitre fort avancé. Je ne saurois cependant vous indiquer le tems ou il pourra estre fini. On n'a cessé d'y ajouter jusqu'à present ; et vraisemblablement cela ira de mesme jusqu'à la fin.« [ANOM *15 DFC 27*, »Etat des fortifications et des bâtiments civiles, par M. De Lalanne, Port-au-Prince, 15 avril 1755«]; »Les nouvelles cazernes du Cap sont bien avancées; et j'espère que la gar-

166

ginal plan is in the Archives Nationales d'Outre-Mer in Aix-en-Provence [ANOM F/3/296/E11, "Plan de la Place Royale et des façades des islets formant la dite Place à l'Entrée de la Ville…," signed Calon de Felcourt (8 November 1780)]. Moreau does not mention Artau's first name but he appears in some notary documents, e.g. ANOM *DPPC NOT SDOM//371*, "Accord entre M Artaud et C Angard" (8 September 1786). In 1777 a newspaper advertisement noted that the architect had "seven carpenter Negroes" working for him [*Affiches Américains* (7 June 1777): 276]. Artaud is last mentioned in the same newspaper in 29 June 1803 (p. 212).

27 Moreau de Saint-Méry, *Description*, I, 446–47. See also: Pinot, "Saint-Domingue," 119.

28 A drawing of the fountain survives [ANOM *F3 296 E69*, "Fontaine nouvellement construite. Place Royale 1789"]

29 ANOM *15DFC360A*, "Plan et élévation du projet d'un corps de caserne à faire au Cap" (1752); ANOM *F3 296 E2*, "Perspective des Cazernes du Cap en 1783"; Médéric Louis Élie Moreau de Saint-Méry, *Recueil de vues des lieux principaux de la colonie françoise de Saint-Domingue* (Paris, 1791): pl. 3.

30 Built quickly, because the troops were housed in insalubrious rental properties at a lower elevation near the harbour, it was described as "very advanced" already in 1755 and ready for use in June 1756: "Par le compte qui vous sera remis de ce plan l'ouvrage vous paraitre fort avancé. Je ne saurois cependant vous indiquer le tems ou il pourra estre fini. On n'a cessé d'y ajouter jusqu'à present ; et vraisemblablement cela ira de mesme jusqu'à la fin." [ANOM *15 DFC 27*, "Etat des fortifications et des bâtiments civiles, par M. De Lalanne, Port-au-Prince, 15 avril 1755"]; "Les nouvelles cazernes du Cap sont bien avancées; et j'espère que la garnison y sera logée dans le courant du mois prochain." [ANOM *15 DFC 33*, "Détail des ouvrages faits au petit Goave, au Port au Prince au cap &c, par M. De Lalanne, Port-au-Prince, 6 avril 1756]. On the barracks see also Moreau, *Description*, I, 423–24.

31 Moreau de Saint-Méry, *Description*, I, 424.

nison y sera logée dans le courant du mois prochain.«
[ANOM *15 DFC 33*, »Détail des ouvrages faits au petit
Goave, au Port au Prince au cap &c, par M. De Lalanne,
Port-au-Prince, 6 avril 1756]. Zur Kaserne siehe auch
Moreau, *Description*, I, 423–24.

31 Moreau de Saint-Méry, *Description*, I, 424.

32 Moreau nennt sowohl diese als auch die inneren Säulen
ionisch und in der Zeichnung sind sie auch als solche
dargestellt, die heutigen jedoch sind dorisch. Sie wurden entweder ausgetauscht, was angesichts der Nähe
des Baus zu den Originalentwürfen unwahrscheinlich
ist, oder Moreau unterlief schlicht ein Fehler: Er ver-
wechselt dorisch und ionisch auch an anderer Stelle in
seiner Beschreibung, etwa in seiner Besprechung des
Place Montarcher-Brunnens, der ebenfalls dorisch war
und sogar als solcher in seinem Buch illustriert war
(siehe Moreau de Saint-Méry, *Description*, I, 357).

33 Charles-Marie Vincent schrieb 1795 über die Kaserne,
zwei Jahre nachdem die Stadt zum ersten Mal abge-
brannt war: »Ce bel édifice est en assez bon état, l'on a
soin d'y faire les nombreuses réparations que nécessite
souvent le grand nombre d'individus qui l'habitent.«
[ANOM *15DFC 239*, f. 5a]

34 William Woodis Harvey, *Sketches of Hayti; from the Expulsion of the French, to the Death of Christophe* (London,
1827): 188.

35 Das Armeekorps aus Ingenieuren wurde regelmäßigen
Namensänderungen unterzogen: Nach 1743 wurde es
als das *Génie militaire* bezeichnet, in den 1750ern war es
als das *corps du Génie* bekannt, und nach 1776 wurde es
das *corps royal du Génie* genannt [Anne Blanchard, *Les
ingénieurs du 'Roy' de Louis XIV à Louis XVI* (Montpellier,
1979): 215–25]. Die Literatur zu Vauban ist gewaltig.
Für einige neuere Studien siehe: Martin Barros et al.,
Vauban: L'intelligence du territoire (Paris, 2007); Janis Langins, *Conserving the Enlightenment: French Military Engineering from Vauban to the Revolution* (Cambridge MA,
2004): 47–76; Association Vauban, *Vauban et ses successeurs en Briançonnais* (Paris, 1995).

36 Blanchard, *Les ingénieurs*, 181–213.

32 Moreau calls these and the interior columns Ionic and they are so depicted on the drawings but they are Doric today. Either they were replaced, which seems unlikely given how closely the structure relates to the original blueprints, or Moreau simply made a mistake: he confuses Doric and Ionic elsewhere in his description, as in his discussion of the Place Montarcher fountain, which was also Doric and even illustrated as such in his book (see Moreau de Saint-Méry, *Description*, I, 357).

33 Charles-Marie Vincent wrote about the Barracks in 1795, two years after the first time the city was torched: "Ce bel édifice est en assez bon état, l'on a soin d'y faire les nombreuses réparations que nécessite souvent le grand nombre d'individus qui l'habitent." [ANOM *15DFC 239*, f. 5a]

34 William Woodis Harvey, *Sketches of Hayti; from the Expulsion of the French, to the Death of Christophe* (London, 1827): 188.

35 The army corps of engineers underwent regular name changes: after 1743 they were called the *Génie militaire*, in the 1750s they were known as the *corps du Génie*, and after 1776 they were called the *corps royal du Génie* [Anne Blanchard, *Les ingénieurs du 'Roy' de Louis XIV à Louis XVI* (Montpellier, 1979): 215–25]. The literature on Vauban is massive. For some recent studies see: Martin Barros et al., *Vauban: L'intelligence du territoire* (Paris, 2007); Janis Langins, *Conserving the Enlightenment: French Military Engineering from Vauban to the Revolution* (Cambridge MA, 2004): 47–76; Association Vauban, *Vauban et ses successeurs en Briançonnais* (Paris, 1995).

36 Blanchard, *Les ingénieurs*, 181–213.

37 Blanchard, *Les ingénieurs*, 316.

38 Katie Scott, *The Rococo Interior* (New Haven and London (1995): 242–46; Michel Gallet, *Les architects parisiens du XVIIIe siècle* (Paris, 1995): 65–67.

39 On the lack of a guild system see: James Pritchard, *In Search of Empire: The French in the Americas, 1670–1730* (Cambridge, 2004): 97–98. Christophe Charley's claim that "dans les colonies françaises, il n'y a pas d'architectes civils" is simply incorrect [Christophe Charley,

37 Blanchard, *Les ingénieurs*, 316.

38 Katie Scott, *The Rococo Interior* (New Haven und London (1995): 242–46; Michel Gallet, *Les architects parisiens du XVIIIe siècle* (Paris, 1995): 65–67.

39 Zum Mangel eines Gildensystems siehe: James Pritchard, *In Search of Empire: The French in the Americas, 1670–1730* (Cambridge, 2004): 97–98. Christophe Charlerys Behauptung, dass »dans les colonies françaises, il n'y a pas d'architectes civils« ist schlicht falsch [Christophe Charlery, »Maisons de maître et habitations coloniales dans les anciens territoires français de l'Amérique tropicale,« *In Situ* 5 (2004): 8].

40 *Affiches Américaines* (3. September 1766): 312 ; *Affiches Américaines* (24. Dezember 1766): 439–40; *Affiches Américaines* (2. April 1777): 163; *Affiches Américains* (21. Juni 1777): 299; *Affiches Américaines, Supplément* (7 janvier 1784): 1. Sieur Lacroix gab seine Annonce im *Supplément aux Affiches Américaines* auf (22. February 1777): 8.

41 Bailey, *Architecture and Urbanism in the French Atlantic World*, 5. Kapitel.

42 Die Tradition war besonders in Neuspanien verbreitet. Siehe Ilona Katzew, *New World Orders: Casta Painting and Colonial Latin America* (New York, 1996) und Magali Carrera, *Imagining Identity in New Spain: Race, Lineage, and the Colonial Body in Portraiture and Casta Paintings* (Austin, 2003).

43 John D. Garrigus, *Before Haiti: Race and Citizenship in French Saint-Domingue* (New York, 2006): 2–3; Stewart R. King, *Blue Coat or Powdered Wig: Free People of Color in Pre-Revolutionary Saint Domingue* (Athen und London, 2001): ix–xii; David Patrick Geggus, *Haitian Revolutionary Studies* (Bloomington, 2002): 172; Molefi Kete Asante und Ama Mazama, *Encyclopedia of Black Studies* (Thousand Oaks, 2005): 260; McClellan, *Colonialism & Science*, 59–61.

44 Dominque Rogers, »Les libres de couleur dans les capitales de Saint-Domingue : fortune, mentalités et intégration à la fin de l'Ancien Régime (1776–1789)« (Doktorarbeit, Université Michel de Montaigne, Bordeaux III): 616–17.

"Maisons de maître et habitations coloniales dans les anciens territoires français de l'Amérique tropicale," *In Situ* 5 (2004): 8].

40 *Affiches Américaines* (3 September 1766): 312 ; *Affiches Américaines* (24 December 1766): 439–40; *Affiches Américaines* (2 April 1777): 163; *Affiches Américains* (21 June 1777): 299; *Affiches Américaines, Supplément* (7 janvier 1784): 1. Sieur Lacroix listed his advertisement in the *Supplément aux Affiches Américaines* (22 February 1777): 8.

41 Bailey, *Architecture and Urbanism in the French Atlantic World*, chapter 5.

42 The tradition was particularly prevalent in New Spain. See Ilona Katzew, *New World Orders: Casta Painting and Colonial Latin America* (New York, 1996) and Magali Carrera, *Imagining Identity in New Spain: Race, Lineage, and the Colonial Body in Portraiture and Casta Paintings* (Austin, 2003).

43 John D. Garrigus, *Before Haiti: Race and Citizenship in French Saint-Domingue* (New York, 2006): 2–3; Stewart R. King, *Blue Coat or Powdered Wig: Free People of Color in Pre-Revolutionary Saint Domingue* (Athens and London, 2001): ix-xii; David Patrick Geggus, *Haitian Revolutionary Studies* (Bloomington, 2002): 172; Molefi Kete Asante and Ama Mazama, *Encyclopedia of Black Studies* (Thousand Oaks, 2005): 260; McClellan, *Colonialism & Science*, 59–61.

44 Dominque Rogers, "Les libres de couleur dans les capitales de Saint-Domingue : fortune, mentalités et intégration à la fin de l'Ancien Régime (1776–1789)" (PhD dissertation, Université Michel de Montaigne, Bordeaux III): 616–17.

45 On Pironneau, see also Rogers, "Libres de couleur," 188–89.

46 *Affiches Américaines de Saint-Domingue* (4 April 1803): 112 ; *Affiches Américaines de Saint-Domingue* (7 April 1803): 116.

47 ANOM *DPPC NOT SDOM//176* (Cap-François, Notary Bordier, 1779–80), "Testament de Cecile N.L." (4 February, 1780); *DPPC NOT SDOM//180* (Cap-François, No-

45 Zu Pironneau, siehe auch Rogers, »Libres de couleur,«
    188–89.

46 *Affiches Américaines de Saint-Domingue* (4. April 1803):
    112 ; *Affiches Américaines de Saint-Domingue* (7. April
    1803): 116.

47 ANOM *DPPC NOT SDOM//176* (Cap-François, Notar
    Bordier, 1779–80), »Testament de Cecile N.L.« (4. Feb-
    ruar, 1780); *DPPC NOT SDOM//180* (Cap-François,
    Notar Bordier, 1782), »Testament de la Ve. Seurié«
    (23. April 1782).

48 *Almanach Royal d'Hayti pour l'année bissextile 1815* (Cap-
    Henry, 1814): 114.

49 Zu Provoyeur, siehe auch Philippe Girard, *Toussaint
    Louverture: A Revolutionary Life* (New York, 2016): 75–76;
    Rogers, »Libres de couleur,« 187–88.

50 Girard, *Toussaint Louverture*, 75; Rogers, »Libres de cou-
    leur,« 188.

51 Érick Noël, *Etre noir en France au XVIIIe siècle* (Paris,
    2006): 95; Robin Blackburn, *The Making of New World
    Slavery: From the Baroque to the Modern 1492–1800* (Lon-
    don und New York, 1997): 284; Laurent Dubois, »Sla-
    very in the French Caribbean, 1635–1804,« in David
    Eltis und Stanley L. Engerman, Hrsg., *The Cambridge
    World History of Slavery* (Cambridge, 2011): 431, 435,
    442, 448. Die Gesamtzahl für Saint-Domingue zur Zeit
    der Revolution basiert auf den neuesten Zahlen
    [Jacques de Cauna, »D'Aquitaine en Haïti et inverse-
    ment,« in Éric Dubesset und Jacques de Cauna, *Dynami-
    ques caribéennes: pour une histoire des circulations dans
    l'espace atlantique (XVIIIe – XIXe siècles)* (Bordeaux,
    2014): 28].

52 *Supplément aux Affiches Américaines* (16. Juli, 1783): 401.

53 Jacques de Cauna, *Au temps des isles à sucre: histoire d'une
    plantation de Saint-Domingue au XVIIIe siècle* (Paris,
    2003): 113.

54 Cauna, *Au temps des isles à sucre,* 112.

55 Brice Martinetti, »Une habitation à Saint-Domingue
    au XVIIIe siècle: l'indigoterie Belin Desmarais ou les
    rouages d'une microsociété,« in Mickaël Augeron und
    Olivier Caudron, Hrsg., *La Rochelle, L'Aunis et la Sain-*

tary Bordier, 1782), "Testament de la Ve. Seurié"
(23 April 1782).

48 *Almanach Royal d'Hayti pour l'année bissextile 1815*
(Cap-Henry, 1814): 114.

49 On Provoyeur, see also Philippe Girard, *Toussaint Lou-*
verture: A Revolutionary Life (New York, 2016): 75–76;
Rogers, "Libres de couleur," 187–88.

50 Girard, *Toussaint Louverture*, 75; Rogers, "Libres de couleur," 188.

51 Érick Noël, *Etre noir en France au XVIIIe siècle* (Paris,
2006): 95; Robin Blackburn, *The Making of New World*
Slavery: From the Baroque to the Modern 1492–1800 (London and New York, 1997): 284; Laurent Dubois, "Slavery
in the French Caribbean, 1635–1804," in David Eltis and
Stanley L. Engerman, eds., *The Cambridge World History*
of Slavery (Cambridge, 2011): 431, 435, 442, 448. The
total numbers for Saint-Domingue at the time of the
revolution are based on the most recent figures [Jacques
de Cauna, "D'Aquitaine en Haïti et inversement," in
Éric Dubesset and Jacques de Cauna, *Dynamiques cari-*
béennes: pour une histoire des circulations dans l'espace
atlantique (XVIIIe – XIXe siècles) (Bordeaux, 2014): 28].

52 *Supplément aux Affiches Américaines* (16 July, 1783): 401.

53 Jacques de Cauna, *Au temps des isles à sucre: histoire d'une*
plantation de Saint-Domingue au XVIIIe siècle (Paris,
2003): 113.

54 Cauna, *Au temps des isles à sucre,* 112.

55 Brice Martinetti, "Une habitation à Saint-Domingue au
XVIIIe siècle: l'indigoterie Belin Desmarais ou les rou-
ages d'une microsociété," in Mickaël Augeron and Olivier Caudron, eds., *La Rochelle, L'Aunis et la Saintonge*
face à l'ésclavage (Paris, 2012): 149. On the comparative
price of skilled and non-skilled slaves see also King, *Blue*
Coat or Powdered Wig, 103. He found the mean value for
"technical specialists" during the late colonial period to
be 3,162 *livres* (slightly less than for leaders, or *comman-*
deurs, at 3,520 *livres*) and more than 2,618 *livres* for domestics and the overall average of 1,751 *livres*.

tonge face à l'ésclavage (Paris, 2012): 149. Zum preislichen Vergleich zwischen ausgebildeten und unausgebildeten Sklaven siehe auch King, *Blue Coat or Powdered Wig*, 103. Er stellte fest, dass sich der durchschnittliche Wert »technischer Spezialisten« auf 3.162 *livres* bezifferte (etwas weniger als für Anführer, oder *commandeurs*, nämlich 3.520 *livres*) und mehr als 2.618 *livres* für Dienstboten und als der Gesamtdurchschnitt von 1.751 *livres.*

56 ANOM *DPPC NOT SDOM//371*, »Vente sous la faculté de réméré de six mois plusieurs esclaves maréchal de Balande à M Bardinet« (26. August 1786).

57 King, *Blue Coat or Powdered Wig*, xiii.

58 Olivier Caudron, »S'insérer dans une société de Blancs: destins de 'gens de couleur'« in Dubesset und Cauna, *Dynamiques caribéennes*, 89–90. Noël, *Être noir en France*, 116. Érick Noël hat Verweise auf 12 schwarze Tischlergesellen, 11 Zimmerer, und möglicherweise mehr als 16 Steinmetze (*tailleurs de pierre*) in ganz Frankreich gefunden, aus einer Gesamtzahl von 297 im Jahr 1777 eingetragenen Gesellen, darunter ein schwarzer Steinmetz namens Noradin und der freie »*mulâtre*« Pierre Morel, der ein Miniaturmaler war und auch »*des dessins d'architecture*« herstellte, beide wohnhaft in Paris. Siehe auch: Jean-Pierre Sainton, *Histoire et civilisation de la Caraïbe* (Paris, 2012): 172–73.

59 *Supplément aux Affiches Américaines* (9. August 1783); *Affiches Américaines* (16. Februar 1767): 54.

60 Für den Gesamttext der Proklamation siehe David Geggus, *The Haitian Revolution: A Documentary History* (Indianapolis, 2014): 107–09.

61 Jeremy D. Popkin, *You are All Free: The Haitian Revolution and the Abolition of Slavery* (Cambridge 2010): 394; James, *The Black Jacobins*, 301.

62 Pérard, *La Citadelle restaurée*, 44–45; Mangones, »The Citadel as Site of Haitian Memory,« 859.

63 Pérard, *La Citadelle restaurée*, 105–10; Mangones, »The Citadel as Site of Haitian Memory,« 859.

64 Pérard, *La Citadelle restaurée*, 46.

65 Wilson, »The Forgotten Eighth Wonder,« 849.

56 ANOM *DPPC NOT SDOM//371*, "Vente sous la faculté de réméré de six mois plusieurs esclaves maréchal de Balande à M Bardinet" (26 August 1786).

57 King, *Blue Coat or Powdered Wig*, xiii.

58 Olivier Caudron, "S'insérer dans une société de Blancs: destins de 'gens de couleur'" in Dubesset and Cauna, *Dynamiques caribéennes*, 89–90. Noël, *Être noir en France*, 116. Érick Noël has found references to 12 black apprentice joiners, 11 carpenters, and possibly as many as 16 stonecutters (*tailleurs de pierre*) throughout France out of a total of 297 apprentices registered in 1777, including a black mason named Noradin and the free "*mulâtre*" Pierre Morel, who was a miniature painter and also made "*des dessins d'architecture*," both resident in Paris. See also: Jean-Pierre Sainton, *Histoire et civilisation de la Caraïbe* (Paris, 2012): 172–73.

59 *Supplément aux Affiches Américaines* (9 August 1783); *Affiches Américaines* (16 February 1767): 54.

60 For the full text of the proclamation see David Geggus, *The Haitian Revolution: A Documentary History* (Indianapolis, 2014): 107–09.

61 Jeremy D. Popkin, *You are All Free: The Haitian Revolution and the Abolition of Slavery* (Cambridge 2010): 394; James, *The Black Jacobins*, 301.

62 Pérard, *La Citadelle restaurée*, 44–45; Mangones, "The Citadel as Site of Haitian Memory," 859.

63 Pérard, *La Citadelle restaurée*, 105–10; Mangones, "The Citadel as Site of Haitian Memory," 859.

64 Pérard, *La Citadelle restaurée*, 46.

65 Wilson, "The Forgotten Eighth Wonder," 849.

66 E.g., *Bulletin de l'ISPAN* 11 (1 April 2010): 3. On the phases of construction see: Mangones, "The Citadel as Site of Haitian Memory," 859.

67 Harvey, *Sketches of Hayti*, 189–90; John Candler, *Brief Notices of Hayti: with its Condition, Resources, and Prospects* (London, 1842): 32. See also: Henock Trouillot, "Les ouvriers de La Citadelle et de sans-souci," *Revista de historia de América* 98 (July-December 1984): 49.

68 ANOM *15DFC564B*, "Projet d'une place de guerre à peu près centrale pour la partie française de l'Isle de Saint-

66 E.g., *Bulletin de l'ISPAN* 11 (1. April 2010). 3. Zu den Bauphasen siehe: Mangones, »The Citadel as Site of Haitian Memory,« 859.

67 Harvey, *Sketches of Hayti*, 189–90; John Candler, *Brief Notices of Hayti: with its Condition, Resources, and Prospects* (London, 1842): 32. Siehe auch: Henock Trouillot, »Les ouvriers de La Citadelle et de sans-souci,« *Revista de historia de América* 98 (Juli-Dezember 1984): 49.

68 ANOM *15DFC564B*, »Projet d'une place de guerre à peu près centrale pour la partie française de l'Isle de Saint-Domingue, conformément aux ordres de la Cour,« unterzeichnet von Deherine, 1796; *15DFC565B*, »Projet d'une place de guerre à peu près centrale pour la partie française de l'Isle de Saint-Domingue, conformément aux ordres de la Cour,« unterzeichnet von Deherine, 1796. Die beiden Entwürfe sind identisch.

69 »Toujours occupé du soin de fixer un point central de défense et de ralliement, le G.al Du Portal homme du premier mérite porta définitivement ses vues sur un point des hauts de l'Artibonite qui se trouve sur l'habitation Mirault ou il proposa de fortifier un octogone qui seroit un objet de dépense effrayante et plus impossible que jamais en ce moment.« [ANOM *15DFC 233*, »Réflexions sur le Projet d'Etablissement d'une Place de Guerre Centrale dans la Colonie« (4. Dezember 1795): 1b] Zu Vincents Kollaboration mit Christophe siehe: Cole, *Christophe, King of Haiti*, 51.

70 ANOM *15DFC239*, »Etat des Fortifications Permanentes et Passagères...dans les Parties du Nord & de l'Ouest de Saint Domingue,« unterzeichnet von Charles-Marie Vincent (21. September 1798): 3a.

71 Thomas Madiou, *Histoire d'Haïti* III (Port-au-Prince, 1847): 147. Das Hérard-Zitat wurde in Trouillot veröffentlicht, »Les ouvriers,« 50. Für eine weitere Zuschreibung an Henri Barré siehe: Leconte, *Henri Christophe*, 273.

72 Madiou, *Histoire*, III, 55, 92, 101–02, 344. Madiou schreibt erneut den »plan gigantesque« der Citadelle Laferrière Barré zu [S. 212]. 1806 war Barré auch »chef de bataillon«. Für die Zuschreibung an Barré siehe: Gi-

Domingue, conformément aux ordres de la Cour," signed Deherine, 1796; *15DFC565B*, "Projet d'une place de guerre à peu près centrale pour la partie française de l'Isle de Saint-Domingue, conformément aux ordres de la Cour," signed Deherine, 1796. The two plans are identical.

69 "Toujours occupé du soin de fixer un point central de défense et de ralliement, le G.al Du Portal homme du premier mérite porta définitivement ses vues sur un point des hauts de l'Artibonite qui se trouve sur l'habitation Mirault ou il proposa de fortifier un octogone qui seroit un objet de dépense effrayante et plus impossible que jamais en ce moment." [ANOM *15DFC 233*, "Réflexions sur le Projet d'Etablissement d'une Place de Guerre Centrale dans la Colonie" (4 December 1795): 1b] On Vincent's collaboration with Christophe see: Cole, *Christophe, King of Haiti*, 51.

70 ANOM *15DFC239*, "Etat des Fortifications Permanentes et Passagères...dans les Parties du Nord & de l'Ouest de Saint Domingue," signed Charles-Marie Vincent (21 September 1798): 3a.

71 Thomas Madiou, *Histoire d'Haïti* III (Port-au-Prince, 1847): 147. The Hérard quotation is published in Trouillot, "Les ouvriers," 50. For another attribution to Henri Barré see: Leconte, *Henri Christophe*, 273.

72 Madiou, *Histoire*, III, 55, 92, 101–02, 344. Madiou again attributes the "plan gigantesque" of the Citadelle Laferrière to Barré [p. 212]. In 1806 Barré was also "*chef de bataillon*". For the attribution to Barré see: Giselle Hyvert, "Conservation et restauration de la citadelle Laferrière du palais de Sans Souci et du Site des Ramiers," (unpublished report to UNESCO, 1979) 6.

73 Quoted without citation or date by Trouillot, "Les ouvriers," 58.

74 The discovery is mentioned, without any citation, in Pérard, *La Citadelle restaurée*, 105.

75 [Archives Nationales de France (hereafter ANF), *Base de donnés Léonore, Dossier LH/120/89*]. He also appears in ANOM *1COL6*, "Ordonnance du roi nommant à la dignité...de la Légion d'honneur, des officiers supérieurs et

selle Hyvert, »Conservation et restauration de la citadelle Laferrière du palais de Sans Souci et du Site des
Ramiers,« (unveröffentlichter Bericht für die UNESCO,
1979) 6.

73 Ohne Zitat oder Datum von Trouillot angegeben, »Les
ouvriers,« 58.

74 Die Entdeckung wird ohne Zitat von Pérard erwähnt,
La Citadelle restaurée, 105.

75 [Archives Nationales de France (hiernach ANF), *Base de
donnés Léonore, Dossier LH/120/89*]. Er erscheint auch in
ANOM *1COL6*, »Ordonnance du roi nommant à la dignité...de la Légion d'honneur, des officiers supérieurs et
des officiers de la Martinique, de la Guadeloupe, de la
Guyane française, du Sénégal et de l'Inde« (28. April
1821).

76 Wilson, »The Forgotten Eighth Wonder,« 851.

77 Pérard ist die einzige Quelle, die Besse nennt [Pérard,
La Citadelle restaurée, 106].

78 Madiou, *Histoire d'Haïti*, IV, 42, 228–31; Louis-Joseph
Janvier, *Les constitutions d'Haïti*, 1801–1885 I (Paris,
1886): 30, 89, 105. In Césaires Stück *La tragédie du Roi
Christophe* ist Martial Besse der Architekt der Citadelle.
[Aimé Césaire, *La tragédie du Roi Christophe* (Paris,
1963): 64.

79 Wilson, »The Forgotten Eighth Wonder,« 852.

80 Leconte, *Henri Christophe*, 273; Trouillot schreibt über
Leconte: »Außer, dass er Warloppes Grab in einem
Friedhof im nördlichen Haiti ermittelt, führt er seine
Angaben auf keine spezifischen Archive oder Quellen
zurück« [Trouillot, *Silencing the Past*, 62]. Für die War-
loppe-Zuschreibung siehe auch Michael Hall, *Historical
Dictionary of Haiti* (Lanham, 2012): 233.

81 Cole, *Christophe, King of Haiti*, 207.

82 Charles Mackenzie, *Notes on Haiti, Made during a Residence in that Republic* I (London, 1830): 163.

83 Harvey, *Sketches of Hayti*, 191–93.

84 Brown, *History and Present Condition* II, 187–88.

85 Loederer, »A Voodoo Castle in Haiti,« 4. Wilson ver-
gleicht Christophe mit den Pharaonen Ägyptens [Wil-
son, »The Forgotten Eighth Wonder,« 852]. Ebenso

des officiers de la Martinique, de la Guadeloupe, de la Guyane française, du Sénégal et de l'Inde" (28 April 1821).

76 Wilson, "The Forgotten Eighth Wonder," 851.

77 Pérard is the only source to mention Besse [Pérard, *La Citadelle restaurée*, 106].

78 Madiou, *Histoire d'Haïti*, IV, 42, 228–31; Louis-Joseph Janvier, *Les constitutions d'Haïti*, 1801–1885 I (Paris, 1886): 30, 89, 105. In Césaire's play *La tragédie du Roi Christophe*, Martial Besse is the architect who builds the Citadelle. [Aimé Césaire, *La tragédie du Roi Christophe* (Paris, 1963): 64.

79 Wilson, "The Forgotten Eighth Wonder," 852.

80 Leconte, *Henri Christophe,* 273; Trouillot writes about Leconte: "except for locating Warloppe's grave in a cemetery in northern Haiti, he does not tie his data to specific archives or sources." [Trouillot, *Silencing the Past*, 62]. For the Warloppe attribution see also Michael Hall, *Historical Dictionary of Haiti* (Lanham, 2012): 233.

81 Cole, *Christophe, King of Haiti*, 207.

82 Charles Mackenzie, *Notes on Haiti, Made during a Residence in that Republic* I (London, 1830): 163.

83 Harvey, *Sketches of Hayti,* 191–93.

84 Brown, *History and Present Condition* II, 187–88.

85 Loederer, "A Voodoo Castle in Haiti," 4. Wilson compares Christophe directly with the Pharaohs of Egypt [Wilson, "The Forgotten Eighth Wonder," 852]. So do Griggs and Prater, who write "[e]ven in ruin, however, it rivals the Egyptian Pyramids." [Griggs and Prater, *Henry Christophe & Thomas Clarkson*, 51].

86 Derek Walcott, *Henri Christophe: A Chronicle in Seven Scenes* (reprint New York, 2002): 86.

87 Candler, *Brief Notices of Hayti*, 32.

88 Brown, *History and Present Condition* II, 187–88.

89 Mackenzie, *Notes on Haiti*, II, 179–80.

90 Madiou, *Histoire d'Haïti*, III, 147.

91 Beaubrun Ardouin, *Etudes sur l'histoire d'Haiti* VIII (Paris, 1853–60): 459. Trouillot questions that such great numbers worked on the project since Ardouin provides no sources, blaming these exaggerations on Ardouin's

Griggs und Prater, die schreiben, dass »[s]ogar als Ruine, indes, kommt sie den ägyptischen Pyramiden gleich« [Griggs und Prater, *Henry Christophe & Thomas Clarkson*, 51].

86 Derek Walcott, *Henri Christophe: A Chronicle in Seven Scenes* (Nachdruck New York, 2002): 86.

87 Candler, *Brief Notices of Hayti*, 32.

88 Brown, *History and Present Condition* II, 187–88.

89 Mackenzie, *Notes on Haiti*, II, 179–80.

90 Madiou, *Histoire d'Haïti*, III, 147.

91 Beaubrun Ardouin, *Etudes sur l'histoire d'Haiti* VIII (Paris, 1853–60): 459. Trouillot stellt in Frage, dass so viele an dem Projekt beteiligt waren, da Ardouin keine Quellen angibt, und schreibt diese Übertreibungen den republikanischen Sympathien Ardouins zu [Trouillot, »Les ouvriers,« 51]. Siehe auch Leconte, *Henri Christophe*, 351, 368.

92 Pérard, *La Citadelle*, 44–45; Wilson, »The Forgotten Eighth Wonder,« 852. Für eine Besprechung der Geschichten, die Führer über den hohen Preis erzählen, der bei Laferriere und Sans-Souci »mit Geld und mit menschlichem Blut« gezahlt wurde, siehe Trouillot, *Silencing the Past*, 35–36. Siehe auch Philippe R. Girard, *Paradise Lost: Haiti's Tumultuous Journey from Pearl of the Caribbean to Third World Hot Spot* (New York, 2005): 62.

93 Trouillot, »Les ouvriers,« 52, 58; Leconte, *Henri Christophe*, 368.

94 Zitiert in Trouillot, »Les ouvriers,« 56.

95 Der Brief war an General Capois adressiert [Trouillot, »Les ouvriers,« 56–57].

96 Brief vom 14. April 1806 zitiert in Trouillot, »Les ouvriers,« 20. Siehe auch Cole, *Christophe, King of Haiti*, 207.

97 Harvey, *Sketches of Hayti*, 189–90.

98 ANOM *F3/296/B10 bis*, »Isle S. Domingue 1770. Carte du Cap-François et de ses environs,« unterzeichnet von Boisforêt. Siehe auch Moreau de Saint-Méry, *Description*, I, 231. Zu Millot/Milot siehe auch Leconte, *Henri Christophe*, 281.

99 Für Verweise auf die Anzahl und Namen der Paläste

republican sympathies [Trouillot, "Les ouvriers," 51]. See also Leconte, *Henri Christophe*, 351, 368.

92 Pérard, *La Citadelle*, 44–45; Wilson, "The Forgotten Eighth Wonder," 852. For a discussion of the tales told by guides about the heavy price "in currency and in human blood" at Laferriere and Sans-Souci, see Trouillot, *Silencing the Past*, 35–36. See also Philippe R. Girard, *Paradise Lost: Haiti's Tumultuous Journey from Pearl of the Caribbean to Third World Hot Spot* (New York, 2005): 62.

93 Trouillot, "Les ouvriers," 52, 58; Leconte, *Henri Christophe*, 368.

94 Quoted in Trouillot, "Les ouvriers," 56.

95 The letter was addressed to General Capois [Trouillot, "Les ouvriers," 56–57].

96 Letter of 14 April 1806 quoted in Trouillot, "Les ouvriers," 20. See also Cole, *Christophe, King of Haiti*, 207.

97 Harvey, *Sketches of Hayti*, 189–90.

98 ANOM *F3/296/B10 bis*, "Isle S. Domingue 1770. Carte du Cap-François et de ses environs," signed by Boisforêt. See also Moreau de Saint-Méry, *Description*, I, 231. On Millot/Milot see also Leconte, *Henri Christophe*, 281.

99 For references to the number and names of the palaces see Pérard, *La Citadelle restaurée*, 59, 72–73; Cole, *Christophe, King of Haiti*, 207; Griggs and Prator, *Henry Christophe & Thomas Clarkson*, 47; Leconte, *Henri Christophe*, 335–338.

100 Pompée Valentin Baron de Vastey, *An Essay on the Causes of the Revolution and Civil Wars of Hayti* (Cap-Henry, 1819): 137. See also: Garraway, "Empire of Freedom," 9–10; Leconte, *Henri Christophe*, 338. For the 1815 completion date, for which no source is given, see: *Bulletin de l'ISPAN* 11 (1 April 2010): 4.

101 Hérard Dumesle, *Voyage dans le nord d'Hayti, ou, Révélations des lieux et des monuments historiques* (Les Cayes, 1824): 225–26. See also Trouillot, *Silencing the Past*, 61.

102 Brown, *History and Present Condition*, 216.

103 Cole, *Christophe, King of Haiti*, 207; Wilson, "The Forgotten Eighth Wonder," 853.

104 *National History Park – Citadel, Sans-Souci, Ramiers* (http://whc.unesco.org/en/list/180). Accessed 3 Febru-

siehe Pérard, *La Citadelle restaurée*, 59, 72–73; Cole, *Christophe, King of Haiti*, 207; Griggs und Prator, *Henry Christophe & Thomas Clarkson*, 47; Leconte, *Henri Christophe*, 335–338.

100 Pompée Valentin Baron de Vastey, *An Essay on the Causes of the Revolution and Civil Wars of Hayti* (Cap-Henry, 1819): 137. Siehe auch: Garraway, »Empire of Freedom,« 9–10; Leconte, *Henri Christophe*, 338. Für das Datum der Vollendung im Jahr 1815, für das keine Quelle angegeben wird, siehe: *Bulletin de l'ISPAN* 11 (1. April 2010): 4.

101 Hérard Dumesle, *Voyage dans le nord d'Hayti, ou, Révélations des lieux et des monuments historiques* (Les Cayes, 1824): 225–26. Siehe auch Trouillot, *Silencing the Past*, 61.

102 Brown, *History and Present Condition*, 216.

103 Cole, *Christophe, King of Haiti*, 207; Wilson, »The Forgotten Eighth Wonder,« 853.

104 *National History Park – Citadel, Sans-Souci, Ramiers* (http://whc.unesco.org/en/list/180). Abgerufen am 3. February 2017. Für dasselbe Zitat siehe: *Bulletin de l'ISPAN, numéro special Monuments historiques d'Haiti élus au WMF Watch 2012* (5. October 2011): 3.

105 Cole, *Christophe, King of Haiti*, 207; Henock Trouillot, *Le Gouvernement du Roi Henri Christophe* (Port-au-Prince, 1972): 29.

106 Trouillot, *Silencing the Past*, 44. Siehe auch Laurent Dubois, *Avengers of the New World: The Story of the Haitian Revolution* (Cambridge MA, 2004): 294.

107 William St Clair, *The Door of No Return: The History of Cape Coast Castle and the Atlantic Slave Trade* (New York, 2007); Robin Law, *Ouidah: The Social History of a West African Slaving »Port«, 1727–1892* (Athen OH und Oxford, 2004); Alain Sinou, *Le comptoir de Ouidah* (Paris, 1995); Simone Berbain, *Etudes sur la traite des noirs au golfe de Guinée. Le Comptoir français de Juda (Ouidah) au XVIIIè siècle* (Paris, 1942).

108 Harvey, *Sketches of Hayti*, 133.

109 Berger, *A Royal Passion*, 5, 164–68.

110 Brown, *History and Present Condition*, 187.

111 Brown, *History and Present Condition*, 187.

ary 2017. For the same quotation see: *Bulletin de l'ISPAN, numéro special Monuments historiques d'Haiti élus au WMF Watch 2012*, (5 October 2011): 3.

105 Cole, *Christophe, King of Haiti*, 207; Henock Trouillot, *Le Gouvernement du Roi Henri Christophe* (Port-au-Prince, 1972): 29.

106 Trouillot, *Silencing the Past*, 44. See also Laurent Dubois, *Avengers of the New World: The Story of the Haitian Revolution* (Cambridge MA, 2004): 294.

107 William St Clair, *The Door of No Return: The History of Cape Coast Castle and the Atlantic Slave Trade* (New York, 2007); Robin Law, *Ouidah: The Social History of a West African Slaving "Port", 1727–1892* (Athens OH and Oxford, 2004); Alain Sinou, *Le comptoir de Ouidah* (Paris, 1995); Simone Berbain, *Etudes sur la traite des noirs au golfe de Guinée. Le Comptoir français de Juda (Ouidah) au XVIIIè siècle* (Paris, 1942).

108 Harvey, *Sketches of Hayti*, 133.

109 Berger, *A Royal Passion*, 5, 164–68.

110 Brown, *History and Present Condition*, 187.

111 Brown, *History and Present Condition*, 187.

112 Brown, *History and Present Condition*, 205.

113 Vastey, *An Essay*, 137. It was Trouillot who noted that Vastey "anticipated Afrocentrism by more than a century" [Trouillot, *Silencing the Past*, 36]. See also: Baron de Vastey, *Le système colonial dévoilé* (Cap-Henry, 1814): 93; and Garraway, "Print, Publics," 87.

114 Wilson, "The Forgotten Eighth Wonder," 853; Edward E. Crain, *Historic Architecture of the Caribbean Islands* (Gainesville, 1994): 121.

115 Julien Prevost, *le comte de* Limonade, *Relation des Glorieux Evénements qui ont porté leurs Majestés Royales sur le Trône d'Hayti* (Cap-Henry, 1811): 19–20.

116 Quoted in Harvey, *Sketches of Hayti*, 227–30; Griggs and Prator, *Henry Christophe & Thomas Clarkson*, 48–49. See also Cole, *Christophe, King of Haiti*, 256–58.

117 Karl Ritter, *Naturhistorische Reise nach der westindischen Insel Hayti*, (Stuttgart, 1836): 77–79.

112 Brown, *History and Present Condition*, 205.

113 Vastey, An Essay, 137. Es war Trouillot, der anmerkte, dass Vastey den »Afrozentrismus um mehr als ein Jahrhundert vorwegnahm« [Trouillot, Silencing the Past, 36]. Siehe auch: Baron de Vastey, *Le système colonial dévoilé* (Cap-Henry, 1814): 93; und Garraway, »Print, Publics,« 87.

114 Wilson, »The Forgotten Eighth Wonder,« 853; Edward E. Crain, *Historic Architecture of the Caribbean Islands* (Gainesville, 1994): 121.

115 Julien Prevost, *le comte* de Limonade, *Relation des Glorieux Evénements qui ont porté leurs Majestés Royales sur le Trône d'Hayti* (Cap-Henry, 1811): 19–20.

116 Zitiert in Harvey, *Sketches of Hayti*, 227–30; Griggs und Prator, *Henry Christophe & Thomas Clarkson*, 48–49. Siehe auch Cole, *Christophe, King of Haiti*, 256–58.

117 Karl Ritter, *Naturhistorische Reise nach der westindischen Insel Hayti*, (Stuttgart, 1836): 77–79.

118 Siehe Wolfgang Steiner, *Eine andere Art von Malerey: Hinterglasgemälde und ihre Vorlagen 1550–1850* (Augsburg, 2012): 8–17.

119 Vastey gibt ihr beide Namen: Vastey, An Essay, 137.

120 Ritter, *Naturhistorische Reise*, 79.

121 Dumesle, *Voyage dans le nord d'Hayti*, 224–25.

122 Marc Fumaroli, *L'âge de l'éloquence* (Genf, 2009): 217–19.

123 Harvey, *Sketches of Hayti*, 133–35.

124 Mackenzie, *Notes on Haiti*, 170–71.

125 Brown, *History and Present Condition*, 187.

126 Candler, *Brief Notices of Hayti*, 29.

127 Crain, *Historic Architecture*, 121–22.

128 Zu den französischen Bâtiments du Roi siehe: Thierry Sarmant, *Les demeures du Soleil. Louis XIV, Louvois et la surintendance des bâtiments du Roi* (Seyssel, 2003): 90; François Fossier, *Les dessins du fonds Robert de Cotte de la Bibliothèque nationale de France* (Paris, Rom, 1997): 37.

129 Prevost, *Relation des Glorieux Evénements*, 74, 187.

130 *The formation of the new dynasty of the Kingdom of Hayti, formerly the island of Saint Domingo* (Philadelphia, 1811): 14.

131 »Loi pénale militaire,« in *Code Henry* (Cap-Henry, 1812):

118 See Wolfgang Steiner, *Eine andere Art von Malerey: Hinterglasgemälde und ihre Vorlagen 1550–1850* (Augsburg, 2012): 8–17.

119 Vastey gives it both titles: Vastey, *An Essay*, 137.

120 Ritter, *Naturhistorische Reise*, 79.

121 Dumesle, *Voyage dans le nord d'Hayti*, 224–25.

122 Marc Fumaroli, *L'âge de l'éloquence* (Geneva, 2009): 217–19.

123 Harvey, *Sketches of Hayti*, 133–35.

124 Mackenzie, *Notes on Haiti*, 170–71.

125 Brown, *History and Present Condition*, 187.

126 Candler, *Brief Notices of Hayti*, 29.

127 Crain, *Historic Architecture*, 121–22.

128 On the French Bâtiments du Roi see: Thierry Sarmant, *Les demeures du Soleil. Louis XIV, Louvois et la surintendance des bâtiments du Roi* (Seyssel, 2003): 90; François Fossier, *Les dessins du fonds Robert de Cotte de la Bibliothèque nationale de France* (Paris, Rome, 1997): 37.

129 Prevost, *Relation des Glorieux Evénements*, 74, 187.

130 *The formation of the new dynasty of the Kingdom of Hayti, formerly the island of Saint Domingo* (Philadelphia, 1811): 14.

131 "Loi pénale militaire," in *Code Henry* (Cap-Henry, 1812): 27; *Extrait des registres du grand Conseil d'État* (Sans-Souci, 1819): 4.

132 *Almanach Royal d'Hayti pour l'année bissextile 1816* (Cap-Henry, 1815): 73. See also Cheesman, *The Armorial of Haiti*, 62.

133 Leconte, *Henri Christophe*, 273.

134 Cheeseman, *The Armorial of Haiti*, cat. 62. Cheeseman is curiously reluctant to identify Faraud as the chief architect of the Citadelle on the basis of Leconte's attribution to Henri Barré even though the shield and evidence in the almanacs should leave no doubt as to his role. Barré by contrast does not appear in the almanacs.

135 Rogers, "Les libres de couleur."

136 *Affiches Américaines* (6 December 1775): 584.

137 Cheesman, *The Armorial of Haiti*, 90; Leconte, *Henri Christophe*, 273; *Almanach royal d'Hayti; pour l'année bissextile 1820* (Cap-Henry, 1819): 9.

27; *Extrait des registres du grand Conseil d'État* (Sans-Souci, 1819): 4.

132 *Almanach Royal d'Hayti pour l'année bissextile 1816* (Cap-Henry, 1815): 73. Siehe auch Cheesman, *The Armorial of Haiti*, 62.

133 Leconte, *Henri Christophe*, 273.

134 Cheesman, *The Armorial of Haiti*, Kat. 62. Cheesman ist seltsam zögerlich, Faraud aufgrund von Lecontes Zuschreibung an Henri Barré als Chefarchitekten der Citadelle zu identifizieren, auch wenn das Wappen und Belege in den Almanachen keine Zweifel an seiner Rolle lassen. Barré hingegen taucht nicht in den Almanachen auf.

135 Rogers, »Les libres de couleur.«

136 *Affiches Américaines* (6. Dezember 1775): 584.

137 Cheesman, *The Armorial of Haiti*, 90; Leconte, Henri Christophe, 273; *Almanach royal d'Hayti; pour l'année bissextile 1820* (Cap-Henry, 1819): 9.

139 *Almanac Royal d'Hayti pour l'année 1815* (Cap-Henry, 1814): 10; *Almanac Royal d'Hayti pour l'année 1816*, 10.

130 *Almanach Royal d'Hayti, pour l'année bissextile 1820*, 39.

140 *Affiches Américaines* (23. Februar 1788): 104.

141 Prevost, *Relation des Glorieux Evénements*, 86.

142 *Affiches Américaines* (29. August 1768): 124.

143 Anne Pérotin-Dumon, *La ville aux îles, la ville dans l'île: Basse-Terre et Pointe-à-Pitre, Guadeloupe, 1650–1820* (Paris, 2000): 765, 797; Cauna, *Au temps des isles à sucre*, 113.

144 Laurent Dubois, *Avengers of the New World: The Story of the Haitian Revolution* (Cambridge MA, 2004): 228, 270; Amédée Dechambre und Jacques Raige-Delorme, *Dictionnaire encyclopédique des sciences médicales* XXVIII (Paris, 1883): 288; »Jean Théodore Descourtilz,« in Tom Taylor und Michael Taylor, Hrsg., *Aves: A Survey of the Literature of Neotropical Ornithology* (Baton Rouge, 2011).

145 *Affiches Américaines* (25. November 1767): 384.

146 Briefe von Henry Christophe an André (4. März 1806) zitiert in Trouillot, »les ouvriers,« 58–59.

147 Garrigus, *Before Haiti*, 222; Rogers, »Libres de couleur,« 615. Für Dokumente über den Rechtsfall, in dem es um

138 *Almanac Royal d'Hayti pour l'année 1815* (Cap-Henry, 1814): 10; *Almanac Royal d'Hayti pour l'année 1816*, 10.

139 *Almanach Royal d'Hayti, pour l'année bissextile 1820*, 39.

140 *Affiches Américaines* (23 February 1788): 104.

141 Prevost, *Relation des Glorieux Evénements*, 86.

142 *Affiches Américaines* (29 August 1768): 124.

143 Anne Pérotin-Dumon, *La ville aux îles, la ville dans l'île: Basse-Terre et Pointe-à-Pitre, Guadeloupe, 1650–1820* (Paris, 2000): 765, 797; Cauna, *Au temps des isles à sucre*, 113.

144 Laurent Dubois, *Avengers of the New World: The Story of the Haitian Revolution* (Cambridge MA, 2004): 228, 270; Amédée Dechambre and Jacques Raige-Delorme, *Dictionnaire encyclopédique des sciences médicales* XXVIII (Paris, 1883): 288; "Jean Théodore Descourtilz," in Tom Taylor and Michael Taylor, eds., *Aves: A Survey of the Literature of Neotropical Ornithology* (Baton Rouge, 2011).

145 *Affiches Américaines* (25 November 1767): 384.

146 Letter from Henry Christophe to André (4 March 1806) quoted in Trouillot, *"les ouvriers,"* 58–59.

147 Garrigus, *Before Haiti*, 222; Rogers, "Libres de couleur," 615. For documents about the case to grant Jasmin's hospital official status see: ANOM *COL E 229*, "Jasmin, nègre libre de Saint-Domingue, fondateur au Cap-Français d'un hospice pour les gens de couleur" (1788/1789); and Archives Departementales de Gironde (hereafter ADGi), *61 J 5*, "Extrait des Registres de la Société Royale d'Agriculture du 26 mars 1789."

148 "Le Sr Louis chargea Jasmin de diriger plusieurs travaux, et en fut si content, qu'il sollicita son affranchissement dès 1741." [ADGi, *61 J 5,* 1a].

149 The two letters by Henry Christophe are quoted in Trouillot, *"les ouvriers,"* 59.

150 *Gazette Officielle de Saint-Domingue* (3 September 1803): 287.

151 *Almanach Royal d'Hayti pour l'année bissextile 1816*, 107; *Almanach Royal d'Hayti pour l'année bissextile 1815*, 10, 97; *Almanach Royal d'Hayti, pour l'année bissextile 1820*, 39, 120: Prevost, *Relation des Glorieux Evénements*, 107. On Béliard see also: Cheesman, *The Armorial of Haiti*,

die Verleihung des offiziellen Status an Jasmins Krankenhaus ging siehe: ANOM *COL E 229*, »Jasmin, nègre libre de Saint-Domingue, fondateur au Cap-Français d'un hospice pour les gens de couleur« (1788/1789); und Archives Departementales de Gironde (hiernach ADGi), *61 J 5*, »Extrait des Registres de la Société Royale d'Agriculture du 26 mars 1789.«

148 »Le Sr Louis chargea Jasmin de diriger plusieurs travaux, et en fut si content, qu'il sollicita son affranchissement dès 1741.« [ADGi, *61 J 5*, 1a].

149 Die zwei Briefe Henry Christophes werden in Trouillot zitiert, »*les ouvriers,*« 59.

150 *Gazette Officielle de Saint-Domingue* (3. September 1803): 287.

151 *Almanach Royal d'Hayti pour l'année bissextile 1816*, 107; *Almanach Royal d'Hayti pour l'année bissextile 1815*, 10, 97; *Almanach Royal d'Hayti, pour l'année bissextile 1820*, 39, 120: Prevost, *Relation des Glorieux Evénements*, 107. Zu Béliard siehe auch: Cheesman, *The Armorial of Haiti*, 150, 202; Griggs und Prator, *Henry Christophe & Thomas Clarkson*, 243.

152 ANOM *COL E 147*, »Dufresne de Pontbrillant, Julien Guillaume, propriétaire d'une habitation à Saint-Domingue et ses héritiers« (1785).

153 Zur Familie Dardan in Bordeaux, siehe: Philippe Maffre, *Construire Bordeaux au XVIIIe siècle* (2013): 27, 36.

154 Maffre, *Construire Bordeaux*, 59; ADGi, *C 4466*, »Status des Maîtres,« 3; *Supplément aux Affiches Américaines* (30. August 1777): 420.

155 Das Dokument gibt nur seinen Nachnamen an, die Signatur jedoch ist identisch mit einer Joseph Dardans in einem Brief vom 26. Mai 1781. [ADGi, *C 4466*, »Corporations, charpentiers, maçons et architectes, orfèvres, 1673–1780, doc 13« (14. April, 1765); ANOM *COL E 108*, Brief vom 26. Mai 1781] Am 30. April 1765 unterzeichnet Dardan im Beratungsbuch der Gilde mit seinem Namen, am 11. Juni 1768 wird er zum Büttel gewählt, und am 17. Dezember 1770 nimmt er an seiner letzten Sitzung teil. Seine Signatur fehlt bei dem nächsten Treffen am 15. April [ADGi, *C 1757* »Déliberations, Co-

150, 202; Griggs and Prator, *Henry Christophe & Thomas Clarkson*, 243.

152 ANOM *COL E 147*, "Dufresne de Pontbrillant, Julien Guillaume, propriétaire d'une habitation à Saint-Domingue et ses héritiers" (1785).

153 On the Dardan family in Bordeaux, see: Philippe Maffre, *Construire Bordeaux au XVIIIe siècle* (2013): 27, 36.

154 Maffre, *Construire Bordeaux*, 59; ADGi, *C 4466*, "Status des Maîtres," 3; *Supplément aux Affiches Américaines* (30 August 1777): 420.

155 The document only gives his surname however the signature is identical to that of Joseph Dardan in a letter of 26 May 1781. [ADGi, *C 4466*, "Corporations, charpentiers, maçons et architectes, orfèvres, 1673–1780, doc 13" (14 April, 1765); ANOM *COL E 108*, letter of 26 May 1781] Dardan also signed his name in 30 April 1765 in the Company's book of deliberations, is elected bailiff on 11 June 1768, and attends his last meeting on 17 December 1770. His signature is missing at the next meeting of 15 April [ADGi, *C 1757* "Déliberations, Comunauté des Maîtres Architectes de Bordeaux" (1769–90): 1, 2, 15, 16].

156 "Ses affaires l'ayant appelé au Cap, il résolut d'y fixer sa résidence et de s'y livrer aux fonctions de son art, qu'il avoit exercé pendant plusieurs années à Bordeaux." [ANOM *COL E 108 no 13*, "Dardan, Joseph Antoine, maître-maçon et architecte juré en la ville de Bordeaux, ancien grand voyer de la ville et banlieue du Cap, à Saint-Domingue," Letter of 1 February 1783, fol. 1]. See also : Maffre, *Construire Bordeaux*, 27–29, 33–36. Dardan's departure date from Bordeaux (1771) is mentioned in a legal proceedings from 1793 [ADGi, *2 E 785*, "Titre de famille Dardan" (1 August, 1793), document 2, f. 1a].

157 In the minutes of the 17 November and 6 September 1770 meetings he was simply listed as "*absent*" [ADGi, *C 1757* "Déliberations, Comunauté des Maîtres Architectes de Bordeaux" (1769–90): 22, 23].

158 *Affiches Américaines, Supplément, Avis Divers* (5 mars 1774): 9, p. 2.

munauté des Maîtres Architectes de Bordeaux« (1769 90): 1, 2, 15, 16].

156 »Ses affaires l'ayant appellé au Cap, il résolut d'y fixer sa résidence et de s'y livrer aux fonctions de son art, qu'il avoit exercé pendant plusieurs années à Bordeaux.« [ANOM *COL E 108 no 13*, »Dardan, Joseph Antoine, maître-maçon et architecte juré en la ville de Bordeaux, ancien grand voyer de la ville et banlieue du Cap, à Saint-Domingue,« Brief vom 1. Februar 1783, fol. 1]. Siehe auch: Maffre, *Construire Bordeaux*, 27–29, 33–36. Dardans Abreisedatum von Bordeaux (1771) wird in einem Gerichtsverfahren von 1793 erwähnt [ADGi, 2 E 785, »Titre de famille Dardan« (1. August, 1793), document 2, f. 1a].

157 In den Protokollen der Sitzungen vom 17. November und 6. September 1770 wurde er einfach als *»absent«* verzeichnet [ADGi, *C 1757* »Déliberations, Comunauté des Maîtres Architectes de Bordeaux« (1769–90): 22, 23].

158 *Affiches Américaines, Supplément, Avis Divers* (5 mars 1774): 9, p. 2.

159 ANOM *COL E 108 no 13*, Brief vom 1. Februar 1783; Brief vom 13. November, 1785. Für Dokumente über seine Berufung, siehe: ANOM *COL E 108*, Brief vom 9. September 1786.

160 »Les talents du supliant ne se sont point bornés dans la Ville de Bordeaux à la simple architecture. Il a encore été choisi pour mesurer les chemins de la dépendance, allignements et nivellements de la ditte Ville, au lieu et place de son Père, commis par le Bureau de la Voyerie pour ces sortes d'opérations que sa vieillesse l'a empêché de continuer.« [ANOM *COL E 108 no 13*, Brief vom 1. Februar 1783, fol. 3a]

161 ADGi, *2 E 785, Titre de famille Dardan* (1. August, 1793), 2a, 3b, 4b. Es wird vermerkt, dass »la portion e Joseph Dardan rester dans les mains de l'acquéreur pour y produire l'intérêt si mieux il n'aime la déposer dans les mains du Receveur des consignations ou dans celle de tout autre officier public solvable...« [5b] Hinsichtlich der Briefe seiner Eltern: »1e. Avoir parfaitement connu le dit Joseph Dardan ainé architecte frère des susnom-

159 ANOM *COL E 108 no 13*, Letter of 1 February 1783; Letter of 13 November, 1785. For documents on his appeal, see: ANOM *COL E 108*, letter of 9 September 1786.

160 "Les talents du supliant ne se sont point bornés dans la Ville de Bordeaux à la simple architecture. Il a encore été choisi pour mesurer les chemins de la dépendance, allignements et nivellements de la ditte Ville, au lieu et place de son Père, commis par le Bureau de la Voyerie pour ces sortes d'opérations que sa vieillesse l'a empêché de continuer." [ANOM *COL E 108 no 13*, Letter of 1 February 1783, fol. 3a]

161 ADGi, *2 E 785, Titre de famille Dardan* (1 August, 1793), 2a, 3b, 4b. It notes "la portion e Joseph Dardan rester dans les mains de l'acquéreur pour y produire l'intérêt si mieux il n'aime la déposer dans les mains du Receveur des consignations ou dans celle de tout autre officier public solvable…" [5b] Concerning his parents' letters: "1e. Avoir parfaitement connu le dit Joseph Dardan ainé architecte frère des susnommés, et savoir qu'il partit de ce lieu au mois de Septembre mil sept cent soixante-onze, pour les colonies, que depuis il n'a plus reparu en cette ville; qu'ils savent de plus que ses parents lui ont écrit plusieurs lettres et qu'ils n'ont jamais oui dire qu'ils eussent reçu de réponse." [ADGi, *2 E 785*, Letter from Bordeaux, 29 July, 1793].

162 *Gazette Officielle de Saint-Domingue* (4 July 1803): 216; (6 July 1803): 220.

163 *Affiches Américaines de Saint-Domingue* (14 April 1803): 124; *Affiches Américaines de Saint-Domingue* (24 March 1803): 100; *Affiches Américaines de Saint-Domingue* (26 May 1803): 172; *Affiches Américaines de Saint-Domingue* (2 June 1803): 180; *Affiches Américaines de Saint-Domingue* (4 July 1803): 216; *Affiches Américaines de Saint-Domingue* (7 April 1803): 116. Robard alone is not listed in the *Déclarations de Départs* for 1803, however he may have left even earlier. Robard was active as early as the 1780s and appears in notarial documents of the period: ANOM *DPPC NOT SDOM//181*, "Bail d'emplacement et bâtiments Srs Maitre et le Cardinal au S. Robard" (8 De-

més, et savoir qu'il partit de ce lieu au mois de Septembre mil sept cent soixante-onze, pour les colonies, que depuis il n'a plus reparu en cette ville; qu'ils savent de plus que ses parents lui ont écrit plusieurs lettres et qu'ils n'ont jamais ouï dire qu'ils eussent reçu de réponse.« [ADGi, *2 E 785*, Brief aus Bordeaux, 29. Juli, 1793].

162 *Gazette Officielle de Saint-Domingue* (4. Juli 1803): 216; (6. Juli 1803): 220.

163 *Affiches Américaines de Saint-Domingue* (14. April 1803): 124; *Affiches Américaines de Saint-Domingue* (24. März 1803): 100; *Affiches Américaines de Saint-Domingue* (26. Mai 1803): 172; *Affiches Américaines de Saint-Domingue* (2. Juni 1803): 180; *Affiches Américaines de Saint-Domingue* (4. Juli 1803): 216; *Affiches Américaines de Saint-Domingue* (7. April 1803): 116. Nur Robard wird nicht in den *Déclarations de Départs* von 1803 aufgeführt, allerdings mag er noch früher abgereist sein. Robard war bereits in den 1780ern aktiv und taucht in notariellen Unterlagen der Zeit auf: ANOM *DPPC NOT SDOM//181*, »Bail d'emplacement et bâtiments Srs Maitre et le Cardinal au S. Robard« (8. Dezember 1782); DPPC *NOT SDOM//187*, »Marché Le Sr.a Barganger et le Sr. Robard« (2. Juni 1784).

164 Zu Dessalines' Einnahme Cap-François' siehe Popkin, *You are all Free*, 394.

165 Laurent Dubois, »Avenging America: The Politics of Violence in the Haitian Revolution,« in David Patrick Geggus und Norman Fiering, Hrsg., *The World of the Haitian Revolution* (Bloomington und Indianapolis, 2009): 120–21.

166 Girard, *Paradise Lost*, 56–57.

167 Der Almanach von 1815 nennt als »Peintres du Roi« die »Messieurs Revinchal, Frédéric Toucas, Baptiste, Manuël, Beaumy, Châtel, Bazile, Charles« [*Almanach Royal d'Hayti pour l'année bissextile 1815*, 113]. Siehe auch Lerebours, *Haïti et ses peintres*, I, 94; Leconte, *Henri Christophe*, 326.

168 Zu de Cotte und Boffrand, siehe: Germain Boffrand, *Book of Architecture* (Caroline van Eck Hrsg.; Aldershot,

cember 1782); *DPPC NOT SDOM//187*, "Marché Le Sr.a
Barganger et le Sr. Robard" (2 June 1784).

164 On Dessaline's capture of Cap-François see Popkin, *You
are all Free,* 394.

165 Laurent Dubois, "Avenging America: The Politics of
Violence in the Haitian Revolution," in David Patrick
Geggus and Norman Fiering, eds., *The World of the Haitian Revolution* (Bloomington and Indianapolis, 2009):
120–21.

166 Girard, *Paradise Lost,* 56–57.

167 The 1815 Almanac names the "Peintres du Roi" as "Messieurs Revinchal, Frédéric Toucas, Baptiste, Manuël,
Beaumy, Châtel, Bazile, Charles" [*Almanach Royal
d'Hayti pour l'année bissextile 1815,* 113]. See also Lerebours, *Haïti et ses peintres,* I, 94; Leconte, *Henri Christophe,* 326.

168 On de Cotte and Boffrand, see: Germain Boffrand, *Book
of Architecture* (Caroline van Eck ed.; Aldershot, 2002);
Fossier, *Les dessins du fonds Robert de Cotte,* 47–53; Robert Neuman, *Robert de Cotte and the Perfection of Architecture in Eighteenth-Century France* (Chicago and London, 1994): 3–5; Wend von Kalnein, *Architecture in
France in the Eighteenth Century* (New Haven and London, 1995): 8–34; Michel Gallet, *Les architectes parisiens
du XVIIIe siècle: dictionnaire biographique et critique*
(Paris, 1995): 72–79; 146–158; Robert Neuman, "French
Domestic Architecture in the Early 18th Century: the
Town Houses of Robert de Cotte," *Journal of the Society
of Architectural Historians,* 39, 2 (May, 1980): 128–44.

169 Bruno Kissoun, *Pointe-à-Pitre: urbanisme et architecture
religieuse, publique et militaire XVIIIe-XIXe siècles* (Cla-
mecy, 2008): 139; Marie-Emmanuelle Desmoulins et al.,
Basse-Terre, patrimoine d'une ville antillaise (Pointe-à-
Pitre, 2006): 146–47; Pérotin-Dumon, *La ville aux Iles,*
plate 7.13.

170 Boffrand, *Book of Architecture,* 30–37; Kalnein, *Architecture in France,* 28–30.

171 Neuman, *Robert de Cotte,* 193–98; 204–14.

172 Neuman, *Robert de Cotte,* 67–72.

173 Kalnein, *Architecture in France,* 112–14.

2002); Fossier, *Les dessins du fonds Robert de Cotte*, 47–53;
Robert Neuman, *Robert de Cotte and the Perfection of
Architecture in Eighteenth-Century France* (Chicago und
London, 1994): 3–5; Wend von Kalnein, *Architecture in
France in the Eighteenth Century* (New Haven und Lon-
don, 1995): 8–34; Michel Gallet, *Les architectes parisiens
du XVIIIe siècle: dictionnaire biographique et critique*
(Paris, 1995): 72–79; 146–158; Robert Neuman, »French
Domestic Architecture in the Early 18th Century: the
Town Houses of Robert de Cotte,« *Journal of the Society
of Architectural Historians*, 39, 2 (Mai, 1980): 128–44.

169 Bruno Kissoun, *Pointe-à-Pitre: urbanisme et architecture
religieuse, publique et militaire XVIIIe-XIXe siècles* (Cla-
mecy, 2008): 139; Marie-Emmanuelle Desmoulins et al.,
Basse-Terre, patrimoine d'une ville antillaise (Pointe-à-
Pitre, 2006): 146–47; Pérotin-Dumon, La ville aux Iles,
plate 7.13.

170 Boffrand, *Book of Architecture*, 30–37; Kalnein, *Architecture in France*, 28–30.

171 Neuman, *Robert de Cotte*, 193–98; 204–14.

172 Neuman, *Robert de Cotte*, 67–72.

173 Kalnein, *Architecture in France*, 112–14.

174 Neuman, *Robert de Cotte*, 141–42; Georges Pillement, *Les
hôtels du Faubourg Saint-Germain* (Paris, 1950): 33, 59,
XVI, LIII.

175 Leconte, Henri Christophe, 343.

176 David R. Coffin, *The Villa in the Life of Renaissance Rome*
(Princeton, 1979): 281–302.

177 Leconte, *Henri Christophe*, 343.

178 BNF, *Département Estampes et photographie, FT 4-VA-422*.

179 Jean-Marie Pérouse de Montclos, *L'art de France de la
Renaissance au siècle des Lumières (1450–1770)* (Paris,
2004): 259; Anthony Blunt, *Art and Architecture in France
1500–1700* (London, 1979): 227; Sebastiano Serlio, I
Sette libri dell'architettura. *Libro Terzo* (1540): 120.

180 Die angegebenen Maße sind die von Leconte veröffent-
lichten [*Henri Christophe*, 343]; Siehe auch Hyvert,
»Conservation et restauration,« 18.

181 Leconte, *Henri Christophe*, 344.

182 Für Definitionen von *opus incertum* und *opus mixtum*

174 Neuman, *Robert de Cotte*, 141–2; Georges Pillement, *Les hôtels du Faubourg Saint-Germain* (Paris, 1950): 33, 59, XVI, LIII.

175 Leconte, *Henri Christophe*, 343.

176 David R. Coffin, *The Villa in the Life of Renaissance Rome* (Princeton, 1979): 281–302.

177 Leconte, *Henri Christophe*, 343.

178 BNF, *Département Estampes et photographie, FT 4-VA-422.*

179 Jean-Marie Pérouse de Montclos, *L'art de France de la Renaissance au siècle des Lumières (1450–1770)* (Paris, 2004): 259; Anthony Blunt, *Art and Architecture in France 1500–1700* (London, 1979): 227; Sebastiano Serlio, *I Sette libri dell'architettura. Libro Terzo* (1540): 120.

180 The measurements given are those published by Leconte [*Henri Christophe*, 343]; See also Hyvert, "Conservation et restauration," 18.

181 Leconte, *Henri Christophe*, 344.

182 For definitions of *opus incertum* and *opus mixtum* see: Nikolas Davies et al., *Dictionary of Architecture and Building Construction* (Oxford, 2008): 258.

183 The interior walls were plastered as well, and surveyors have also found traces of pale pink, blue, red, and black paint. [Hyvert, *Conservation et restauration*, 19].

184 Christian Goguet and Frédéric Mangones, *L'architecture de la ville historique du Cap Haïtien* (Port-au-Prince, 1989): 24–25. I am very grateful to Fréderick Mangones for making this rare book available to me.

185 Goguet and Mangones, *L'architecture*, 44.

186 ANOM *F3 296 E9*, "Plans, profil et elevation du Magasin Royal du Cap, le Cap le 30 aoust 1737," signed Delalance.

187 For the dimensions, see: Hyvert, "Conservation et restauration," 19.

188 "1ᵉ Que le prix de la construction de l'église sur le plan en rotonde était beaucoup élevé pour les circonstances actuelles ou se trouvent les habitans de cette paroisse. 2ᵉ. Que l'on ne trouverait pas d'ouvriers capables d'exécuter un pareil projet." [Archives Departementales de Guadeloupe (hereafter ADGu), *E. Dépôt 13.5,* "Délibéra-

siehe: Nikolas Davies et al., *Dictionary of Architecture and Building Construction* (Oxford, 2008): 258.

183   Die Innenwände waren ebenfalls verputzt, und Gutachter haben auch Spuren von hellrosa, blauer, roter und schwarzer Farbe entdeckt [Hyvert, *Conservation et restauration*, 19].

184   Christian Goguet und Frédéric Mangones, *L'architecture de la ville historique du Cap Haïtien* (Port-au-Prince, 1989): 24–25. Ich bin Fréderick Mangones für die Bereitstellung dieses seltenen Buches sehr dankbar.

185   Goguet und Mangones, *L'architecture*, 44.

186   ANOM *F3 296 E9*, »Plans, profil et elevation du Magasin Royal du Cap, le Cap le 30 aoust 1737,« unterzeichnet von Delalance.

187   Für die Maße, siehe: Hyvert, »Conservation et restauration,« 19.

188   »1ᵉ Que le prix de la construction de l'église sur le plan en rotonde était beaucoup élevé pour les circonstances actuelles ou se trouvent les habitans de cette paroisse. 2ᵉ. Que l'on ne trouverait pas d'ouvriers capables d'exécuter un pareil projet.« [Archives Departementales de Guadeloupe (hiernach ADGu), *E. Dépôt 13.5*, »Délibération sur le plan de l'Eglise (Pointe-à-Pitre)« (18. Dezember 1806), f. 15]. Siehe auch Kissoun, *Pointe-à-Pitre*,113; Bruno Kissoun, »Les prémices de l'architecture métallique en Guadeloupe: la construction de l'église Saint-Pierre et Saint-Paul de Pointe-à-Pitre aux XIXe siècle,« *In Situ: Revue des patrimoines* 6 (2005): 2; *Camille Fabre, De clochers en clochers: Saint Pierre Saint Paul* (Pointe-à-Pitre, 1978): 7; R. P. Ballivet »Nos paroisses de 1635 à nos jours…La Pointe-à-Pitre 2e Partie: Les églises,« *L'écho de la Reine de Guadeloupe* 77 (1927): 97.

189   ANOM *19DFC/180/B*, »Projet de Chapelle [Saint-Louis],« unterzeichnet von Courtois, 1820.

190   Eine Fotografie von 1931 beweist, dass der steinerne Unterbau zum Zeitpunkt der Restauration intakt war, die Kuppel aber vollständig verschwunden war [Archives Nationales d'Haïti (hiernach ANH), *11.242*, »Direction Générale des Travaux Publics. 4 Août 1931. Vue générale de Milot prise du Palais de Sans-Souci.«]

tion sur le plan de l'Eglise (Pointe-à-Pitre)" (18 December 1806), f. 15]. See also Kissoun, *Pointe-à-Pitre,*113; Bruno Kissoun, "Les prémices de l'architecture métallique en Guadeloupe: la construction de l'église Saint-Pierre et Saint-Paul de Pointe-à-Pitre aux XIXe siècle," *In Situ: Revue des patrimoines* 6 (2005): 2; Camille Fabre, *De clochers en clochers: Saint Pierre Saint Paul* (Pointe-à-Pitre, 1978): 7; R. P. Ballivet "Nos paroisses de 1635 à nos jours...La Pointe-à-Pitre 2e Partie: Les églises," *L'écho de la Reine de Guadeloupe* 77 (1927): 97.

189 ANOM *19DFC/180/B*, "Projet de Chapelle [Saint-Louis]," signed Courtois, 1820.

190 A 1931 photograph shows that the stone substructure was intact at the time of the restoration but that the dome had completely disappeared [Archives Nationales d'Haïti (hereafter ANH), *11.242,* "Direction Générale des Travaux Publics. 4 Août 1931. Vue générale de Milot prise du Palais de Sans-Souci."]

191 Leconte, *Henri Christophe*, 340.

192 Nicolas Courtin, *Paris au XVIIIe siècle* (Paris, 2013): 21; Kalnein, *Architecture in France*, 237–39.

193 The church is illustrated in Volume I, *deuxième cahier*, plate IV. This book was used by French colonial designers elsewhere, as in Marie-Philippe Deroisin's Church of Saint-Louis in Saint-Louis, Senegal, 1827–28 (Designed 1826). See Bailey, *Architecture and Urbanism in the French Atlantic World*, chapter 14.

194 Walter Szambein, "Bernin et l'architecture néoclassique française (1750–1830)," in Chantal Grell and Milovan Stani eds., *Le Bernin et l'Europe: du baroque triomphant à l'âge romantique* (Paris, 2002): 154; Robert Rosenblum, *Transformations in Late Eighteenth-Century Art* (Princeton, 1969): 123.

195 Cole, *Christophe: King of Haiti*, 192; Ardouin, *Etudes sur l'histoire d'Haiti* VII, 412–13. Vergniaud Leconte is the only source to indicate that it was a temporary structure [Leconte, *Henri Christophe*, 259, 267].

196 Cheesman, *The Armorial of Haiti*, 5; Leconte, *Henri Christophe*, 421–27.

191   Leconte, *Henri Christophe*, 340.

192   Nicolas Courtin, *Paris au XVIIIe siècle* (Paris, 2013): 21; Kalnein, Architecture in France, 237–39.

193   Die Kirche ist in Band I, *deuxième cahier*, Tafel IV illustriert. Dieses Buch wurde auch andernorts von französischen Planern der Kolonialzeit verwendet, etwa in Marie-Philippe Deroisins Kirche von Saint-Louis in Saint-Louis, Senegal, 1827–28 (1826 entworfen). Siehe Bailey, *Architecture and Urbanism in the French Atlantic World*, Kapitel 14.

194   Walter Szambein, »Bernin et l'architecture néoclassique française (1750–1830),« in Chantal Grell und Milovan Stani Hrsg., *Le Bernin et l'Europe: du baroque triomphant à l'âge romantique* (Paris, 2002): 154; Robert Rosenblum, *Transformations in Late Eighteenth-Century Art* (Princeton, 1969): 123.

195   Cole, *Christophe: King of Haiti*, 192; Ardouin, *Etudes sur l'histoire d'Haiti* VII, 412–13. Vergniaud Leconte ist die einzige Quelle, die andeutet, dass es sich um einen temporären Bau handelte [Leconte, *Henri Christophe*, 259, 267].

196   Cheesman, *The Armorial of Haiti*, 5; Leconte, *Henri Christophe*, 421–27.

197   Gabriel García Marquez, *Der Herbst des Patriarchen* (Curt Meyer-Clason, Übers., Berlin 1979): 1–3.

198   Fischer, *Modernity Disavowed*, 246.

199   Césaire, *La tragédie du Roi Christophe*, 16. Die Hervorhebungen sind meine eigenen.

200   Césaire, *La tragédie du Roi Christophe*, 66. Siehe auch Luís Madureira, *Cannibal Modernities: Postcoloniality and the Avant-garde in Caribbean and Brazilian literature* (Charlottesville und London, 2005): 164.

201   Girard, *Paradise Lost*, 66–67. Girard merkt allerdings an, dass die Auswirkungen von Boyers Entscheidung übertrieben wurden, um die anhaltenden finanziellen Sorgen Haitis zu erklären.

197 Gabriel García Marquez, *The Autumn of the Patriarch* (Gregory Rabassa, trans., reprint London 1996): 1–3.

198 Fischer, *Modernity Disavowed*, 246.

199 Césaire, *La tragédie du Roi Christophe*, 16. The italics are my own.

200 Césaire, *La tragédie du Roi Christophe*, 66. See also Luís Madureira, *Cannibal Modernities: Postcoloniality and the Avant-garde in Caribbean and Brazilian literature* (Charlottesville and London, 2005): 164.

201 Girard, *Paradise Lost*, 66–67. Girard notes however that the impact of Boyer's move has been exaggerated to explain Haiti's enduring financial woes.

Abbildungsnachweis Illustrations:
Fotografien des Autors (2017) Photographs by the author (2017):
Abb. 1–2, Abb. 6, Abb. 8–10, Abb. 12, 14–15, Abb. 19–27, Abb. 29–30 | Abb. 3:
© Josefina del Toro Fulladosa Collection, Alfred Nemours Collection, University of Puerto Rico, Fig. Río Piedras Campus | Abb. 4: © London, Royal College of Arms, Ms JP 177 | Abb. 5: © Bibliothèque Nationale de France, CP 149, 4, 23 | Abb. 7: © Archives Nationales d'Outre-Mer, Aix-en-Provence, F3 296 E2 | Abb. 11: © Archives Nationales d'Outre-Mer, Aix-en-Provence, 15dfc564b | S. 10/11, Abb. 13: © Bayerische Staatsbibliothek, It.sing. 883 m | Abb. 16–18: © Zentralinstitut für Kunstgeschichte, 4° CA 242/725 R | Abb. 28: © Archives Nationales d'Outre-Mer, Aix-en-Provence, 15dfc335a

Umschlagabbildung Cover illustration:
    Philipp Reitsam, München Munich

Herausgeber Editor:
    Ulrich Pfisterer
Lektorat deutsch Copyeditor of the German texts:
    Tobias Teutenberg
Lektorat englisch Copyeditor of the English texts:
    Julian Hermann
Übersetzung englisch–deutsch Translation English—German:
    Julian Hermann
Übersetzung dt.–englisch (Vorwort) Translation German–English (Preface):
    Marisa Mandabach
Gestaltung, Satz und Layout Design, type setting, and layout:
    Edgar Endl, Deutscher Kunstverlag
Druck und Bindung Printing and binding:
    Grafisches Centrum Cuno, Calbe

Bibliografische Information der Deutschen Nationalbibliothek:
Die Deutsche Nationalbibliothek verzeichnet diese Publikation in der
Deutschen Nationalbibliografie; detaillierte bibliografische Daten
sind im Internet über http://dnb.dnb.de abrufbar.
Bibliographic information published by the Deutsche Nationalbibliothek:
The Deutsche Nationalbibliothek lists this publication in the Deutsche
Nationalbibliografie; detailed bibliographic data are available on the
Internet at http://dnb.dnb.de.

© 2017 Deutscher Kunstverlag Berlin/München
Paul-Lincke-Ufer 34 · 10999 Berlin
ISBN 978-3-422-07466-8